Subjects Matter

Subjects Matter

Every Teacher's Guide to Content-Area Reading

Harvey Daniels
Steven Zemelman

HEINEMANN
Portsmouth, NH

Heinemann

361 Hanover Street
Portsmouth, NH 03801–3912
www.heinemann.com

Offices and agents throughout the world

The authors and publisher wish to thank those who have generously given permission to reprint borrowed material:

Excerpt from *E=mc²: A Biography of the World's Most Famous Equation* by David Bodanis. Copyright © 2000 by David Bodanis. Reprinted by permission of Walker and Company.

Mary Ehrenworth, for permission to include the poem that appears on pp. 270–271.

Library of Congress Cataloging-in-Publication Data
Daniels, Harvey. 1947–
    Subjects matter : every teacher's guide to content-area reading / Harvey Daniels, Steven Zemelman.
      p.   cm.
Includes bibliographical references and index.
    ISBN 0-325-00595-8 (alk. paper)
   1. Content area reading—United States.   2. Reading (Middle school)—United States.
3. Reading (Secondary)—United States.   I. Zemelman, Steven.   II. Title.
   LB1050.455.D36 2004
   428.4'071'2—dc22
                                                      2003024143

Editors: Leigh Peake and Lisa Luedeke
Production management: Patricia Adams
Production coordination: Abigail M. Heim
Typesetter: Technologies 'N Typography
Interior and cover design: Joyce Weston Design
Photographs: Robb Hill
Manufacturing: Louise Richardson

Printed in the United States of Americal on acid-free paper
    08   RRD   10 9

To our mothers: Carol Atwood Daniels and Ethel Kissin

With 176 years of mothering between them (and still counting), these *grandes dames* bring new meaning to the term "lifelong learning." Thanks, Moms, for giving us the gift of language, an ear for a story, and the love of books.

Contents

Acknowledgments

The two of us have now written five books together, and we are still friends. Remarkably, on this summer's canoe trip with the guys (our 12th), we each had several perfectly good chances to drown the other, but didn't even try. So, we'd like to begin by saluting the longevity of our partnership. It has been great to teach, write, and grow up (not old) together. We couldn't have done it without us.

Now that we have patted ourselves on the back(s), we can talk about where this book *really* came from. Like all our other books, this one is built on the wonderful ideas of working teachers, people who are already making reading real for their students every day. We have visited their classrooms, observed their strategies, talked through their plans, interviewed their students, looked at their materials, and tried to carefully and faithfully write down what they do. Our job is not so much to generate brand-new ideas as it is to spread rare but promising practices to a wider audience. In fact, we have often thought of ourselves as "the delivery boys" of education, writing and speaking about great things we have seen in real classrooms.

So we are especially happy to thank the following outstanding educators for giving of their time, classrooms, and teaching strategies: Melissa Bryant-Neal, Mike Cannon, Matt Feldman, Theresa Hernandez, Sonja Kosanovic, Mike Myers, and Peter Thomas at Best Practice High School; Sushma Sharma at the South Shore Small School for Entrepreneurship; Terrence Simmons, Karon Stewart, and Kelly Vaughan at the South Shore Small School for the Arts; Brenda Dukes and Kenya Sadler at the Foundations School; Jacqueline Sanders at the Nia School; Vanessa Brechling and Sarah Lieberman at Perspectives Charter School; Scott Sullivan at Highland Park High School; Nancy Steineke, Jeff Janes, and Mike Dwyer at Victor J. Andrew High School; Margaret Forst at Lake Forest High School; Ralph Feese, Don Grossnickle, and Katy Smith at Addison Trail High School; Kathleen McKenna at Baker Demonstration School; Jodie Bonville and Jude Ellis, our confederates in upstate New York. And thanks to our fellow author Jim Burke, who kindly gave permission for us to use his textbook guide on pages 150–151.

The recommended book list in Chapter 4 was built with input from scores of teachers, including the faculty at Best Practice High School and the staff of the Walloon Institute. Extra-special help, including specific book blurbs, was supplied by Dagny Bloland, Barbara Dress, Nancy Steineke, Elaine Daniels, Rich Katz, Scott Sullivan, Angela Whetstone, Mike Myers, Matt Feldman, Arthur Hyde and our Pet pals at Texas Instruments. Kylene Beers, one of the profession's top experts on books for adolescent readers, vetted the final list, adding some wonderful titles and helping us balance the reading levels.

Marilyn Bizar, the Chair of Secondary Education at National-Louis University, probably should have written this book herself, since she knows more about reading than the two of us put together. But in the arcane rotation of co-authorship that has guided us three friends through a half-dozen books, this was Marilyn's hiatus, during which she led the growth of a very successful secondary MAT program at the University. The good thing, Marilyn, is that the mistakes aren't your fault.

Over the years, we have grown a wonderful professional family of about 20 people, all of us irreverent readers and almost indefatigable school reformers. Sometimes this crew is known as the Center for City Schools, sometimes as the Walloon Institute faculty, and at other times, simply the world's most ill-behaved book club. All of these people have contributed in some way to the contents of this book. But mainly, they are our friends. They give us the energy to keep writing, and regular reality-checks to make sure we don't think we are some kind of big stuff. Hugs all around to Marilyn Bizar, Jim Vopat, Nancy Steineke, Mike and Susan Klonsky, Nancy Doda, Barbara Morris, Yolanda Simmons, Toni Murff, Marianne Flanagan, Pete Leki, Jessica Swanson, Linda Bailey, Lynnette Emmons, Natasha Schaefer, Sara Nordlund, Melissa Woodbury, Brenda Bell, Mary Hausner, Barbara Dress, Pat Bearden, Kathy Daniels, Alice Perry, Lea Mc Donald, and the Walloon Gopher Crew under DJ Marny D. If for some peculiar reason you'd ever like to meet these people, come and join us at the Walloon Institute; together, we conduct teacher seminars around the country each summer.

In 1996, against all odds and good sense, we gathered with several veteran teachers to establish a new small public school on the west side of Chicago. Working with a cross-section of the city's kids, in a system with a drop-out rate of 50%, Best Practice High School now sends 80% of its graduates to college. This remarkable achievement is due to one thing: the brilliance, courage, and self-sacrifice of 28 amazing teachers. Though they must spend every day of their professional lives swimming upstream, coping with an unending onslaught of central-office mandates, bureaucratic interference, and doubting administrators, these brave educators consistently provide first-rate instruction and personal care to our wonderful, talented students.

After writing five books for Heinemann, and being officially counted among the "old-timers" (thanks a lot, Lesa Scott), we expect, but are not de-sensitized to, the TLC treatment which newborn books receive in Portsmouth. This time around, we were extra lucky to be assigned the editorial duo of Lisa Luedeke and Leigh Peake, who put a whole new spin on the "good cop, bad cop" routine (all good cop). We know that when all the skilled people in copy-editing, design, production, marketing, and sales are done with their fine work, there'll be no one but the authors to blame for the shortcomings of the final product. As it should be.

When we first started writing books together, we both had a houseful of children—well, two each seemed like a houseful to us. Now we have four grownup kids scattered from San Francisco to Santa Fe, from St. Paul to west-ern Massachusetts. And we continue to learn so much from their learning, as they build lives centered on dance, music, art, and forensic science. So the nests are empty now, but luckily they still contain the two best literary part-ners any writer could hope for. Elaine and Susan, thanks, one more time, for making our books (and our lives) so much better.

Walloon Lake, Michigan
Evanston, Illinois
August 2003

CHAPTER ONE
Reading for Real

A McDonald's restaurant in downtown Chicago, Wednesday, lunchtime. On the street out front, a sidewalk preacher testifies to passersby with the aid of a portable P.A. system. Inside, the store is filled with shoppers, tourists, well-pierced students from the Art Institute, and traders from the nearby commodities exchange wearing their distinctive yellow-numbered vests. Customers contentedly chew their Big Macs and chicken nuggets. The air is thick with conversation and the smell of french fries.

The door swings open and two teenage boys walk in. They're big kids, about 17 or 18 years old, one Hispanic and one African American. They weave through the tables and up to the crowded window where people are ordering. Michael is carrying a stack of blue flyers, which he quietly places on the counter, so customers can easily pick one up while waiting for their food.

The flyer is headlined "What's in the Meat We Love?" and depicts the headless carcass of a steer, hanging upside down, just as it would in a slaughterhouse. Below is a grinning likeness of Ronald McDonald, swinging a butcher knife high over his head, with a caption underneath asking "Who profits from the killing floor?" The text warns readers of the prevalence of food-borne illnesses, especially those carried by the beef served in fast-food restaurants. As its source, the flyer cites the book *Fast Food Nation: The Dark Side of the All-American Meal* by Eric Schlosser.

Customers waiting for their burgers gradually become aware of the handout, and a few idly pick one up. Reactions differ: some look disgusted, some annoyed, some amused. There is a growing audience now, as the boys begin walking from table to table. Antonio approaches a middle-aged white woman who's eating alone, reading a book. He asks if she is familiar with *e coli* poisoning. Has she heard about the notorious cases of fast food restaurants sickening their customers? "No," she patiently replies, looking down at her lunch, spread out on its yellow paper wrapping. Does she know that every day in America, 200 people are sickened—and 14 die—from bacteria commonly found in hamburger meat? From his back pocket, Antonio pulls out his copy of *Fast Food Nation* and points out some key statistics on page 195. She leans down to read the page, heavily over-lined in yellow, with cryptic annotations in the margins.

"See," he concludes, gesturing at her lunch, "it tastes good and it's quick to get, but it could be a manure sandwich, is what I'm saying."

The woman nods, but seems a little stunned by all this passionate attention to her health. Or perhaps she's put off by Antonio's barnyard analogies.

Meanwhile, the 30-ish manager has been alerted to the disturbance by his counter crew. He scoops up the leftover flyers and walks up behind Antonio, tapping him on the shoulder.

"You can't bother my customers like this," he says firmly, "and you can't hand these out either." He calmly dumps the sheaf of blue flyers into a nearby wastebasket, right on top of the ketchup-soaked napkins and empty soda cups. Antonio and Michael look at each other, silently deciding whether to raise the ante.

Discretion rules, and they shrug as the manager points to the way out. They go, but not quickly and not quietly. All the way to the door, as the manager herds him along, Antonio half-playfully hollers health warnings over his shoulder:

"Listen up, listen up people!"
"Coming soon—the new truth about McDonald's!"
"You gotta know what your food contains!"
"You might be having an *e coli* sandwich for lunch up in here!"

And finally, at the door, he gives the manager one for the road: "You gonna put me out because I'm tellin' the truth?"

Michael and Antonio are students at Best Practice, a small public high school we helped to design and open in Chicago in 1996. At BPHS, we believe in reading—real reading—in all content areas, across the curriculum. The boys' truth-squad assault on the McDonald's at State and Jackson happened after they had spent a month reading about the fast food industry and how it affects our health, agriculture, values, laws, economy, and society. The unit was designed by a cross-disciplinary team of senior teachers representing science, social studies, English, and special education, with help from faculty in math, technology, art, and ourselves, the university partners.

Like other lessons at Best Practice High School, the fast food project was built on the assumption that teenagers should not be "getting ready" to be life-long learners—but should be acting like them **right now.** The school's faculty believe that feeding students a steady stream of textbook chapters is not a healthy reading diet—or a grownup one. So they supplement kids' intake with generous servings of newspapers, magazines, websites, and nonfiction trade books—the same range of texts that thoughtful, curious members of the adult community around them might read.

In the fast food unit, the kids read widely and dug deep. First, each student received the paperback edition of *Fast Food Nation*. Reminiscent of Upton Sinclair's *The Jungle,* but ranging even more widely, Schlosser's book is an old-fashioned muckraking exposé which lambastes every link in the chain of industrialized agriculture, up to its ultimate crudescence in fast food restaurants. We used some grant funds to buy every student their own copy for two reasons: first, we simply wanted them to own the book, since our kids generally don't own a lot of books; and second, because we planned to use some reading strategies that required kids to actively mark up, overline, and annotate the text.

But the book was just the start. For scientific background (and also because it is mandated in the citywide curriculum), the kids read the biology textbook's chapters on nutrition, digestion, viruses, and bacteria. Each student also read several magazine articles, including a *Fortune* magazine piece about lawsuits brought (and dismissed) against fast food restaurants for causing obesity, one from *Science* magazine debunking the "fat myth" and arguing that fat may actually be good for you, and another from *Harper's* about how fast food companies intentionally target poor urban neighborhoods. Students also chose from six articles about animal cruelty downloaded from the PETA (People for the Ethical Treatment of Animals) website, sparking lively discussion about whether, for example, harvesting eggs or milking cows is really animal abuse. The more the kids and teachers dug into the topic, the more relevant sources seemed to pop up—in books, articles, and websites everywhere. One juicy favorite was the American Restaurant Association's stinging rebuttal called "The Truth About Fast Food Nation," a Web-based press release quoting the book's few negative reviews and pounding home the point that Schlosser wanted to deny people "the food they love."

The faculty didn't just assign all these readings and hope that kids would comprehend them. All year long, they had been teaching specific, practical **thinking strategies** that help kids to dig meaning out of a document in any content field. As a result, these kids knew how to:

Visualize ideas and situations in the text

Make connections

Ask questions

Draw inferences
Evaluate and determine what's important
Notice and analyze the author's craft
Recall ideas
Self-monitor while reading

Further, the teachers embodied these thinking strategies in concrete **tools** that helped students understand and remember what they read. In this unit, for example, the teachers made use of text coding tools, book clubs, dialogue journals, bookmarks, post-it notes, text annotation, admit slips, and exit slips, among others. With these kinds of scaffolding, students were able to enter some very challenging texts, make sense of them, monitor their thinking, bring ideas back to discussions, and apply what they had read to their own lives.

And, of course, there were lots of classroom and community-based activities that grew out of and extended the readings. Kids made anthropological observations at fast food joints, interviewed restaurant workers, kept personal diet journals, searched the Web for nutrition information, and joined in two elaborate simulations, one about life as a teenage employee in a fast food restaurant and another that dramatized the unionization of a slaughterhouse. The outcome of all this reading and experience was 80 kids with a lot of questions, concerns, and opinions. And that made things pretty easy when it came to the culminating experience—finding a public audience with whom to share ideas and concerns about the fast food industry.

Not all the kids chose "in-your-face" actions like Michael and Antonio. Jaisy, who was upset by the working conditions of immigrant employees in modern meat-packing plants, very diplomatically wrote her Congressman:

> *Dear Representative Davis,*
> *My class and I are reading* Fast Food Nation. *This book addresses a lot of issues, however, the one I find to be most disturbing is the conditions of slaughterhouses, especially for the cleanup crews. That portion of the book was really hard for me to read. The descriptions were way too vivid for my liking! I am writing you because I want to know what the average person can do to increase the chances of workers having good working conditions in slaughterhouses. . . . I plan to make every effort to convince you to take action to better the conditions in the slaughterhouses. If you haven't read* Fast Food Nation, *I strongly urge you to; that will be the strongest influence over you.*
> *Sincerely,*
> *Jaisy R. Geans*

Jaisy also created a petition made up of direct quotes from the book, and then solicited signatures around the school and the neighborhood. Jaisy brought her own special style to the petition process: she'd approach you in the hall, hand you the petition, and ask you to read the quotes. After about ten seconds, she'd start asking: "Isn't that awful? Isn't that just terrible?" And when you'd nod, she'd command, "Well, sign it, then!!"

Shawn's group wrote and illustrated a picture book called "What's in Your Happy Meal?" *(See the cow. See Jack kill the cow. See the french fries soaked in grease.)* They met with an interested teacher in the elementary school downstairs about visiting a first-grade class to read the book at story time and talk about fast food with the children. But they decided the younger children would be too upset with the idea of killing animals—but the teenagers were too, which is why they wrote the book. Indeed, of all the issues encountered during the unit, this was the one with the greatest emotional wallop; adolescents could care less what their cholesterol is, but once they learn what goes on in a slaughterhouse, it can change their thinking forever.

Another group of kids documented their own miserable school lunches by taking digital photos of each item being served and collecting wrappers from the other food sold in the cafeteria. Using these assorted materials, they created a huge collage and superimposed it on the U.S. Department of Agriculture's "food pyramid," the chart which specifies the officially recommended diet for Americans. Enhancing the 3–D effect were some napkins and plastic "sporks," hanging from the corner of the piece.

To drive home their point, the kids drew multicolored arrows from each cafeteria item (hot dogs, nachos with cheese sauce, Snickers bars) to the appropriate step on the food pyramid. The graphic was dramatic: almost all the arrows pointed to the top of the pyramid—to fats and oils, sugars, and red meat, categories from which people are advised to eat very sparingly. Fruits and vegetables, which are supposed to dominate a healthy diet, were virtually absent from the school food residue. The collage sparked a lively and still ongoing discussion about upgrading the food served in our own school.

Some of these projects may seem a little naive, heavy-handed, even—what's the word we're looking for—adolescent? Admittedly, hectoring innocent diners in a restaurant or reminding six-year-olds that their lunch began as Bossie does seem a little aggressive. But the thing was, these teenage readers were actually angry and concerned. They had learned things that really got them thinking, got them agitated, got them activated. The self-reflections at the end of the unit showed how deeply many students (admittedly not all—hey, this is a real school) were affected by what they learned.

I really don't like eating McDonald's anymore. Before I read this book I had already stopped eating beef and pork, and this book really makes you wanna quit.

After this book, now at a fast food restaurant I don't eat the burgers—only apple pies and fries (I'm not going to starve myself)!

For about $1\frac{1}{2}$ weeks I couldn't eat meat. However, that really sucked because I didn't have too much to eat without meat. Finally, I was pushed to the edge of hungriness and I ended up eating a chicken sandwich. I will definitely be more conscious of what I eat.

Will this change my eating habits? No way, except that I'll think about the facts and laugh ironically before I eat a delicious mean Burger King or McDonald's.

Ever since I read *Fast Food Nation* I only ate fast food one time. I thought differently about it and started to reduce my fast food servings.

I can't really eat any meat without thinking about the animal it used to be.

Read This for Friday

Mr. Cosgrove's biology class, Thursday, second period.

"All right. . . . Jamie, sit down, please. All right. Everyone, before the bell rings, let me give the assignment for tomorrow. I want you to read Chapter 17 in the textbook, and answer the questions at the end of the chapter. You're gonna turn those in at the start of class tomorrow, so be sure to use our regular format—name, date, and period in the upper right—you know the drill. Now, a word to the wise. Are you listening, Kathy? I would suggest that you pay special attention to the section on photosynthesis, because we might have a quiz on that one of these days. O.K.? Did everyone hear that? I said, we might have a pop quiz on photosynthesis sometime very soon. Any questions? O.K. See you tomorrow."

Cut to Friday. The kids straggle in, and after a gentle reminder, begin hunting in their backpacks for the homework. As usual, Jamie whines, "Oooh, Mr. C, can I go to my locker? I think I left my homework in there." As Mr. Cosgrove roams the aisles, collecting papers, a few routine excuses pop up. ("I had soccer last night." "I think it's on my kitchen table.") But most of the kids have done the work—and here comes Jamie back from his locker, triumphantly clutching a crumpled sheet of notebook paper.

Flipping through the stack, Mr. Cosgrove is not especially displeased. Though some students' responses are more complete than others, almost every kid has written down something for each of the 12 questions from the textbook.

"O.K., gang," Mr. Cosgrove announces, "Remember my words to the wise yesterday—it's quiz time. Please clear your desks."

Pro forma resistance immediately breaks out. "Aw, Mr. C—that's not fair! You only said *maybe* a quiz!" "But we just had a quiz on Tuesday!" Inevitably, the 10-item multiple-choice quiz is distributed, and the kids gradually quiet down and bend to the task. There's some background sighing and pencil-tapping, and a few students gaze steadily up in the air, as if the correct answers might suddenly appear on a ceiling tile. When Steve calls time and collects the test papers, he notices a lot of blank, unanswered questions.

Once the quizzes are stacked on his desk, it is time for some class discussion. "So, guys," Steve asks, "What's the big picture here? Why is photosynthesis so important to life?" Twenty-seven eighth graders simultaneously look down at their desktops, apparently finding something utterly fascinating in the grain of the wood. "Who wants to start us off? Why is photosynthesis so important?" Mr. C scans the room, but no eye contact seems to be available, no glimmer of volunteerism emerges. Call on one of the reliable ones, Steve thinks. Christine, maybe. But as he gazes her way, she drops her pen on the floor and turns, in ultra-slow motion, to retrieve it. The silence is profound.

"Geez, guys, give me a break here. We read this stuff last night, you just had it on the quiz." Blank stares.

"O.K., why don't you take your books out and open up to Chapter 17 again." The kids heft the six-pound science books back onto their desks, opening to the chapter.

"O.K., everybody with me now? Alright, here's an easy one: what's the green stuff that is the key to photosynthesis?" There's the sound of pages flipping. And flipping. And flipping.

"Come on, you gotta know this."

More silence, and then, finally, a first tentative hand is raised.

"Uh, would that be carbon dioxide?" wonders Diane.

The phrase "pulling teeth" flashes through Mr. Cosgrove's head. For a split-second, he sees himself in a white dentist's smock, holding a shiny pair of pliers in one hand; the students arrayed before him resemble rows of deeply impacted, unpullable teeth—definitely **not** of the "wisdom" type.

"All right, guys, maybe this just isn't a good day for a discussion. Tell you what, let's just turn to Chapter 18 and start reading that for tomorrow. I'll give you the last 15 minutes of class to get a head start on the homework. And be ready for a quiz on Monday."

Later, grading the tests, Mr. C tallies two As, four Bs, seven Cs, seven Ds, and eight Fs. All the kids needed was to get six out of 10 answers half-way right. Sixty percent! Was that too much to ask? Apparently, even sitting at home last night, with the textbooks right in front of their noses, students couldn't memorize the most straightforward points—even the ones sitting right there in bold-face type. They read it, but they just didn't get it.

Not only do they not get it—they don't seem to care. And this bothers Steve Cosgrove most of all. Steve went into teaching because he loved science—and especially ecology. Back in college, he took an advanced ecosystems course, where he studied global warming with a group of classmates. His life changed that day when he read about scientists who drilled into air pockets in Antarctica to find samples of the atmosphere trapped centuries ago. They proved that in the year 1700 the earth's air had a third less carbon dioxide than it has now. When he read that study, Steve was stunned, concerned—and hooked.

Here at Cutler Middle School, Steve's goal in teaching has never been just to push kids through the textbook, or help them pass a state assessment—though he cares about both of those necessary outcomes. Steve hopes for more. He wants his students to really understand how the earth works, how life interlocks, how thin and fragile the biosphere really is. He wants to awaken in young people a sense of wonder at the complexity of life. He hopes that they will feel concern, maybe get involved, see themselves as stewards of the environment, friends of the planet. But these kids, they can't even (or *won't* even) read the book.

Why Content Teachers Care About Reading

Studies consistently show that most of us are like Steve: that we middle- and high-school teachers chose our profession mainly because we loved a **subject**—physics, mathematics, art, history, political science, biology, chemistry, literature, a language. Elementary teachers, on the other hand, most commonly say they elected teaching because they "like being with children." That's a big difference. It doesn't mean we secondary types don't like young people (most of us are quite fond of them, actually), but we have another quite powerful dynamic going on in our heads: we care deeply about a particular field, a body of knowledge, a special set of tools and procedures, an intellectual tradition, a heritage.

Looking back over our careers, we can feel the truth of this. We didn't sign up for this occupation, go to school for four or five years, get ourselves certified, and agree to this pitiful pay scale, just to push some state assessment score up a half a percent. Our imagination wasn't fired by some list of 3,000 state standards to be met in the first semester of ninth grade. We got into this job because we were fascinated by a field, usually our college major, and we wanted to transmit that excitement to young people. We wanted students to share our enthusiasm, our engagement, our wonder at the beauty and importance of ideas. We had something powerful and precious to share: *knowledge.*

We imagined students catching our fever of ideas. We pictured them exploring a Civil War battlefield on a summer vacation, or looking through a telescope in their back yard, or writing their own software on a home computer, or sketching a great artwork in a museum gallery, or authoring their own collection of poems. After having us as teachers, after we had lit the fire, we saw our students moving on to take more courses in math, in science, in literature, in art. We envisioned them going on to major in our subject in college—the greatest compliment a secondary teacher can get. They would make our subject a special part of their own lives, just like we did; some would even join the field, make a contribution, become fellow travelers, our colleagues and peers.

But even in these professional fantasies, we were realistic. We knew we'd never get them all; not every student would commit their working life to our subject area. However, we expected every kid to grasp the big ideas, to respect the field, to remain curious about it through life. When our ex-students read the daily paper, they'd scan for stories about the subject and understand the basic issues. Perhaps some would subscribe to *Scientific American, American Heritage,* or *Harper's.* Others would work through books of math puzzles, just for fun. Maybe they'd read popular books in the field: *Zero: Biography of a Dangerous Idea, Founding Brothers: The Revolutionary Generation, Nickel and Dimed, Salt: A World History, The Future of Life, Into the Wild,* or *Bodega Dreams.* And who knows? Maybe at least a small number of our alumni might be the kind of people who join in monthly book discussion groups, meeting with friends to talk about the latest novels or nonfiction trade books.

Of course, between our long-term dreams and the immediate realities, things can intrude. Here sit our students before us, first period, today. Before they can become lifelong learners and pillars of their intellectual communities, there might be a few obstacles to overcome. Maybe these kids aren't ready to explore genetics at the level that excites us. Maybe, right at this moment, they are grappling with personal or developmental issues that tower higher than the pyramids. Perhaps their previous experience in school hasn't delivered them to our classrooms ready to tackle tariffs. And quite possibly, state standards, mandated curricula, departmental exams, and tests, tests, tests, are undermining our own ability to teach with passion and personality.

Yes, there are a lot of obstacles to young people falling in love with math, science, history, language, and the arts. But that doesn't mean that our idealism is sentimental and misplaced, or that we should give up the dream that binds us to this profession. It is right and reasonable to hope that kids can have a lifelong engagement with at least one, hopefully several fields of knowledge—and that they'll pursue it through reading.

Why the Public Is Concerned

We teachers are not the only people worried about knowledge, learning, and reading in middle and high school. As we write this book, a bright spotlight is being shined on the nation's public schools—and especially those at the secondary level. The country's president, governors, legislatures, researchers, task forces, think tanks and media are casting a cool, appraising eye at our schools—and apparently, finding little to like.

There are some problems that simply cannot be denied. Our high school drop-out rate, nationally about 11%, has dire personal and social consequences for millions of young people. In Chicago, where we work, the drop-out rate is listed at 50%, though many insiders peg the number closer to 60%. If you look over the enrollment records of a typical Chicago high school, you might find 600 freshmen listed, 450 sophomores, 300 juniors—and just 150 seniors left to march at graduation. And these tragic outcomes are replayed in big-city school systems around the country, where most of America's 3.9 million dropouts between age 16 and 24 can be found.

Among the great majority of teenage students who do stay in school, their scores on standardized achievement tests yield disappointing results and evoke many worrisome headlines. Some recent findings from the National Assessment of Educational Progress ("our nation's report card") are emblematic of the problem:

☞ In civics, just 24% of American eighth graders and 30% of seniors scored at the "proficient" level or above.

☞ NAEP science scores show no gains for eighth graders since 1996, while scores for high school seniors have dropped from 150 to 147.

☞ NAEP mathematics scores show modest gains for both eighth and 12th graders over the past 10 years, but a recent dip among seniors.

☞ Ten-year score trends on NAEP history and geography assessments show scores up slightly for eighth grades, but flat for high school.

Of course, each one of these tests—whatever its content area—requires, before anything else, that students be able to *read* passages, tables, problems, charts, and questions.

Now, educators might like to quibble about the validity of such measures. And, indeed, a few indefatigable researchers remind us of the very mixed picture presented by these imperfect measures (Bracey 2001; Allington 2000, 2002). One prominent example: both eighth and 12-grade reading scores were not down, but up significantly in the last national assessment. Still, in a political sense, the inconclusive findings and dubious validity of these tests may not matter very much, since most parties to educational policymaking have long since bought in to the idea of a decline. Nor do self-exculpating interpretations from inside the profession have much clout with a public already pre-sold on the idea that the public schools are a mess.

International educational comparisons don't offer much comfort, either. These studies sometimes show American kids performing at the middle, or even the bottom of world achievement levels. A much-quoted example was the *Trends in International Mathematics and Science Study* (TIMSS 2003), which tested young people from dozens of countries. The exam listed U.S. high school students toward the bottom of the pack, besting only students from Cyprus and South Africa. United States teenagers performed at about the same level as their age-mates from Russia, Italy, and the Czech Republic, but well below those in New Zealand, Canada, and all the Scandinavian countries. When the U.S. public and its policymakers read such reports, they are disappointed—and potentially, energized to act.

Again, professional educators might like to rebut such data. We'd remind critics that America's secondary schools are more broadly inclusive than those in other countries, that they enroll a higher proportion of young people, for more years than most nations attempt (Bracey 2001). We might also point out that America's top echelon schools compare favorably with the best in the world. On the same TIMSS exam that showed dismal results for average U.S. teenagers, a consortium of affluent suburban schools around Chicago voluntarily took the same test, and scored the equivalent of second in the world in math and fifth in science. This proud "first in the world coalition" inadvertently highlighted the fact that only when you average in the results from America's embarrassingly large proportion of poor, underserved school communities do test scores get "dragged down" to sub-world-class levels. But what a sad defense that is. And, as teachers, we know that all of our kids can do better, know more, be more engaged—and we certainly do not deny that some American schools have a really long way to go.

In addition to the "scientific evidence" provided by standardized tests, both foreign and domestic, there is a robust industry of public school debunking, with think tanks, pundits, and publications deployed in loud, unanimous doom-saying. Among these is the formulaic but always headline-worthy genre of "Shocking things today's students don't know" (Henriksson 2001; Ravitch and Finn 1989). These critics stun and alarm the public with news that, say, 54% of high school seniors don't know who dueled with Aaron Burr back in 1804 (or was it 1805?). Though student-bashing critiques are designed more to incite than to enlighten, they do inadvertently raise some interesting educational issues. Here's one: the "stuff-kids-don't-know" anthologizers want us to infer that vital facts are being deleted and our nation's history being dumbed-down by craven educators. But in fact, every single kid who attended an American high school in the last century probably was taught about Aaron Burr and Alexander Hamilton. The problem is: *they don't remember it.* Now, that is an educational puzzle worthy of attention. That's why making sure that kids *remember* and *think about* what they read in school is the focus of much of this book.

Looking at the adult community outside the schools, our country ain't exactly a hotbed of literacy, either. Department of Labor studies consistently show that tens of millions of American adults are "functionally illiterate." The spread of Barnes and Noble, Borders, and Amazon.com notwithstanding, the percentage of Americans who actually buy and read books remains relatively constant. We are not growing a bigger citizenry of readers; we are just changing the location where the readers gather, and adding a half-decaf-half-skim latte to the experience. Are you math teachers tired of hearing citizens (often the parents of your own students) tell you: "Oh, I hated math in school." Well, English teachers are almost as accustomed to hearing the same folks happily declare: "Oh, I'm just not a reader." Perhaps this kind of insecurity is what explains the popularity of the "Idiot's Guide" and "For Dummies" series of books.

So, while there are many things we might like to change about literacy practices in the wider culture—and in the distorted world of standardized tests—we've got to start where we are. And making reading a more meaningful, more effective, and more long-lasting learning experience is something that we teachers can start tackling today, in our very own classrooms.

Two Visions of Reading

So what's the difference between our two opening stories of reading and learning, and how do they help us take on this troubling national puzzle? Well, to begin with, one of these stories really happened and the other was made up. Steve Cosgrove is not a real teacher, and there is no Cutler Middle School, as far as we know. We created "Steve's" story to display some common problems that teachers of all subjects struggle with when we assign content-area reading "the regular way." We tried to portray Steve as a nice person and a hard worker, because that's what teachers are. He's approaching reading the way he was taught in his methods class, and probably the same way he experienced it in his own schooling, in middle school, high school, and college. Admittedly, we did engineer every conceivable problem into Steve's classroom; here's hoping none of us ever encounters a real class as discouraging as his photosynthesis-proof group!

Obviously, we think the fast food reading story has a lot more to recommend it—and not only because it is about our own students, whom we love even when they go a little over the top. If your teaching experience is like ours, you might agree that we don't see young people, teenage readers, this engaged very often. When we assign students to read pages 234–245 in the textbook and answer the questions at the end of the chapter, they hardly ever get on a bus and go share their learning with fellow citizens across town. And maybe you also feel the way we do—that we'd prefer to see students overly worked up than not worked up at all. We'd rather help a kid simmer down and find productive outlets for her rage, than to try to wake her up in the back row of the classroom, where she is snoozing face-down on a textbook.

Still, we realize that the fast food unit may sound a bit idealized, kind of complicated, and even a little unrealistic to people working in "normal" middle and high schools. We can almost hear you thinking: "Hey, excuse me, but I **do** have a textbook to get through. I have a curriculum to cover. It is mandated by the district and I can just barely cram it into the school year as it is. My kids have to take a departmental exam and a state assessment. If they don't do well, both the school and I could be in trouble. And even if I wanted to, where would I find the time to bring in all these other readings and activities? I've got my hands full with my own subject area without trying to cook up some cross-disciplinary project with my colleagues. We don't have any common planning time, anyway. And what about materials and money? I mean, you bought a book for every kid? What budget line did that $900 come out of? And, really, so what if kids write their congressman or make collages? I'm here to teach the subject, not reform people's diets or stir up a controversy." O.K., O.K. We hear you! We're not saying that the fast food unit is what content-area reading must look like every day—or that this is where you begin. It isn't where we began, either.

At BPHS, the teachers of algebra, math, English, history, geometry, art, chemistry, Spanish, biology, and music have been working their way slowly and unevenly into big, complex units like these, which we now undertake for about 10 weeks per year. The rest of the time, our faculty are deployed in separate-subject teaching, just like middle schools and high schools everywhere. We have plenty of constraints, too, including citywide curriculum guides, local tests, and a brutal state assessment—and all our scores wind up in the *Chicago Tribune,* which ranks and compares us to the other 91 high schools in the city.

Nevertheless, when our faculty are working alone in their content-area classes, when they are leading kids through required curriculum and textbook chapters, they model and reinforce that same repertoire of thinking strategies, choose from the same range of materials, use the same reading tools, and structure the same kinds of classroom activities that we draw upon in the big thematic units.

The Goals of This Book

There are two main problems with reading in secondary subject fields: first, students are reading the wrong stuff and second, they don't understand what they read. Other than that, everything is fine! Students consume a drastically unbalanced and unhealthful reading diet, with negative side effects like low test scores, ignorance of vital information, and negative attitudes toward reading. They read too many textbooks, and not enough "real" books and articles. And while we assign plenty of reading, we don't teach kids how to understand and remember what they do read. There are specific and documented mental processes that effective readers use: questioning, predicting, connecting, visualizing, synthesizing, and more (Harvey 2000; Zimmerman and Keene 1997). But these thinking skills are not being consistently taught or used in middle and high school courses.

This book addresses both of these issues. We want to make sure that your students possess the cognitive strategies they need to understand the core written information in your field—and that you, the teacher, have a repertoire of tools and structures to make this happen. And further, we want to be sure that your students are exposed to the best possible samples, those just-right texts and critical documents that can ignite genuine interest and curiosity about your subject matter.

Below is a preview of the changes we will argue for in the coming pages, what we mean by the *what* and the *how* of content reading experiences. As you look at these lists, you can think back over our two opening stories, the fast food unit and the attempted photosynthesis lesson.

In the coming pages, we will show how content teachers can take steps—carefully and thoughtfully—toward more promising reading activities. In the next chapter, we'll look at how our own brains work when we read so we can explain the tricks of the trade to students. Reading is not some unknowable

Successful Content-Area Reading—*What* Is Read

- Kids still use the textbook as a basic source of information, but they also venture far beyond it.

- The subject matter includes authentic, interesting, and current issues that affect young people's daily lives.

- Instead of relying upon a single authority, students consult a variety of sources and voices on the topic, constructing their own understanding of what is fact, what is true, what is right. The students are not only reading about settled facts and closed questions. They are also reading in the arena of the unsettled, the debatable, the still-emerging.

- Students sample a wide variety of genres including textbooks and other reference works, newspapers, magazines, websites, and popular trade books.

- Reading selections have a range of lengths, from short newspaper and magazine pieces to whole books.

- There's a premium on current information; many of the pieces used in a given unit were recently published (or posted).

- Many of the readings take an interdisciplinary approach, using the tools of multiple disciplines, combining science, statistics, history, biography, and more.

Successful Content-Area Reading—*How* It Is Read

☞ The purpose for reading is not just to pass a test or get through the textbook. The students' work is to gather information, construct meaning, and apply knowledge about important issues.

☞ The teacher selects some, but not all, of the readings; students also make choices of their own.

☞ Not every student reads the same texts. There are some common readings and some "jigsawing" of related but different texts.

☞ Teachers teach (and kids use) a repertoire of specific thinking strategies that help them enter, understand, and apply the material they read.

☞ Teachers offer students practical tools that help them process different kinds of texts.

☞ Teachers organize classroom structures and activities that deepen student engagement with key written materials.

☞ Reading is seen as a social, rather than a solitary activity; there is plenty of collaborative work in pairs, teams, Book Clubs, or inquiry groups.

☞ Instead of an exclusive focus on "right answers," there's also room for debate and discussion, for differences of opinion and interpretation.

☞ Instead of receiving a string of 180 daily reading assignments, students do their subject area reading as part of longer, coordinated themes or inquiries.

☞ Reading is linked to action in the real world: young readers engage in research, documentation, correspondence, and advocacy.

☞ The assessment of kids' reading relies less on quizzes and worksheets, and more on complex performances, products, and exhibitions.

"black box" of cognition; it's actually quite easy to surface our own reading strategies, to name them, and then show them to students. Next, we need a new and more healthful diet of reading materials for young people—and we won't just generalize. We'll give you lists of the specific books, magazines, journals, and websites that have energized the curiosity of many young readers, across the whole range of content areas. We'll tell you about teachers who have integrated these new materials into their curricula, alongside the textbook, in harmony with the local curriculum guide, and with success on high-stakes tests.

We'll also share a repertoire of practical classroom structures and strategies that help kids understand and remember what they read—whether it comes from a textbook, a newspaper, or a novel. Some of the most powerful of these strategies take only a few minutes of class time to implement, and can reap huge dividends in comprehension. We'll cover a wide range of activities, from quick getting-started exercises to structures that guide kids through longer, harder texts. We'll show you how to make sure that kids enter texts thinking, demanding clarity along the way, and connecting their learning to real-life issues. We'll describe how to build whole units around "real" books in your own subject area—or even to create interdisciplinary units, planned and co-taught with colleagues from other departments. And we'll be sure to translate all these ideas to kids who struggle with reading. And yes, we'll face up to that scary old bugaboo, assessment, too.

If you're wondering about our authority: yes, we do have scientific research showing that these practices work—and plenty of it. In these times, it is vital to show that suggested classroom activities really enhance student learning, that they have been validated by both quantitative and qualitative research of careful design. Happily, there is more than 60 years of research showing the value of a varied reading diet and careful reading-as-thinking instruction, as measured by standardized test scores as well as improved reading habits and attitudes. In the interest of getting right to the classroom stuff, we have placed our research chapter toward the back of the book. But for people who want to see the proof right away, or for administrators or parent leaders who must consider policy questions first, you may want to begin with Chapter 12, and return to the instructional ideas later.

Improving reading in middle and high school can be a victory for everyone involved, a rare win-win-win deal. To meet the state mandates and pass standardized tests in any subject area, as well as to find personal meaning in a field, young people must be able to read key materials fluently, skillfully, strategically, and critically. To fulfill our entirely reasonable dream that every kid will fall in love with at least one discipline of knowledge, students must encounter each field's most galvanizing, tantalizing, and accessible documents. This means we teachers must do more than just "assign" reading, and we must help our students venture well beyond the textbook. But what an energetic and hopeful adventure this can be, with payoffs for all: for schools, to show the public what their students can do; for the kids, to lock in lifelong reading skills and maybe find a passion; and, for us teachers, to realize that vision we always dream of—"the light going on"—in lots of kids' heads, and maybe hooking a few of them on the ideas that changed our own lives. Sound good? Let's get to work.

Notes

Allington, Richard. 2002. *Big Brother and the National Reading Curriculum: How Ideology Trumped Evidence.* Portsmouth, NH: Heinemann.

Allington, Richard. 2000. *What Really Matters for Struggling Readers: Designing Research-Based Programs.* Portsmouth, NH: Heinemann.

Bracey, Gerald. 2001. *The War Against America's Public Schools: Privatizing Schools, Commercializing Education.* New York, NY: Pearson, Allyn & Bacon.

Daniels, Harvey, Marilyn Bizar, and Steven Zemelman. 2001. *Rethinking High School: Best Practice in Teaching, Learning, and Leadership.* Portsmouth, NH: Heinemann.

Harvey, Stephanie. 2000. *Strategies That Work: Teaching Comprehension to Enhance Understanding.* York, ME: Stenhouse.

Henriksson, Anders. 2001. *Non Campus Mentis: World History According to College Students.* New York, NY: Workman.

National Assessment of Educational Progress, the Nation's Report Card http://nces.ed.gov/nationsreportcard/. Accessed August 25, 2003.

Ravitch, Diane and Chester E. Finn. 1989. *What Do Our 17-Year-Olds Know? A Report on the First National Assessment of History and Literature.* New York, NY: Harper-Collins.

Schlosser, Eric. 2001. *Fast Food Nation: The Dark Side of the All-American Meal.* New York, NY: Harper-Collins.

Third International Mathematics and Science Study. 1999. http://nces.ed.gov/timss/results.asp. Accessed August 25, 2003.

Zimmerman, Susan and Ellin Keene. 1997. *Mosaic of Thought: Teaching Comprehension in a Reader's Workshop.* Portsmouth, NH: Heinemann.

CHAPTER TWO
How Smart Readers Think

We often complain that students "can't read" (or *won't* read) the materials in our subject areas. And indeed, if flunked quizzes, unfinished homework, and low test scores prove anything, then we have plenty to worry about. And we do worry. Sometimes in the faculty lounge, agonizing about this problem, when we hit a really low moment, we'll cast aspersions down upon our colleagues in the lower grades: "Weren't they supposed to learn to read in elementary school?" we'll wonder.

To figure out what skills our students are missing, let's look at ourselves as skillful, experienced, mature readers. Now, don't give us that "aw, shucks, not me" stuff, apologizing because you haven't read a novel in 10 years or guiltily copping to your T.V. habit. Let's give ourselves some credit. We are grownups who have done tons of reading in our lives, inside and outside of school. We've successfully digested enough written material to earn at least a bachelor's degree, maybe even a master's. Every day we deal with reams of text: the morning paper (if we have time), memos from the principal or the department chair, the textbook and all the supplementary materials we use in class, students' work, magazine or journal articles—it really adds up when you inventory everything. So it's true: teachers have print-heavy jobs, and we do know a lot about reading, understanding, and remembering a wide variety of written material, whether we're highly conscious of it or not.

So, please read the following text:

> The Batsmen were merciless against the Bowlers. The Bowlers placed their men in slips and covers. But to no avail. The Batsmen hit one four after another along with an occasional six. Not once did their balls hit their stumps or get caught.

O.K., that was a trick, sorry. But we think you might have just learned a few things about yourself as a reader. What did you notice about your own thinking process? How was your comprehension? Your attitudes or feelings? Many teachers with whom we have read this passage "live" have found it to be difficult in some ways, and a somewhat irritating experience as well. We certainly don't want to irritate you, so here's some help: it's about cricket. You know, that goofy sport that the British are so obsessed with? Now, go back and read the passage again.

Makes a little more sense now, right? And since no reading exercise would be complete without a quiz, it's time for the questions-at-the-end-of-the-chapter. Please answer:

1. Who were merciless against the Bowlers?
2. Where did the Bowlers place their men?
3. Was this strategy successful?
4. Who hit an occasional six?
5. How many times did the Batsmen's balls hit a stump?

See, you got 100%! Congratulations! What? You say you didn't *really* understand it? Hmmm. Now we're starting to see content-area reading from a kids-eye view: how students can read every word on a page without deep understanding; how they can sometimes pass tests on concepts they don't really grasp; how they can go through a whole book or a unit, and end up with no long-term memory of what they have studied at all.

Reading Lessons

How can our own reading of the cricket passage help us as teachers of math, science, art, English, or history? We know that much of the knowledge in our subject fields is stored in print, and we urgently want that material to be open, available, readable for our students. So exactly what do we need to know about the mental process called *reading* to help students access our content?

☞ **Reading is more than "decoding."** In the cricket passage, were there any letters that you couldn't sound out? Any words you had never seen before? Probably not. Whatever makes this passage hard to read goes way beyond phonics, phonemics, or decoding skills. This is important to remember, especially these days, when there is a national frenzy over phonics in elementary schools, and a tendency for that obsession to creep up through the grades. Sometimes, middle and high school teachers wonder if kids who struggle with a textbook or novel might be suffering from a lack of phonics. But "phonics" just means the sound-symbol correspondence between spoken and printed language. Beginning readers learn which letters in English can make each of the 40 sounds used in the spoken language. This task is supposed to be completed by the end of second grade, and for the great majority of American kids, it is. True, a small fraction of students (no more than 5% nationally) manage to arrive in middle school or even high school with lingering decoding problems, and those few kids should have long since been identified for services from the special education department. In other words, if large numbers of our older students are having trouble reading content-area texts, it is not because they were shorted on phonics in elementary school and now can't "sound the words out"—any more than your problems with the cricket passage two minutes ago were phonetic in origin.

☞ **Reading is an active, constructive process.** If this chapter's "test passage" had been a paragraph about teaching teenagers in America, instead of about cricket, you might have sailed through it without stopping, with genuinely high comprehension, and with no particular awareness of your reading process. Sometimes we call such smooth, unobstructed reading "clicking," meaning that you are just clicking along through the text. So instead, to make your reading process more conscious and visible, we assigned you a "hard" passage, one that for most Americans has more clunk than click.

As you were trying to read the cricket piece, you could probably *feel* yourself thinking—maybe even struggling or battling for meaning. Instead of clicking, you were clunking, getting this visceral sense of "I don't get it." If you're like us, the first clunk came pretty early and many more followed. And your reading process probably became more conscious—or at least your feelings about it did. You can look back on it now, remembering the stops and starts, the moves you made, the tricks you tried to get the passage to make sense. You may have found yourself trying to picture what was going on, re-reading to clarify meaning, making educated guesses (maybe it's about a game), comparing to your own experience (is it like baseball?), looking for word roots or alternate meanings (maybe the slips aren't underwear), posing questions (what's a cover?), and more.

All these mental acrobatics remind us that readers actively build and construct meaning from a text. The meaning does not simply reside on the page, ready to be understood whole, nor is it a message simply "sent" by an author and "received" by reader. The "message," if you think about it, is merely patterns of ink on a page. These squiggles have to be built into meaningful concepts by the mind of a hard-working reader.

☞ **Good readers have a repertoire of thinking strategies they use to comprehend texts.** Those tricks you used, trying to make sense of the cricket text, weren't random and they weren't spontaneous. You were actually drawing from a set of specific thinking skills that you have developed and used through your life as a reader. There are many ways to label these strategies (Harvey 2000; Zimmerman and Keene 1997) and no one set of terms is authoritative. The following box shows our own list.

Thinking Strategies of Effective Readers

☞ **visualize** (make mental pictures or sensory images)

☞ **connect** (connect to own experience, to events in the world, to other readings)

☞ **question** (to actively wonder, to surface uncertainties, to interrogate the text)

☞ **infer** (to predict, hypothesize, interpret, draw conclusions)

☞ **evaluate** (to determine importance, make judgments)

☞ **analyze** (to notice text structures, author's craft, vocabulary, purpose, theme, point of view)

☞ **recall** (to retell, summarize, remember information)

☞ **self-monitor** (to recognize and act on confusion, uncertainly, attention problems)

Do these feel real to you? Are you aware of having used one or more of these mental tools while trying to crack the cricket passage? Maybe, because the passage forced you to work extra hard at comprehending, you were aware of this thinking.

But based on the bulk of your reading experience, you might doubt that these cognitive choices actually exist in your head. "That's not how it feels to me," you might say. "Usually, I don't use all those different strategies. When some printed material comes into my life, I just read it." Fair enough. In fact, that's how reading does work, much of the time. As a mature reader, your mental strategies have become mainly automatic and unconscious. Have you ever noticed how you can drive your car across town to a friend's house, day-dream all the way, and still arrive at your destination without much conscious attention to the steering wheel, brake pedal, turn signal, or rear-view mirror? To survive and arrive, you had to constantly monitor the movements of other cars behind, beside, and ahead of you; calculate stopping distances; time merges onto the busy expressway. While at the wheel, you are simultaneously dealing with issues of time, space, physics, and potentially, life and death— and all the while, you're wondering who's bringing the guacamole. The same happens with reading: you can "drive" through some text without explicit selfawareness, especially when the topic is as familiar as the directions to your friend's house. But this doesn't mean that, driving or reading, you aren't really thinking. In both cases, you are using complex cognitive strategies, very actively and creatively at the unconscious level.

However, if you're heading off to visit a *new* acquaintance, in a new neighborhood, then your awareness is elevated. Maybe you study the map or directions first. You have to watch closely, questioning the street signs to make sure you don't miss any crucial turns. You're noticing the stores and subdivisions and comparing them in your head with the sort of area you visualized your new friend living in. You're watching the odometer and inferring how much farther you need to go before the next landmark. If you do get lost, you start looking for someone to ask for help (unless you are a male). And if you have been driving someone else's car, an unfamiliar vehicle where you don't know how the pedals and switches and mirrors work, then you have had to pay extra-conscious attention to every stop, turn, merge, and acceleration. Now this is likely what your students are consciously doing as they navigate the unfamiliar territory of the textbook.

But back to our reading passage. Even though we know the text is about cricket, and we have deployed a pretty sophisticated array of comprehension tools to open it up (consciously or unconsciously), we still don't really understand what it says. And look out! Here comes some more:

> Inverarity viciously pulled Brown into the gully but was sent retiring to the pavilion by a shooter from Cox. Jones in slips and Chappel at silly mid on were superb, and Daniel bowled a maiden over in his first spell. Yallop took his toll with three towering sixes but Thompson had little to do in the covers. Grant was dismissed with a beautiful yorker and Jones went from a brute of a ball. . . .

Whew. This must be how students feel with our textbooks, running their eyes over every word but just not getting it, dutifully "doing the reading," but not making satisfactory meaning. What else is missing?

☞ **Prior knowledge is the main determinant of comprehension.** To look deeper into what makes content-area reading hard, let's use a couple more passages. Try this one first:

> With hocked gems financing him, our hero bravely defied all scornful laughter that tried to prevent his scheme. "Your eyes deceived" he had said. "An egg not a table correctly typifies this unexplored planet." Now three sturdy sisters sought proof. Forging along sometimes through calm vastness, yet more often over turbulent peaks and valleys. Days became weeks as many doubters spread fearful rumors

about the edge. At last from somewhere, welcomed winged creatures appeared signifying momentus success.

Probably another puzzler for many of us. It has some familiar problems too, like common words that don't make sense. But now reread the passage using this one clue: Columbus.

Now it clicks just fine, right? That's because you have ample prior knowledge about Columbus and his explorations. When you were reading the passage for the second time, you were using the fund of information in your head about Columbus. Your prior knowledge did not need to be complete or perfectly authoritative to help you read. Indeed, your prior knowledge might even include some ideas that are not correct (Columbus captained the *Pinta*) notions that others might dispute (Columbus was humane to the native peoples he met), or just plain misconceptions (Columbus sailed the ocean blue in 1482).

But you have more in your head than just a bunch of prior knowledge. Notice that a one-word clue opened up the whole passage for you, giving the key to a dozen terms that, a minute earlier, were deeply mysterious. What that key actually opened was your *schema* for Christopher Columbus. Cognitive researchers have found that we human beings store our knowledge in mental patterns called *schemata* (don't worry, we don't have to explain this to the students). It helps to think of a schema as a web that stores and connects all the information in your mind related to a given topic. You have a schema in your head for your mother, one for hospitals, another for football, for weddings, for rivers, and for Star Wars movies. Most of us adult Americans have a schema for Columbus, which both contains and interconnects all the bits and pieces of information we have about the explorer: words, pictures, stories, maps, images, readings, attitudes, and feelings.

So what just happened was that we helped you "switch on" your schema for Columbus, which allowed you to comprehend the passage. It turned out that all the information you needed to read that passage was right in your head, but until the right schema was activated, you "couldn't read" the passage. The same happens with students at times: approaching any given reading, they may actually have some good prior knowledge to build on, a usable schema to attach information to, **but they don't activate it**—with the result that they do not understand or remember the material. That's why this book later describes many specific ways of activating kids' prior knowledge and switching on their related schemata, so they can take in new information, remember, and understand. We need to give kids the "Columbus key" so they can read in all our content areas.

But the definition of reading is really shifting now. The ability to get meaning from print is dependent on what we already know. Those same brain scientists believe that the only way we can learn new information is by attaching it, connecting it, and integrating it with information we already have. You have to assimilate the information into an existing schema or revise an old one to make the new stuff fit. Either way, you have to work with what is already in the mind; you can't build on nothing.

Build on nothing? Hey, that's what I do every day in my classroom. My students *don't know* algebra (history, chemistry, British literature)—that's why they're here! Do these kids have any schemata for federalism or the conservation of matter? Doesn't look like it to me. They're enrolled in my courses, for crying out loud, because they don't know this stuff.

O.K. Let's take that description of our students' predicament seriously. How can you read stuff if you don't know something about it already? How do you operate (as our students often must) when the content is largely unfamiliar, and it's not easy to connect with things you already know? Let's shed some light on this with one last (we promise!) reading experiment.

The following paragraph was written by a well-known biochemist to describe one of his research interests, and posted on his university website:

MS$_2$ **Phage Coat Protein–RNA Interaction** This system is being studied for several reasons: (1) it is an example of a sequence-specific RNA-protein interaction, (2) it participates in a well-behaved in vitro capsid assembly reaction, and (3) it is a good model system to study how protein finds a target on a large RNA molecule. Available are an X-ray crystal structure of the RNA-protein complex and an NMR structure of the free RNA hairpin target. Current efforts focus on understanding how the thermodynamic details of sequence-specific "recognition" is achieved. We have made mutations in all the amino acids believed to make contact with the RNA and are evaluating the affinity of the mutant proteins to the normal RNA target as well as to targets that have single atom changes in either the bases or the phosphodiester backbone. It is already clear that nearly all the contacts predicted by the co-crystal structure contribute to the total free energy of binding. Thus, unlike several protein-protein interfaces that have been analyzed in a similar way, there are no "hot spots" that dominate the affinity. However, we have several examples where affinity and specificity are defined by structural elements of the RNA in its free form. (Uhlenbeck, "Research Interests")

Hey, could you science teachers please explain this to the rest of us? We used all of our sophisticated adult reading strategies on this passage—we questioned, we inferred, we analyzed like crazy, we even visualized some dancing double helices—but we still don't understand what this research is about. Maybe *your* capsid assembly reactions are well-behaved, but ours are acting like morons! Perhaps we just don't have the phosphodiester backbone for reading as tough as this.

All biochemical jokes aside, what makes this passage hard to read is the **content**. We're not lost in Professor Uhlenbeck's paragraph because some hapless elementary teacher forgot to teach us a dipthong 20 years ago. The problem is, it's too damn hard. "Hard," meaning we don't have enough background knowledge—a good enough schema of this discipline—to build much meaning upon. There's no "Columbus key" to this passage for most of us, is there? Would it have helped if we gave you the clue "RNA research" for this passage? Probably not much, since, except for biochemists, that clue would not switch on a large enough web of pre-existing information in our heads, the way it did before.

We need more help. We need someone to get us ready for readings like this by giving us an overview, telling us beforehand what some of the words mean, drawing us a picture, showing us a model, giving us explanations—or maybe, taking us much further back, to the "basics" of this field. So, perhaps this underscores our belief that having kids read mostly text like this is an incomplete experience, or even a wrong approach to our subject fields. Once again, that is what the rest of this book will try to do: show you how, with textbooks and novels, with lab reports and census tracts, to build up to the more challenging material in your field. Soon, you'll be guiding your students to seek out the larger concepts that underlie the technical details, to find connections with examples they do understand, to actively search for related readings more at their level of knowledge that will begin to bridge the gap, and to feel confident and curious enough to pursue such inquiry.

☞ **Reading is a staged and recursive process.** Take a quick look back at the MS_2 passage again, and see if you can remember how you worked your way through it even if you didn't understand it fully. What steps did you take, first, second, third, and so on after that? Your thinking steps may be hard to reconstruct (especially in sequence) because so much of it was unconscious. But we'll venture that you can identify some things you did before, during, and after reading. Before you hit the text, we purposely gave you an introduction about Dr. Uhlenberg and his research, hoping to get you thinking, searching for prior knowledge, and hunting for the right schema to activate. On your own, you might have scanned the title and started digging deeper for background information on RNA—or maybe you started preparing yourself mentally: "Oh-oh, this is gonna be really technical science stuff." Then, as you worked your way into the passage itself, clicking and clunking along, you might have noticed yourself stopping, maybe going back and re-reading, and so on. While your schema for DNA research may be very rickety and full of holes and blank spots, you probably started building on whatever scraps you *do* have (unless you simply gave up!). You may have read at some time in the past about how DNA and RNA molecules are long sequences of amino acids that work like letters in a code, and now seeing the words "sequence-specific recognition" and "target," you started making some dim guesses, whether right or wrong, about using certain chemicals to locate a significant spot on the RNA molecule. Later, if your biochemistry teacher clarified it all, you'd recall these guesses and either congratulate yourself for being smarter than you thought, or replace your mistaken surmise with something better—"Oh, now I get it!"

We could walk you through all the stages—right up to the after-reading part, but you'd probably end up cursing us and our cutesy little reading tests. The point is: There are activities that skillful readers typically engage in *before* they start reading, other things they do *while* reading, and still other things they do *after* they have read a passage, all focused on the process of using, expanding, or altering what they know to make sense of new information. They do everything every time, but as we have learned, much of it is done unconsciously. Plus, just to make things extra complicated, smart readers don't just go through these activities in 1–2–3 order, but hop back and forth between stages, especially when the reading is complex or unfamiliar. You might have noticed this recursiveness in your own reading just now. If we want to put this staged model of reading in a simple linear order, the sequence of tasks might look like those shown in the box on the next page.

There are many reading-process diagrams like this one, and until we have traced all the participating neurons, no one version will be deemed "correct." But all the models shed a pretty dramatic light on the customary "read this for Friday" approach to reading in middle and high school. If the real task of reading, of making meaning from content-area texts, involves a complex series of cognitive operations like those listed in the box, it's no wonder that kids are often adrift. Inadvertently, we may be leaving them alone with many more jobs to do than we realized—and with much less support than they need.

All through this chapter we have been using ourselves—grownup school teachers—as a handy example of how mature readers develop. But we now have to warn that there are limits to the generalizability of our experience.

Stages of Reading

Before Reading

    Set purposes for reading

    Activate prior knowledge

    Develop questions

    Make predictions

During Reading

    Sample text

    Visualize

    Hypothesize

    Confirm/Alter predictions

    Monitor comprehension

After Reading

    Recall/Retell

    Evaluate

    Discuss

    Reread

    Apply

    Read more

After all, as people who chose careers in education, we are not exactly "normal." That's not a slam—just a reminder that we were probably pretty successful students in school. We might have been better-than-average readers and students from the beginning, perhaps starting off with some out-of-school advantages (parents who read, or books in our homes, or a burning interest in a subject ignited at an early age). If we had struggled terribly with reading, and failed in school as a result, we probably wouldn't have elected to spend our whole working lives there.

But we stayed—and as adult teachers, we command an amazing array of mental processes. Look at all we can do: We can use our phonics skills. We can predict, activate our prior knowledge, sample, reread, and confirm. We can generate and revise hypotheses. We can monitor our own reading process and try a variety of ways to construct meaning. We can tap into a large repertoire of cognitive strategies—visualizing, questioning, connecting, analyzing, evaluating. We can work in a staged and stepwise manner. For crying out loud, we even have thousands of interlocking schemata in our heads that we can activate at will. Who knew?

For many educators (most definitely including ourselves), these operations were never explicitly named or taught in our own schooling. Instead, we cobbled together our inventory of reading/thinking skills from a mix of inconsistent school instruction and a lot of real-life trial-and-error experience. And we certainly didn't finish acquiring all these self-taught reading powers back in elementary school—we were still working on them in middle and high school. In fact, we recognize that our reading skills were honed in college and into adult life—and are still growing today.

But now, as we gaze out into our classrooms, we are **not** facing rows and rows of future teachers sitting there; they are not ranks of little us-es eagerly looking forward to a life of book work. Instead, we face a normal distribution of kids for whom neither reading nor school necessarily comes easy. So, yes, whatever subject we teach, we do need to understand reading a little better, including what makes it so hard for kids when they step into our disciplines and try to read our subject matter without some of the advantages and predilections that we enjoyed.

What Does It Mean for Our Teaching?

If we understand that reading is not just "receiving a message," but actively building meaning upon prior knowledge using staged, strategic thinking, then we will teach differently. Instead of saying "Read this for Friday" and popping out a quiz on the appointed day, we will first provide pre-reading activities that help kids activate their thinking, get ready for new vocabulary, and start making predictions about the text. Knowing that prior knowledge is the strongest determinant of understanding, and that new knowledge can only be built upon existing knowledge, we know better where to begin—with students' conceptions and misconceptions about our subject, whatever they are, and with connections to ideas that the kids *do* know about within their own experience. We will work harder to activate, develop, build upon, shape, and add to our students' prior knowledge.

While students are reading, we will provide them with tools and activities that help them question, interpret, harvest their responses as they go, using us and their classmates to clarify ideas. And after students have read, we will talk over ideas to clarify, confirm, and deepen understanding. Maybe we'll even *transmediate,* which means moving ideas from one domain of expression (writing) into another (drawing, drama, dance), to ensure deep comprehension.

In short: understanding what we do now, we will *teach* reading, not just assign it, though that doesn't mean we are turning into reading teachers. We are specialists—science, math, history, art, music, foreign language people—to the bone. The difference is, we'll break the work up into steps for kids, and provide help along the way. We'll be using methods, tools, activities, and procedures that help our students understand and remember our content better—and maybe even, dare we hope, get interested in it. Which is right back where we started.

So what do we tell the children? Let's keep most of this to ourselves, O.K.? Middle- and high-school students do not need to know all this reading terminology, cognition, and research. They can pursue schema theory in a college psychology course someday, if they want. For now, there are only a couple of elements we need to name, teach, and use explicitly in class. One is the list of thinking strategies on page 24. Students do need to know, consciously, that smart readers use a variety of different cognitive lenses to spot the meaning in tough texts. And later, in Chapter 5, we'll introduce a family of specific reading activities—things like "written conversation," "KWL," and "It Says/I Say"—that everyone in the classroom should know how to operate. If teachers and kids share this modest vocabulary, these few key concepts, you can start to build a strong, energetic, high-performing community of readers in any subject, and across a school.

Notes

Harvey, Stephanie and Anne Goudvis. 2000. *Strategies That Work: Teaching Comprehension to Enhance Understanding.* York, ME: Stenhouse.

Uhlenbeck, Olke. "Research Interests." Interdepartmental Biological Sciences, Northwestern University. http://www.biochem.northwestern.edu/ibis/faculty/uhlenbeck.htm. Accessed August 25, 2003.

Zimmerman, Susan and Ellin Keene. 1997. *Mosaic of Thought: Teaching Comprehension in a Reader's Workshop.* Portsmouth, NH: Heinemann.

CHAPTER THREE
Why Textbooks Are Not Enough

Next week, Jane Woodbury starts as a freshman at Walloon Lake High School. So this morning, following the instructions in a letter sent home to families, Jane and her mother have appeared at the school bookstore with an empty backpack. After enduring a short wait in line—and after Mom writes a large check—Jane's bag is stuffed with thick, glossy textbooks. As a set, they are stunningly heavy, more than 30 pounds.

Jane has been issued one textbook for each subject, along with some accompanying workbooks, a lab manual for science, and a couple of paperback novels for English class. The big textbooks are jammed with facts, lists, charts, information, photographs, places, dates, formulas, problems, sidebars, study questions and more study questions, and if you drop one, each weighs enough to break your foot. This is not an exaggeration. According to the TIMSS international comparison of mathematics and science education, American students have the heaviest and thickest textbooks in the world. Our textbooks have become so weighty, in fact, that the American Academy of Orthopedic Surgeons has issued a warning about the rising incidence of injuries among young people toting an ever-heavier burden of textbooks in their backpacks (2001).

Jane's experience is repeated all across the country, in public schools and private, in poor and rich neighborhoods. In a profound sense, textbooks **are** school. In the secondary grades, "reading" usually means reading a textbook. In some states, the predominance of textbooks among instructional materials is even enshrined in law. Many states have special "adoption commissions" that approve or ban the purchase of specific textbooks. Until recently in Illinois, it was actually illegal to spend state book money on anything but commercially published school textbooks—no state funds could be spent on novels or trade nonfiction books. Charles Dickens, Stephen Hawking, and Steven Ambrose need not apply in the Land of Lincoln.

So why do textbooks hold this seemingly unassailable place in classroom practice—and in school budgets? What exactly are the benefits and shortcomings of these ubiquitous and potentially injurious objects? What are kids risking their backs for?

The Central Role of Textbooks

If you are reading this page, you probably use a textbook in your classes every day. When you teach math, or Spanish, or earth science, or almost anything else in a secondary school, textbooks are a basic part of life. And for many teachers, the content-area textbook is a treasured asset. The book may be one that you helped select, after an extensive search process—reviewing all the competition, making a thoughtful match-up with your local curriculum, and (if you served on the adoption committee) even lobbying for this book over others. The textbook may have become a trusted companion over the years, traveling with you through your career. By now, you know its chapters, charts, diagrams, photographs, and study questions backwards and forwards. You may even have seen the book evolve through several editions, and once in a while (if you are as shallow as we are) you may have enviously fantasized about the royalty checks piling up in the authors' mailboxes.

On the other hand, the textbook used in your classes may be less of a choice and more of an imposition. The book may have been selected by others, as a departmental or district adoption that you had no voice in, or that was already picked when you joined the faculty. Maybe this particular text doesn't suit your teaching style, or your way of approaching the field, or your idea of what's really important. Perhaps the book has flaws, gaps, and problems that drive you nuts. Maybe it skimps on information in a key area, or introduces vocabulary too fast, or is just plain out of date. It might be somebody else's favorite—but not yours. In fact, if you think about it, none of us ever finds the absolutely perfect textbook, even when we pick it ourselves.

How you use your textbook may also be under your control—or it may be tightly constrained. Some teachers are free to "pick and choose" from the textbook, inviting kids to dig deeper into some chapters, while skipping or scanning others. They can dip into the textbook occasionally, use it mainly as a reference book, or even make it a supplement to other materials and activities. Other teachers are more locked into the textbook, perhaps because they love it, or because they lack any other materials to choose from. Still others may be trapped by coverage mandates, enforced by departmental or district-wide end-of-semester examinations. Some teachers are even required to keep their students on the same textbook page—literally, not metaphorically—with other students in the same course, or even in schools across the district.

Somewhat ironically, English teachers are less likely to have a single textbook play such a central role in their classes. While they may use a literature anthology or a skills textbook part of the time, language arts teachers often assign students separate novels, plays, or poetry. This may reflect a fundamental difference between fields. Yes, language arts does have *some* content: a canon of literature, the techniques of literary craft, grammar, and the conventions of language use. But most English instruction is focused on processes (reading, writing, speaking, and listening) rather than a hierarchical body of knowledge. The English curriculum is more of a spiral than a pyramid; kids practice the same basic processes year after year, at (we hope) increasingly sophisticated levels. But in highly structured fields like math or science, you must know arithmetic before you can do algebra; you must know some biology before you can understand genetics. Those bodies of knowledge, those big building-blocks of information, need a place to live—and that's what textbooks are for, among other things.

So, love 'em or hate 'em, textbooks are a very big part of our reality in middle and high school. They may not be perfect, they may not be the books we would choose, they may require all sorts of supplementing, working-around, and clarifying. But they are here to stay. Yes, a few publishing companies and authors are experimenting with Web-based materials. But those hefty, shiny textbooks will probably continue to be the main storage system for the content of our courses for a long time to come.

We think it is important for teachers to look at contemporary textbooks with a critical eye—and we'll start doing just that in a minute. But the goal of such scrutiny is not to kick educational publishers in their well-bruised shins. What we want to figure out is: how can we teach our content better, so that students learn, remember, and care about our subjects? How can we use textbooks properly and effectively so kids get the most out of them? Chapter 5 of this book (with the gray-tipped edges) is filled with 24 practical activities for helping students understand their textbooks (or any other kind of written material they might encounter in your courses). We didn't include any strategy there unless it had proven effective with all sorts of reading materials, including textbooks. Then further on, in Chapter 6, we offer six more ideas specifically for using textbooks successfully in all subject areas, throughout the year.

The Trouble with Textbooks

We strongly believe that textbooks are overused, and should be supplemented generously or replaced with other reading materials where possible. But before we make the case, we want to be clear: some textbooks are better than others. Way better. Some are severely afflicted by all the problems we are about to describe, while others suffer from just a few. Some defects are specific to individual books, while others are endemic to the species—built into their DNA. So, if you do use a textbook, it is very much worth the trouble to adopt the best one available. Perhaps after you have read what follows, you will have some new criteria to choose by.

Now as we work through our critique, we're mindful that your state probably has a set of standards requiring you to cover 80,000 tons of material, all of which are conveniently included in that big commercial textbook. We've met the textbook reps, too, and they talk a great game. They'll show you a list (a concordance, almost) detailing exactly how their product matches, standard by standard, with all those state requirements and their accompanying tests. Still, this doesn't prove that this salesperson's book will actually teach your content better than another textbook, or, for that matter, that a completely different set of readings, materials, and experiences might meet the standards better than any textbook. The big problem is: to pass the statewide test, the kids have to actually remember the material. Can the textbook rep guarantee that?

So here are some reasons why textbooks are not enough to build our whole courses or our whole classroom lives around. We'll start with the biggest, most intractable problems first, and get on to the minor beefs later.

Textbooks Are Superficial

Recently we visited a Chicago high school where we had the opportunity to look through the stack of textbooks assigned to all juniors. Man, they were massive!

> British Literature—1,152 pages
> Biology—1,164 pages
> French—620 pages
> U.S. History—982 pages
> Advanced Algebra/Trigonometry—890 pages

Now, it may seem odd to accuse five-pound textbooks of being superficial. They certainly seem complete; they feel mighty weighty. And they undeniably provide an avalanche of data, a staggering amount of detail. They are jammed with facts, figures, charts, tables, and graphs.

But strange as it seems, these books just scratch the surface, and that's because they contain *too much* material. Often, the really key concepts, the big ideas of the field, don't stand out clearly, aren't given enough time and depth for students to grasp them. Two pages on slavery, a paragraph on Hiroshima, or a sidebar about Einstein's theory of relativity, just doesn't get the job done. According to the American Association for the Advancement of Science,

> Today's textbooks cover too many topics without developing any of them well. Central concepts are not covered in enough depth to give students a chance to truly understand them. While many textbooks present the key ideas described in national and state standards documents, few books help students learn the ideas or help teachers teach them well.(Roseman, Kulm, and Shuttleworth 2003)

In the drive to include everything, key ideas fade into the background, or are never successfully communicated, or simply don't stick with students.

You may have been a victim of this textbook superficiality when you were a student. If the science teachers will play along for just a minute, we can try an experiment. Probably, somewhere in school, you studied a little about plants, including photosynthesis and related topics, right? You might even recall that little formula $C_6 H_{12} O_6$, the key roles of chlorophyll, the phloem cells, the cambium layer, and so forth. O.K.: here's the question. As an acorn grows from a slender seedling into a 50-foot oak, where does all that mass come from? Think of yourself hefting even a small log cut from such an enormous life form. Where did all that stuff come from?

If your education depended too much on textbooks, you might have answered that all that mass came from nutrients in the ground, or from sunlight, or from water drawn up through the tree's roots. In fact, the great majority of the grown-up oak tree's mass came from the **air**. Remember, trees take in air, extract the CO_2, give off oxygen, and break down the CO_2 to make carbon, the building block of life. And CO_2, like all gasses, no matter how invisible, has mass—plenty of it—which is conserved even when it is changed by chemical processes.

If you got this wrong, don't feel too bad. A team of researchers from the Harvard–Smithsonian Astrophysical Observatory filmed both fourth graders and seniors at MIT trying to answer the same question (Budiansky 2001). Most of the students, both the 21-year-old engineers and the 10-year-olds on the playground, gave similar wrong answers, though both had studied photosynthesis and even knew some of the terminology. This misconception is an example of students (maybe including us) not learning the big, key ideas in a field even while being bombarded by masses of facts and terminology. In this case, the students never got the basic idea of what matter is, how it can be transformed by chemical reactions, and that it is conserved. This misunderstanding, typical of so many that are spawned by our "coverage" model of curriculum and enshrined in textbooks, has real consequences. How can we expect our future citizens to understand (and maybe even protect) the environment they live in, if they don't know basic scientific principles? How are they going to grasp the important facts like this: driving an average American automobile for a year puts 11,450 *pounds* of invisible but very consequential CO_2 into the atmosphere (Environmental Protection Agency 2003)?

Textbooks Are Exceedingly Hard to Read

Ever wonder why *Algebra II* has never topped *The New York Times* best-seller list? Or why no one ever buys a chemistry textbook and stays up all night reading it straight through? *("I just couldn't put it down!")* Maybe that's because textbooks are reference books, not novels or nonfiction trade books. School textbooks belong in the same category with encyclopedias, dictionaries, and thesauruses. They don't attempt to provide the kind of coherent narrative you get in a *Time* magazine article or a good popular biography or exposé. It is not their primary job to tell you a story, or even pay much attention to your readerly morale. Instead, textbooks are designed to inventory huge amounts of information that can be looked up when needed.

In the field of reading research, school textbooks exemplify what is called "inconsiderate" or "unfriendly" text. They are giant storage systems for information. They are intentionally "content-overloaded" with facts, dates, formulas, and taxonomies. They introduce vocabulary and concepts at a blinding rate. They are overtly structured and highly orderly, packing information into labeled slots, as densely as possible. But looking back on how smart readers actually think in Chapter 2, we realize that just being highly organized does not make a textbook any easier to read than a similarly "well-organized" VCR programming manual.

There is nothing wrong with reference books. Personally, we love them, we use them, we cannot live without them. The problem lies in the way textbooks get used in school. In the civilian world, people use reference books mainly when they have an immediate personal need to find a certain chunk of information—what the Third Amendment really says, how the pancreas works, or how to compute the surface area of a sphere. But in school, we often act as if textbooks were novels that kids should plow right through, from cover to cover, remembering and caring about what they read. We virtually pretend that textbooks aren't reference books at all—but rather some strange hybrid text form: long, fact-packed stories that a person can read day in day out, memorizing with fascination, and passing statewide tests upon completion.

No wonder kids "can't read" their textbooks! We start with the content overload, the inherent readability problems of the genre. Add to this the lack of narrative structures that sustain readers in most real-world nonfiction. Then throw in the expectation that kids should read textbooks cover to cover—and remember everything, even if they are reading other textbooks in three or four different courses. Then there's the strategies problem, which we just described in Chapter 2—our habitual failure to teach kids specific cognitive operations for dealing with text, especially needed for tough-going material like textbooks. Already we have a perfect recipe for ineffective and unpleasant reading experiences—and there are still more problems to consider.

Textbooks Are Badly Designed

In recent years, publishers have worked hard to make textbooks more visually interesting and engaging to students. They are well aware that the look of real-world nonfiction has changed dramatically in recent years—think of the evolution of the weekly news magazines from endless blocks of gray to today's lively columns, graphics, and features. And while some may deride *USA Today* as America's "McPaper," its all-color design, clever boxes, and zippy graphics have been well-received by the public and have changed the standard in newspaper design. Even more urgently, the publishers of school textbooks feel they must compete with the hyper-world of the Internet and video games, where kids live much of their lives. After all, how you gonna keep their noses in the chemistry textbook after they've played *"Grand Theft Auto"*?

The problem is that these postmodern designs mostly don't work. Instead of inviting kids into the material, many of today's textbooks are a graphic maelstrom. As one teacher recently lamented: "The publishers try to make these books attractive to kids, to make them look jazzy and up to date. And I understand, with all the boxes and gimmicks, they are trying to give kids multiple points of entry into the text. They're trying to make it feel like a computer or a video game where the kids feel some control. But those pages end up just being confusing and overwhelming. And it's worst for my struggling readers. They can't make any sense of those pages at all."

The American Association for the Advancement of Science concurs. The AAAS, which counts both working scientists and science educators among its members (and publishes the respected magazine *Science*), has taken the lead in assessing contemporary textbooks. In its recent examination of middle-school science texts, the AAAS found their design to be "hyperkinetic" (Budiansky 2001). Reviewers complained that the text was full of sidebars, boxes, and other presumably eye-catching special features bearing such titles as "Flex Your Brain," "EXPLORE!", "Find Out!", and "Minds On!" which distracted from the content. In the following, AAAS reviewers comment on one book, singled out for being less cluttered than most:

> Like all of the standard texts, (it) throws a welter of concepts and terms at students in confusing order. It brings in atoms on the first few pages with the didactic and, to most students, probably incomprehensible assertion that "matter consists of atoms of various weights that interact in accordance with specific principles." This is followed by an "Activity!" (weighing inflated and deflated balloons) that does make a nod at demonstrating that air is matter. But then come two pages of "Science in Literature," a "Mind On!" exercise ("describe, to an alien who has never seen it before, what ice cream is"), a "Multicultural Perspective" tip for the teacher ("Assist students in locating the Dead Sea on a world map"), and then several more pages of didactic assertions about states of matter. The text flits rapidly from one topic to the next—atoms and electrons and the periodic table and acids and bases—nowhere really even attempting to relate the molecular structure of matter to its observable properties. (Budiansky 2001)

It seems that when textbook publishers try to imitate hypertext, the results are more hyper than text.

Textbooks Are Authoritarian

In many schools and subjects, a single commercial textbook constitutes the entire curriculum. At P.T. Barnum High, the United States History course may simply be *The Americans* by Danzer *et. al* (MacDougal-Littel); the Algebra II class might be nothing but *Advanced Algebra* by Senk *et. al* (Scott, Foresman, Addison-Wesley); the content of Spanish 3 can come exclusively from *Ven Comingo!* by Humback and Ozete (Holt Rinehart and Winston); and so forth. For these courses, there may be no other readings, with the possible exception of a companion workbook (called a "consumable" in the business and prized for its profitability). Then, to make this exclusive franchise official, someone types up the textbook's table of contents and slaps a cover on it emblazoned: "P.T. Barnum High School Curriculum Guide: Spanish 3." Or, more often these days, the textbook sales rep does that copying job, supplying matches between his company's book and every single state standard the school labors under.

For a country espousing democracy as its nominal form of governance, this sanctification of "The Textbook" provides a strangely incongruous apprenticeship. When we rely upon a single source for all of a course's content, we are teaching kids to accept one view, one authority; we are saying that it is right to depend upon a single voice, even on complicated, value-driven questions. This is not the way smart and free people read. Instead, they recognize that most of life's biggest questions have not yet been settled, and that science, technology, and even culture proceed on the "best theory to date," not some Final Truth. That's why mature readers use multiple sources to get a balanced view, to hear the alternate theories, to make up their own minds. Whether it is intentional or not, it is unacceptable for schools in a democracy to teach young people that only one view is permitted—of science, of mathematics, of literature, of history, or any subject.

Textbooks Often Are Inaccurate

Textbook companies work very hard to make sure their products are both timely and accurate. They have teams of factcheckers scrupulously verifying information, and writers constantly creating updated editions every few years, to make sure that new findings, breakthroughs, or emerging theories are included. But it simply is not humanly possible to keep current—or to keep correct.

Recently, we visited the wonderful integrated studies program at Addison Trail High School in suburban Chicago. The students and teachers were in the middle of one of the kids' favorite topics of the year—"The Plagues" unit. The ultimate goal is for each student to select and explore one of the many plagues that could afflict the world, from AIDS to biological and chemical warfare. On the day we visited, science teacher Don Grossnickle started his biology class by saying: "Remember last week how we read in the textbook about the bubonic plague? How it was caused by a bacteria spread by rats and fleas? And we studied that cycle of disease transmission? Well, guess what, guys? It looks like the textbook might be wrong."

Don smiled as the kids looked back curiously. "I thought about keeping this a secret, but I knew I had to tell you." And with that, Don handed out the just-arrived issue of *Science News* (published by the Weekly Reader group) to each student. In an article entitled "The Black Plague: Not a Bacteria After All?" kids read about a recently published book in England which argued, quite convincingly, that the bubonic plague was not a bacteria spread by rats but, in fact, a viral hemorrhagic fever—akin to what we now know as Ebola. A lively discussion ensued about how fast science moves, how long-standing theories can get overturned by a single study, and why, as Don put it, "we can't always rely on a textbook that's three or four years old."

But even when they stay timely, textbooks cannot be factually infallible. The *Science News* (Raloff 2001) reported a study of textbook accuracy conducted by John Hubisz of North Carolina State University in Raleigh. In 12 physical science textbooks, Hubisz and his colleagues catalogued 500 pages of errors. Some were trivial, and others were grave. But, as Hubisz warned, all ran the risk of making science appear confusing or even nonsensical to students. Among the flubs:

- One book said: "Unlike fission, fusion doesn't happen spontaneously." Yet fusion reactions power the sun. The sentence should have been amended with: ". . . at temperatures usually found on Earth."

- This book also stated that the acceleration of gravity on the moon is one-sixth that on Earth because the moon's mass is one-sixth of Earth's. In fact, the moon's mass is roughly one-eightieth of Earth's and the initial statement ignored the fact that the acceleration due to gravity is also related to the radius of a body.

- One book defines some elephant vocal sounds at around 400 hertz—below a frequency perceptible to human ears. However, 400 Hz is about the frequency produced by keys on the middle of a piano.

- One text shows a photo of rubber—with a density of 1.19 grams per cubic centimeter—sinking to the bottom of glycerin, which has a density of 1.26 g/cm^3. As the reviewer points out, "It cannot happen!"

- One passage notes that "sound travels faster through warm air than through cold air." Twelve pages later, the same book notes ". . . but sound travels faster in cold air." You can't have it both ways.

Of course textbooks haven't cornered the market on mistakes, which can be found in any medium. But when teachers depend on a single source of subject-matter authority, the risks (and consequences) of errors rise.

Textbooks Are Not Written for Students

Remember that old expression, "You never want to see either sausages or laws being made?" Well, the same thing applies to textbooks. It is an unsightly assembly line, guaranteed to crush the idealism of the innocent. What is your picture of the process? Maybe the recognized experts in the field sit down around a big seminar table and determine what is the essence of the subject, and how it can best be taught to young people? Maybe they bring some actual students in and talk to them about biology or literature? Nah. There are a lot more people at the table than subject matter experts, and their concerns are not mainly about the sanctity of the field. And students? They may be the end-users of textbooks, but they are not the "market," certainly not the decisionmakers.

Obviously, textbook publishing is a business, and the overriding concern, the consideration that trumps all others, is sales and profits. This is no shock, right? Publishers need to create a product that sells, that beats the competition, that rakes in some cash. And in the dicey market called educational publishing, to have a hit, you must please a wide array of people, groups, and agencies who often disagree with each other.

Publishers claim that teachers consistently ask for textbooks with lots of activity kits, workbooks, black-line masters, videotapes, and supplementary goodies. If that's true, shame on us. Then there are the state education agencies, each of which has its own voluminous set of content standards, enforced with an arsenal of high-stakes tests. From the seller's-eye view, it would be pretty dumb to publish a book that didn't try to include everything that the states have embraced. And since all 50 states have different standards, you better cover yourself by throwing in everything. And then there's the Texas–California problem. Because these two states are both lucrative textbook markets, and because they approve only a few books in each subject and then put up money for the schools to buy them, Texas and California have a vastly disproportionate influence on what goes into all American textbooks. For the major publishers, it is simply not worth the multi-million dollar development expense for a new textbook unless you can go for adoption in Texas and California. So these two states' standards have become our *de facto* national textbook standards.

O.K., so now we are watching textbooks being made, just like sausages, and it's not such a pretty picture. The analogy to the meat-packing houses in *Fast Food Nation* is a little close to the bone (as it were). But in light of the strong criticisms we have laid out so far, it is amazing how thorough and cohesive many textbooks still manage to be, given the intense cross-pressures their makers face. Problematic as most contemporary textbooks are, if we view them as just one source of many from which students can obtain and compare information, and if we provide students with enough background information and some strategies to help them make sense of their reading—then maybe we can use them judiciously, productively, and appropriately.

Textbooks Cost Too Much

It is not uncommon for today's school textbooks to be priced at $50, $70, or more. Take five "solids" and you're looking at a $300 bill. This can cause sticker-shock in communities where parents have to foot the book bill, over and above paying their taxes. And in the city high school where we work, the idea of affording current textbooks is simply a joke. Hey, we just got our federal funds cut by 33%, thanks to the No Child Left Behind Act. We're going to be losing a teacher as a result, not buying any textbooks.

But even so, we wouldn't claim that contemporary textbooks are overpriced; after all, with today's standards of weight, thickness, and color, it would be hard to sell these kind of books for much less. The problem is that buying these $70 textbooks for every kid gobbles up the whole instructional materials budget, and squeezes out the possibility of buying anything else. How can we pay for *Fast Food Nation,* subscribe to the newspaper, sign up for *Science News,* or build classroom libraries, when all the dough goes for textbooks?

So What Can We Do?

To free up some money for supplementary materials, one solution is to switch from one textbook per student (which might mean buying 150 copies) to one classroom set (more like 30 copies). This has the wholesome side effect that since the kids now cannot take the textbooks home, you'll get a chance to experiment with more engaging homework assignments. Another tactic is to delay adopting a new text as long as possible, pushing that big expense as far down the road as you responsibly can. This depends on the subject area, of course. At BPHS, our juniors have been getting along just fine with a 1989 textbook in British literature, a field where revolutionary breakthroughs are rare and owning the latest "revised edition" seems less urgent.

If you must buy a textbook, think seriously about foreswearing the extras, goodies, and dealer-installed upgrades. Chances are you can live without the high-profit transparencies, handouts, posters, videos, CD-ROMs, audiotapes, activity cards, and banks of test questions. Jo Ellen Roseman of AAAS's Project 2061 says, "Our reviewers went through all of this material and can say authoritatively: It's not worth it" (2003). We agree.

And, if you're feeling really adventurous, you could stop having textbook-centered courses altogether, for a few weeks or months at a time. That's what we are moving toward at our school, in different degrees for different subjects. Last Friday, we saw Matt Feldman, the senior English teacher, working the one non-broken risograph (a Chicago-style word for copying machine) really hard. He was creating a collection of poems for his afternoon class, but between the machine jamming, and the people waiting impatiently behind him, Matt was getting frustrated. "Now I get it!" he blurted out. "This is why people have textbooks, so they don't have to go through this #!*%$."

But when we looked at Matt's handmade collection, we realized how good it was that there is no senior English textbook at BPHS. From the Library of Congress website and a few other selected sources, Matt had created a gorgeous and distinctive set of poems, all by and about African Americans, perfectly suited to his class, matched to their age and experience, attuned to their previous literary diet, aimed at their interests, today. No textbook could ever do that. Now, that's what we call *teaching*.

No, our faculty at BPHS does not spend the whole year risographing supplementary materials and reading trade books. We have mandates too, subjects to teach and tests to pass. But when we use the textbooks now, we use them much more strategically and sparingly. We focus in on smaller sections of text, taking time (and other materials) to highlight and flesh out the most important concepts. We teach kids specific strategies (to be described in Chapters 5 and 6) that involve them in thinking about, discussing, critiquing, and applying the ideas they've read. We show them how to monitor their understanding and actively seek help and clarification when they are confused or lost. We do the good teaching it takes to convert a passive review-and-quiz approach to richer, more engaging experiences that students will remember and maybe even enjoy.

―

Perhaps now it is clearer than ever why we must change not just **how** we teach reading, but **what** we ask kids to read. We need to use textbooks more appropriately (and sparingly), as the reference books that they are, and also infuse the curriculum with authentic, real-world nonfiction—the kind of informational, expository, persuasive texts that adults really read. Luckily, textbooks are just the foam on the ocean of nonfiction. The world is full of fascinating, important, debatable, and sometimes inflammatory nonfiction, from partisan magazines to primary source materials to revisionist histories—for readers of all ages. Let's take a look.

Notes

American Academy of Orthopedic Surgeons. 2001. "Kids and Backpacks." http://orthoinfo.aaos.org/fact/thr_report.cfm?Thread_ID=105&topcategory=Spine. August. Accessed August 25, 2003.

Budiansky, Stephen. 2001. "The Trouble with Textbooks," *Prism: Journal of the American Society of Engineering Education,* February.

Environmental Protection Agency. 2003. "Clean Energy." http://www.epa.gov/cleanenergy/morefacts.htm. Accessed August 24, 2003.

Raloff, Janet. 2001. "Errant Texts: Why Some Schools May Not Want to Go By the Book," *Science News,* Vol. 159, No. 11, p. 6.

Roseman, Jo Ellen, Gerald Kulm, and Susan Shuttleworth. 2003. "Putting Textbooks to the Test," Project 2061: American Association for the Advancement of Science. http://www.project2061.org/research/articles/enc.htm. Accessed August 24, 2003.

CHAPTER FOUR
Toward a Balanced Diet of Reading

We've argued that teachers should use textbooks more sparingly, more carefully, and with explicit scaffolding strategies—which we'll detail in Chapters 5 and 6. But the corollary recommendation is that young people should be reading content material *in other genres:* newspaper articles, magazines, research reports, websites, primary sources, biographies, and full-length trade nonfiction books. But why? What is to be found in the wider world of reading that students are missing when they only read textbooks? Why is it so urgent that we change their reading diets? Here is an example of how "real" nonfiction text can be a valuable addition the curriculum.

Let's talk about Einstein. A typical physics textbook might give between a paragraph and a page to his world-changing equation, $E = MC^2$. So we can say that the concept is "covered" in school. The trouble is, if you go out on Main Street America today and ask 100 textbook-educated high school graduates what each symbol in Einstein's equation means, 99 of them will not be able to tell you. And the knowledge gap does not just afflict the *recent* alumni. Between us two, Harvey fell into the "normal" 99%, while Steve, who majored in physics (no fair!) knew the right answer. Now, if you further inquire of your random citizens what the equation actually *means* in daily life, most cannot say much at all. Sometimes people, shown the equation, just shrug their shoulders and say "Boom!" This is not what we could properly call "deep understanding."

The noted science writer David Bodanis was worried about this ignorance of Einstein's equation as well. "There are plenty of books that try to explain it," he says, "but who can honestly say they understand them?" So Bodanis took a distinctly non-textbook approach in his book $E = MC^2$, *A Biography of the World's Most Famous Equation.* "Everyone knows that a biography entails stories of the ancestors, childhood, adolescence, and adulthood of your subject," he reasoned. So Bodanis takes each symbol in the equation, one at a time, and tells the story of the people who developed the big idea from its infancy. Believe it or not, his book is a page-turner, a stay-up-all-night-and-finish-it yarn. It takes 113 pages to complete the main biography, but by the time you've

Science

heard all the stories, you feel that the equation, and indeed the theory of relativity itself, has entered your bones forever. How is this different from the textbook treatment? How does Bodanis provide readers both depth of understanding and page-by-page entertainment? Here's what it sounds like.

Toward the end of the book, Bodanis describes a 1938 breakthrough by Lise Meitner. Meitner, a brilliant Jewish scientist, has just been banned from working in Germany and exiled to Sweden. Her nephew, Robert Frisch, also a physicist, comes to visit her at a friend's country home. "After they finished breakfast," Bodanis explains, "they went for a walk in the snow," with Frisch on cross-country skis and his aunt marching briskly beside him on foot. Along the way, the two were talking about the uranium atom and its peculiar properties. As an idea started to dawn, they slowed down.

> Meitner and her nephew weren't physicists for nothing. They had paper with them, and pencils, and in the cold of the Swedish forest, this Christmas Eve, they took them out and began calculating. What if it turned out that the uranium nucleus was so big, and so crammed with extra neutrons in there, that even before you started artificially pushing extra neutrons in, it was already in a pretty precarious state? That would be as if the uranium were a water droplet that already was stretched apart as far as it could go before bursting. Into that over-stuffed nucleus, one more plump neutron was then inserted.
>
> Meitner started to draw the wobbles. She drew as well as she played the piano. Frisch took the pencil from her politely and did the sketches. It was like taking a water balloon, and squeezing it in the middle. The two ends bulge out. If you're lucky the rubber of the balloon will hold, and the water won't burst out. But keep on with it. Squeeze in some more, and when the balloon spreads sideways, let go until it rebounds toward the center and then squeeze in the opposite way. Keep on repeating. Eventually the balloon will burst. Get your timing right, and you won't even have to squeeze very hard.

By the time their walk in the snow had ended, Meitner and Frisch had developed a hypothesis that would change the world.

> The atom was open. Everyone had been wrong before. The way in wasn't by blasting harder and harder fragments at it. One woman, and her nephew, quiet in the midday snow, had now seen that. You didn't even have to supply the power for a uranium atom to explode. Just get enough extra neutrons in there to start it off. Then it would start

jiggling, more and more wildly, until the strong forces that held it together gave way, and the electricity inside made the fragments fall apart. This explosion powered itself. (2001, pp. 109–111)

What's the difference between textbook talk and this best-selling trade book? Of course, Bodanis, like all good nonfiction writers (including the more skillful textbook authors) uses solid organizational patterns. But he gives much more, to make the information readable and memorable.

- content that is important or engaging
- people we can care about
- a narrative structure or chronological line
- places we can visualize
- danger, conflicts, risks, or choices
- value, moral, ethical or political dimensions
- some ideas that reasonable people can debate, dispute, or disagree about

These are the elements of engagement which you'll find in any successful nonfiction book, in any content area, be it mathematics, science, history, economics, or art. In this example, with 113 pages of letters, diaries, conversations, and photographs (but no other formulas or equations) Bodanis brings to life some of the most complex and consequential ideas in scientific, indeed, in human history.

Now, about this time, any workaday teacher might want to interject: "Hey, this $E = MC^2$ stuff may be readable and engaging—maybe my kids would enjoy it. But it is 113 pages long, not three! I'll grant you that the students might understand the equation better if they read this book. Maybe they'd be more able to think through issues that stem from it; nuclear energy, radiation, and all that. But I don't have that kind of time! I have scores of mandated topics—and the state exam covers everything. What am I supposed to do?"

Fair question. Do we make time for the real book or not? Can we risk it? The answer, according to the content-area standards in each of our subject fields (Zemelman, Daniels, and Hyde 1998) is definitely yes. Unlike most state legislatures and education departments, the national curriculum standards consistently say that we should *go deeper into a smaller number of topics*. Which means, yes, we should step outside the textbook for a while, and have our students read $E = MC^2$, or *Material World*, or *The Joy of Pi*, or *War Is a Force That Gives Us Meaning*, or *Genome*, or *The Future of Life*, or *Postville*, or *The Year 1000*.

But it is hard to make yourself put that textbook down and "teach less," giving up so much time for one book, covering just one big idea. Our friends in the social studies department at Stagg High School faced the same reluctance. Overwhelmed and exhausted by the annual race to "get everything in" to their U.S. history courses—and often finding themselves still on World War I in June—the faculty decided to take a drastic step. They went on a weekend retreat with the express purpose of deciding: what are the few absolutely key, core, central, gotta-have-em ideas in all of American history?

25 BOOKS A YEAR?

Back in the 1990s, it seemed like everyone in the field of education was issuing a "standards report." Many of these documents went on to cause various varieties of grief, but one that we admired in many ways was issued by the New Standards Project. Headed by Linda Darling-Hammond and funded by the National Commission on Education and the Economy, the NSP eventually led to a whole new set of tests, probably the most sophisticated and authentic formative assessment tools ever developed—and also the most ahead of their time, since they are now rarely used.

Anyhow, before they ever designed a single assessment, the NSP made this declaration as their number one educational standard: all students in American public schools should read at least 25 books per year. 25 books a year? Huh? In middle and high school, we obviously can never accomplish this with just one

They were committed to identify just 12 vital themes, movements, phenomena. After what Department Chairman Wayne Mraz called "the longest two days of my life," the department came back with what they dubbed "16 Fenceposts of History." (O.K., 12 was too ambitious to hope for.) Each of these big ideas (topics like native peoples, westward expansion, immigration, reconstruction, etc.) became the focus of a two- to two-and-a-half-week unit (the fence rails, if you will). It also left room to mix the textbook, which they still used, with other readings, films, library research activities, and small-group presentations that gave deeper and more textured understanding of the big themes in U.S. history.

A Balance of What?

We aren't just talking about adding a few exciting nonfiction bestsellers here and there. We need to consider: if textbooks aren't enough, then exactly what must be added to achieve a balance? What else should kids, textbook for each of five or six courses! I mean, if you hang on to the regular textbook in every class, that only gives you five or six of the 25—plus students would have spent a huge amount of time on this handful of tough, 1000–page books. Then what? Where are the other 20 books supposed to come from? Maybe a couple of novels in English, but . . .

Obviously, the framers of the NSP standards wanted to see kids reading a wide variety of real books, across the curriculum, in and out of class, assigned and independent, all year long. This innocuous little standard holds the seed of a real revolution. Taken seriously, it changes everything. So it's not surprising it hasn't been widely adopted, and where it has been adopted nominally, it hasn't been faithfully practiced. Maybe this 25 books a year standard is a little *too* radical for most would-be school reformers, and a little too threatening to the textbook publishers, with their stranglehold on instructional materials budgets.

adolescents, teenagers, be reading? What range of genres, styles, length of texts, and so forth, are we looking for? One way to answer this question is to notice what the thoughtful, curious members of the surrounding adult community are reading. Among your local lifelong learners, what's in the literacy diet? Probably you'd find that these thinking grown-ups read from a wide range of genres, in assorted situations, and for varied purposes. They probably read some "required" material for work, some other texts to stay informed as citizens and consumers, still other materials to get practical information, and some other stuff just for fun. And that's just how we should work it in school for kids, creating a balance along a number of continua, including the following:

Textbooks Vs. Other Genres

Here's a list of some genres of text that exist in our culture, roughly arranged from the most dryly factual to the most "made-up."

Reference books
Textbooks
Manuals/Instructions
Contracts/Legal documents
News stories
Feature stories
Historical accounts
Profiles

Editorials

Essays

Reviews

Biographies

Narrated nonfiction

Memoirs

Travelogues/Adventure

Historical novels

Novels

Plays

Poetry

You might debate these classifications, but we'd still argue that a well-educated middle or high school student should be regularly sampling text in all these genres as she moves through her education. And we can't think of a single school subject that doesn't have its own published materials in many of these slots. There are memoirs of historical figures, biographies of mathematicians, profiles of artists, reviews of literature, reference books on artists—heck, we could probably even find a contract with a scientist (a patent, for example).

Most of these genres are familiar and employ everyday terminology. Perhaps the only unfamiliar term is "narrated nonfiction," which refers to informational texts where the content is delivered through a personal voice. Like this: "Imagine you are standing at the edge of the ice-field, looking up at your first glacier." While this pattern may sound a little childish, it's a trusty tool of magazine writers everywhere: "Nicole Kidman sits at a back table in Starbucks, absently stirring her latte and talking about dreams. She looks much smaller, paler, and more fragile than on the big screen. . . ." You know the drill.

Choice Vs. Assigned

Usually, all school reading is assigned by a teacher. But real readers, lifelong readers, assign themselves. Sure, they may have jobs that provide some "required" reading. But in their wider lives, deciding what to read is a definitive act of literacy. Will it be *The New York Times* or the *Chicago Tribune? Time* or *Mother Jones?* A novel or a biography?

It should be just the same for adolescent students in school. In every subject area, some reading materials should be chosen by kids for themselves, selections that reflect their own view of the topic, their own connections and interests. Of course, young people will need practice and guidance in choosing books, articles, and Internet resources for themselves—after all, they may have experienced nothing but dependence, at least in school. So we'll help with a gentle hand, keeping in mind that giving kids choices is not a matter of "letting" them decide a few things; on the contrary, the flip side of choice is responsibility. When we invite students to find valuable reading materials for themselves, we are "requiring" them to do all the jobs that real readers do. We're refusing to spoon-feed them by locating, copying, handing out, and explaining every single piece of text they need to understand the Civil War. We're also saying, "You cannot choose to read nothing" and forthrightly enforcing that rule. With choice, we expect students to shoulder some work—and we'll explicitly show them how.

Fiction Vs. Nonfiction

In the content areas (English being the allegedly "content-free" exception) we are mostly concerned with creating a more balanced diet of nonfiction, and especially sampling a wider range of genres. This is a realistic adjustment in many ways; after all, 84% of what American adults actually read is nonfiction. And most high-stakes standardized tests contain predominantly nonfiction reading passages—as much as 80% on many of the big-name exams.

But there are times when fiction also has a very special place in science, math, history, and other content fields. Remember the big worry in Chapter 1 about the Hamilton-Burr duel? Well, *Burr* by Gore Vidal is one of a thousand historical novels that includes tons of factual background information, and makes both a person and a period come alive—and provides a detailed if not definitive account of the famed duel. Mark Slouka's recent novel *God's Fool,* about the world-famous conjoined twins Chang and Eng, provides a vibrant picture of life and culture in first half of the 19th century in Asia, Europe, and America, and culminates with a chilling view of the Civil War. And for a page-turner about the development of the Atomic bomb, including personal pecadillos of Robert Oppenheimer and his band of ego-driven physicists at Los Alamos, you can't top *Stallions' Gate* by best-selling novelist Martin Cruz Smith. We don't always need to match novels one to one with a particular fencepost; we can also use fiction simply to set the stage, to entice curiosity. If you are a science teacher trying to prime kids for a unit on time, space, or astronomy, an Arthur C. Clarke short story could provide a great sci-fi blastoff.

English class is where kids get their official doses of fiction and poetry, and maybe that's O.K. But perhaps we could re-balance the diet a bit here, too,

History

Science

opening up English to more nonfiction. After all, some of today's most cele-brated, cutting-edge writing is nonfiction appearing in progressive magazines and edgy websites. And the hot book-length genre for the past few years has been memoir, which brings the tools of fiction to autobiography. Dare we sug-gest a little Dave Eggers in place of Jonathan Edwards?

Classics Vs. Contemporary Works

There are always steamy debates about whether kids should read "classic" works, or dig into contemporary young adult literature instead. In this end-less and tiresome controversy, authoritative prescriptions abound. In his book *The Educated Child* (2002), former U.S. secretary of education William Bennett recommends 60 books for middle-school students. The list is heavily skewed toward the oldies including titles like *Great Expectations, National Velvet, A Boy of Old Prague, The Scarlet Pimpernel,* and *A Gathering of Days: A New England Girl's Journal, 1830–32.* Of the 60 authors on the list, by our quick tally, 56 are dead, 40 are (or rather, were) males, and 52 are of European descent. There's one Asian, one Hispanic, one Arab, and a handful of African-Americans on the list, including Booker T. Washington and, uh. . . . Sorry, but we just can't stop thinking how fun it would be to watch William Bennett try to teach *National Velvet* to some actual teenagers, like our kids at BPHS. Maybe he'd start by showing the black-and-white movie, starring teen heart-throb Elizabeth Tay-lor. But we digress.

Diane Ravitch, earlier cited as an expert on students' failure to remember historical facts, has a newer book that strongly endorses a diet of classic, or at least old, literature (2003). Among the titles she suggests for high school are John Millington Synge's *Riders to the Sea,* Rudyard Kipling's *L'Envoi to the Seven Seas,* and Richard Henry Dana Jr.'s *Two Years Before the Mast.* She scoffs at contemporary young adult literature with its focus on "evanescent" teenage-life issues. "A child who is suffering because of a death in the family," she sniffs, "is likely to gain more comfort from reading a poem by John Donne or Ben Jonson or Gerald Manley Hopkins than by reading banal teen fiction about a death in the family." Take that, Judy Blume! And, oh yes, topping the recommended reading list for eighth grade is (surprise!) Diane Ravitch's own collection, *The American Reader: Words That Moved a Nation.*

Anyway, the question is: do Bennett's or Ravitch's lists provide an appro-priate and balanced reading experience for contemporary American teenag-ers? We surely don't think so. We are big subscribers to the "windows and mir-rors" theory of book selection, which Ravitch mentions but misunderstands.

Some of what kids read in school should hold up a mirror to them, by including their story, their culture, their experience. This is a way of saying, you and your family are important, you are part of us, part of our country and culture. But other books should act as windows, where kids look out not at their own reflection, but upon other peoples, other time periods, other stories, and values, and ways of life.

We sure don't see many mirrors on Bennett's or Ravitch's lists, especially for the African American and Hispanic and, come to think of it, the white students we teach. Once again, it's all about balance. To bind young people to school and to reading, we need to invite them in, make them welcome, honor their heritage, and address their current interests. And, as educators, we also need to stretch them, to broaden their knowledge, enrich their experience, widen their world view, and grow their fund of information. Yes, we know that occasionally contemporary kids can identify deeply with protagonists in way-back times and far-off places. But if the school mainly assigns distant, alien, and anachronistic books (like the tales of long dead, upper-class British adults who populate the Bennett–Ravitch lists) you are pushing many kids away. You are saying, in effect and not by accident, "Hey buddy, this ain't your place."

Hard Vs. Easy

While some reading should be challenging, students can also learn plenty of content (and increase their reading ability) when the text itself doesn't constantly trip them up. Today, too many students (some labeled "special ed" and others not) spend their entire school day staring at text they *cannot read*—and many times, it's a textbook. Now if a student spends six hours a day not being able to read what we put in front of him, what is the most likely consequence? That the kid rededicates himself to reading and to school? Or that he just feels kicked out of a club he doesn't want to join anyway?

We'll say it loud and clear: kids need to read stuff they can read. This is non-negotiable. Some time during every school day, students should be reading comfortable, fun, interesting text that they can zoom through fluently, without hesitation. If this means bringing third-grade materials into a ninth-grade room, fine. Let's start collecting that easy stuff right now.

If you are worried about pandering, under-challenging, or other concerns, think about it this way. Scratch a lifelong reader, someone who has grown up to be a sophisticated consumer of text, and you'll almost always find some Nancy Drew, Hardy Boys, or even—yike!—comic books in their background. Maybe this even describes us. But like most grownups, we tend to forget parts of our own history, like the fact that young readers often grow by reading lots and lots of really easy, sometimes formulaic materials. So have faith. If we spend part of every school day helping kids to enjoy some reading, whether inside our content areas or out, we are giving a great and lasting gift.

Short Vs. Long

Kids' school experience already features plenty of l o n g selections, as embodied in the subject matter textbooks and novels we typically assign. But among real readers, a lot of important information comes from short clips, articles, reports, web pages, charts, tables, and pamphlets, too. Whatever our teaching field, we need to build a collection of these quick-reads. That means constantly scouring newspapers, magazines, and websites for relevant pieces for our kids, realizing that every school subject gets "covered" in the popular press, if we know where to look. Then we can feed class discussions with articles about air pollution in the community, the role of serotonin in brain function, the latest genetic engineering breakthrough, racial quotas in police department hiring, or a controversial art exhibit.

The Internet can really help you build this kind of collection. Most major city newspapers now have free electronic editions, with printer-friendly articles ready to be used in class two minutes from now. Many teachers we work with prefer www.newyorktimes.com for this service, which gives their kids access to "America's newspaper of record" every day. Some teachers also use the well-designed, mostly higher-order discussion questions that accompany some articles on the *Times'* educational website. You may prefer your hometown paper, especially for local news—including events that kids can experience or investigate firsthand. For example, some of our kids at BPHS have been using www.chicagotribune.com to keep track of a highly controversial gentrification project that is eating up their own neighborhood, displacing relatives and friends—and getting a well-earned drumbeat of mostly bad publicity.

Building a collection of short articles about your subject is helpful in many ways. To begin with, you'll want to use subject-related short selections when you teach kids the specific reading strategies outlined in Chapters 5 and 6. Obviously, your new-found inventory of "shorties" allows you to dip your toe into the water and step away from the textbook for brief experiments. You can add some "real" reading to the subject without committing large chunks of class time, and see how you like it. Also, on any given day, short articles allow for a quick in-class read and immediate discussion that leaves no one out. This can bring reluctant readers (or kids who haven't done the homework) into the conversation.

Primary Vs. Secondary Sources

Many school textbooks are "secondary" sources, which means that their content has been gathered from other materials (sometimes other textbooks), and then combined, reshaped, interpreted, and presented by the authors. Sometimes these texts are published as anthologies, where the original source of each section is cited directly in the text; more often, information is simply combined and delivered with assorted sources embedded in each other, and no way to tell where any specific information came from.

Further, suffusing any textbook is the author's subjectivity. There is no such thing as "just the facts." Consciously or not, willfully or not, no matter how hard they try to be "unbiased," secondary-source authors always infuse the books they create with their own attitudes, views, and cultural stance. This doesn't mean there is anything wrong with secondary sources, by the way. We all depend upon them daily, from the spell-checkers on our computers to the "pill book" we consult to see which of our prescriptions might be interacting.

Primary sources are something else; they are the "raw material" of knowledge. Though we most easily see the importance of primary source materials in the humanities, especially history, they can be just as valuable in science and mathematics. Think of looking at the actual lab notes from a famous experiment, or reading the journal of a path-finding mathematician. Whatever the subject, when students go back to these uninterpreted materials, they have a rare chance to really construct knowledge, build theories, and develop conclusions. Working with primary sources puts kids more in the role of a real scholar, "doing" the subject, not just hearing the summaries and conclusions of others.

The University of California Library provides this list of key primary sources, many of which can be gathered and put to use in your classes:

Diaries, journals, speeches, interviews, letters, memos, manuscripts, and
other papers by participants or observers
Memoirs and autobiographies
Records of, or information collected by, government agencies

Records of organizations

Published materials (books, magazine and journal articles, newspaper articles)

Photographs, audiorecordings, and moving pictures or video recordings

Ideas and images conveyed in the media, literature, film, popular fiction, or textbooks

Research data such as anthropological field notes, the results of scientific experiments, and other scholarly activity

Artifacts of all kinds: physical objects, buildings, furniture, tools, appliances and household items, clothing, toys

While collecting such materials is a lot more work than adopting a single textbook, help is available through a variety of websites and your friendly school librarian. And, to their credit, some of the better history textbooks do now include sidebars and samples of primary text materials alongside their secondary-source backbone.

Multiple Texts Vs. Single Sources

As we move away from dependence on a single textbook, one of the wonderful possibilities is to show students the range of views, the variety of theories, the different schools of thought that make intellectual life in our subject interesting, controversial—dare we say, exciting. Is global warming a real threat or does it just represent normal variations in the temperature of the earth's atmosphere? Does evolution proceed at a steady pace or by divine design? Should we revere Jefferson as a philosopher of human freedom or revile him as a hypocritical slave-owner? How important was Fibonacci's contribution to mathematics compared to other innovators'? Which is the finest of Shakespeare's tragedies? None of these questions can be intelligently addressed unless we consult multiple authorities. As you gather nonfiction articles, it is especially useful to gradually create sets of pieces that take different angles on the same topic.

Using the recommended book list at the end of this chapter, for example, students could sample the assorted slants of Michael Moore and Ariana Huffington on the state of the U.S. government. Or they could get different views of the Holocaust by reading *Anne Frank: A Biography* (about a family of victims) and *Stones from the River* (about a German family who hides and saves Jews). Or students might compare Edward Wilson's guardedly hopeful predictions about our biosphere in *The Future of Life* to the apparently well-documented doom and gloom scenarios clogging the popular media. Getting both sides (or the many sides) of the story is an adult-life skill that cannot be learned and practiced too early.

Building a Classroom Library

The outward manifestation of our break with the one-textbook curriculum is the classroom library, a growing assortment of interesting reading materials collected and offered to our students. What we are trying to create here is something like the living room of a big, eclectically literate family, a place where all manner of books, magazines, clippings, articles, brochures, and newspapers surround us. Some of this material will pertain directly to the subject at hand (algebra, history, etc.) while other parts of the collection can be deliciously random, chosen merely because it interests some, or many, teenagers.

So where do you get all this stuff? First of all: take your time and don't begin the process by spending lots of your own money. A good start is to go through old magazines, save newspaper articles, and scan the Internet. We know, hearing this, you may want to smack your forehead, thinking of all the years you've recycled or thrown away all those magazines, AKA valuable teaching materials. Well, don't grieve; just start bringing things to school tomorrow. And trust us, you can get kids going with even a small number of items. Later on, you'll be glad you got started when you did.

If your school or department has a budget line for supplementary materials—boy, are we jealous—and you better claim the money before we do. For the rest of us, it's beg, borrow, or steal—not necessarily an arduous or unpleasant process. We begin in our own homes, gathering up everything that might possibly fit in our classroom library. Sometimes we hit up relatives and neighbors for discards; and other times we scrounge garage sales, where 25-cent books aren't unheard of. If your students still participate in a book club like Troll, Scholastic, or Tab (middle-school teachers know all about this), the teacher gets points for everything kids order, which you then use to build your classroom library. Plus, you can ask kids to donate the books they've ordered (after they read them, of course, and write a review to guide future readers.) Remember, too, that students and their families can be a major source of materials. Some of our teacher buddies give a tear-jerking appeal for castoff books and magazines at every Fall parents' night, and then welcome the parade of kids schlepping in useful materials for days afterwards.

Now, before you start placing an order or rummaging around your basement, here are a couple of quick considerations about *what* to get. No matter what grade your classes may officially represent, almost any actual group of students includes a very wide range of reading levels. So you'll need to find not just books for different interests but for different difficulty levels as well. While many high school kids can simply read adult trade books (David Bodanis' $E=MC^2$ is written at a much easier reading level than a science textbook), we also need plenty of books that are just right for younger middleschoolers, for kids who struggle with reading generally, or for anybody who's just seeking an informative "easy read."

Where do we find such hard and easy, content-related, and generic materials? Twenty years ago, it was really tough to find rich nonfiction selections for young people—and at that time, it hadn't yet occurred to us to have the older kids simply read adult books. But now, through the publication of new materials (and by simply broadening our search) the gap has largely been closed. At the end of this chapter is an annotated bibliography of 150-plus nonfiction books (and some historical novels) that we and our teacher friends have used with success. But now, just to get warmed up, let us tell you about a few of the books that content-area teachers have used to get kids hooked on reading, as they begin to stock their nascent classroom libraries.

Starting at the easier, general-interest end of the spectrum, there are many nonfiction collections that

KEY INGREDIENTS OF A CLASSROOM LIBRARY

1. Interesting trade books, histories, and biographies of people in your field—and if you collect some titles in sets of three-to-five copies of each, students can read and discuss them in groups.

2. Current articles clipped from magazines and newspapers. For example, today's paper included an environmental science piece on the destructiveness of Louisiana crawfish when transplanted to an Italian lake—a typical example of the problems that occur when alien species invade an ecological system.

3. General interest magazines like *Time, Newsweek, U.S. News and World Report, Scientific American, Harpers', Atlantic, The Utne Reader, Popular Science, Popular Mechanics,* which carry stories about many of the topics covered in secondary schools. Anything the teacher has a hobby in should come in also—photography, travel, fishing, whatever. Don't forget the "easy reading" dictum; that means *People, The Enquirer,* punk rock zines, fashion magazines, and car and motorcycle rags should all be welcome. We know, we know; just lower your standards and bring it all in.

continued

feature shorter, engaging pieces. The National Geographic's *Reading Expeditions* is a set of colorful, engaging 40-page booklets; among the most discussable titles are *Feeding the World, The Human Machine, The Great Migration,* and *Kids Care for the Earth.* A similar line of magazine–books from *Time for Kids* offers high-interest, well-illustrated nonfiction that parallels what appears in contemporary news magazines. DK books (whose motto is "showing you what others only tell you") offers a huge line of gorgeously illustrated, browse-worthy books on a range of fascinating topics, including architecture,

4. Educational magazines on school topics, like *ChemMatters, Science News, Discover Magazine, Chance Magazine* (on statistics), and *Dell Math Puzzles and Logic Problems,* for math, *America's Civil War,* and *American History,* both lively history magazines from Primedia—and go to www.thehistorynet.com for a list of another dozen magazines focused on particular historic periods or events.

5. Website lists (or bookmarked on your classroom computers) keyed to various major topics in your course. For example, on radioactivity, BPHS chemistry teacher Mike Cannon has bookmarked www.physics.isu.edu/radinfo/risk.htm, which includes a group of articles on risks of exposure to radioactivity, www.aip.org/history/, which offers short bios of scientists who explored radioactivity, and www.heartcenteronline.org, which explores the medical applications of radioactivity. Math teachers can find great puzzles at the "Interactive Mathematics on the Internet" site, http://wims.unice.fr/, and fascinating instructions for making and learning about a wide variety of beautiful polyhedra at www.georgehart.com/virtual-polyhedra/vp.html.

cavemen, government, crime scenes, tai chi, dinosaurs, religions, fishing, and Batman.

If you can get past the unfortunate name, the *Uncle John's Bathroom Readers* are a terrific source of quickie nonfiction, much of it worth discussing and none of it having to do with bathrooms. Each *Uncle John* book contains hundreds of short (one-paragraph to three-page) fact-filled pieces on a weird and wide array of fascinating topics: Why does popcorn pop? Who planned the White House? Where did the Miss America pageant come from? Why do wintergreen Life Savers make sparks when you bite them in the dark? Was Henry Ford really an anti-semite? The *Uncle John* series is now up to 13 volumes, all of which ought to sit right beside the encyclopedias in every middle-school classroom.

The Guinness Book of World Records deserves a place in every classroom (you may want several copies) and not just because kids are fascinated with its contents. Many of the listings, from world-changing events to goofy stunts, are filled with math and science content—after all, every record requires some form of measurement. The annual editions of *The World Almanac* and *Ripley's Believe It or Not* feed the same curiosity about numbers and statistics. In a more applied-technology vein, our colleague Dagny Bloland, who teaches some of the most academically capable kids in Chicago, says that among the most popular books in her eighth-grade classroom are the *Chilton's Auto Repair Manuals* she has collected from gas stations and other donors.

More grownup in content and reading level are the collections *In Short* and *In Brief,* both edited by Judith Kitchen and Mary Jones, which include fine writers reflecting on assorted topics: how hummingbirds fly, the nature of attention deficit hyperactive disorder (ADHD), and why white people can't cook. A collection of longer pieces, *The Best American Magazine Writing, 2001,* features Robert Kurson's look back at his favorite teacher, who turns out to be a serial killer. There are several similar "best-of" nonfiction collections issued each year. The *2002 Best American Science Writing* was an especially strong edition, with pieces about the physiology of blushing, the nature of altruism, and the grounds for ecological optimism. Dave Eggers, who a few years ago wrote the best-selling novel, *A Heartbreaking Work of Staggering Genius,* has assembled collections called *Best American Non-Required Reading,* with short and often funny pieces skillfully addressing a youthful audience.

There are tons of historical novels aimed at younger readers, and there's no better core for a thematic unit than a book like *Morning Girl* (on exploration and conquest) or *Out of the Dust* (about the dustbowl and depression). The literature on the Holocaust, immigration, and the history of different American ethnic groups is especially well-recognized and available. But no matter what the issue, there seem to be "Young Adult" novels addressing almost any topic today. Amid the recent news reports on Islamic fundamentalism, our colleague Nancy Steineke was able to quickly build a collection of four illuminating YA novels with Islamic protagonists and settings.

As we create our classroom libraries, we are serious about something for everyone, especially our "reluctant readers." To be sure we hook the boys, we're quick to stock the room with Gary Paulsen's fiction and nonfiction, *Into Thin Air* and *Into the Wild,* both by Jon Krakauer, *The Perfect Storm* and *Fire* by Sebastian Junger, and *The Last River* by Todd Balf. All are adventure stories with tons of science information and strong narrative lines. For girls, we often go back to Nancy Drew, pile up the Babysitter's Club, stock plenty of Judy Blume, and even a few romances, if they want 'em.

As young readers grow stronger, the whole world of adult nonfiction opens up. Some of our partner schools in Chicago have been discussing selections from *Remembering Slavery* by Ira Berlin, Marc Favreau, and Steven Miller, a compilation of interviews from former slaves from all parts of the South. The autobiographical accounts, which were transcribed by the Federal Writers Project in the 1930s, provide first-person testimony, sometimes harrowing, sometimes puzzling, from the era of American slavery. The students we work with have also had lively conversations about *There Are No Children Here,* by Alex Kotlowitz, the all-too-real account of two brothers growing up in a Chicago housing project. *The Big Test* by Nicholas Lehman gives kids a chance to learn about the peculiar origins of the S.A.T. test they will someday face. Dava Sobel's books *Longitude* and *Galileo's Daughter* each dramatically recounts an invention that changed the world. Patrick Diamond's *Guns, Germs and Steel* offers a chilling and persuasive theory of why Caucasians have been able to dominate and exploit the other peoples of the world for two millennia.

And on and on. As they say, so many books, so little time!

A few final management tips: It will take some classroom organization to keep your library from being permanently borrowed out of existence. Appoint a student as librarian in each class, to keep track of everything. Organize the storage space so that books and articles can be returned to easily identified locations. And remind students how important it is to maintain materials in good condition for their classmates. Finally, try to accept the notion that a "stolen" book may be the highest possible compliment, and keep on collecting.

Notes

Bennett, William, Chester Finn, and John Cribb. 2000. *The Educated Child: A Parent's Guide from Preschool Through Eighth Grade.* New York, NY: Free Press.

Bodanis, David. 2001. $E = MC^2$: *A Biography of the World's Most Famous Equation.* New York, NY: Berkley Publishers.

Ravitch, Diane. 2003. *The Language Police. How Pressure Groups Restrict What Students Learn.* New York, NY: Knopf.

Zemelman, Steven, Harvey Daniels, and Arthur Hyde. 1998. *Best Practice: New Standards for Teaching and Learning in America's Schools.* Portsmouth, NH: Heinemann.

Great Books for Middle and High School

This is a selective, annotated bibliography of books tied to topics in the middle- and high-school curriculum. First, we introduce 20 special books that have already proven effective in many content-area classrooms. Next, we more briefly highlight a longer list that fellow teachers and students from around the country have used and recommended. We have focused mainly on recent trade nonfiction, biographies, and historical novels, since these genres are most relevant to teachers of science, math, social studies, foreign language, and the arts. English teachers may find some new fiction and memoirs here— as well as some fresh nonfiction titles to their repertoires.

The books listed here might become part of your students' reading diets in several ways. If you have a single copy in your classroom library, the book can be used for individual independent reading. If you have three or four copies, the set can be used for subject-area Book Clubs (see Chapter 9). With 25 or 30 copies, you can use the title as a whole-class book, for a special unit, perhaps supplementing or replacing a textbook section. Many of these books are especially well-suited for interdisciplinary units planned by teachers from different content areas, such as the fast food story described in this book's opening pages. If you are asking "Where do I get these books and who pays for them?" please see page 63, where we talk about the process of building a classroom library.

You might be wondering: aren't some of these books *too hard* for my students? Aren't they above many kids' reading levels? While we have tried to provide a varied distribution of difficulty, our list contains plenty of adult books. This reflects our strong belief that adolescent readers have been underestimated for too long, trapped between bland baby books and dull textbooks, all supplied by educational publishers. Students' so-called "reading levels" are officially determined by pencil-and-paper tests on boring, unchosen, synthetic-for-school passages. But who knows what some kid's reading level is when he chooses his own books? Even for a student who struggles with reading, if a book focuses on a real, burning interest, and especially if he can read it with some friends, creating a conversation that drives the reading, a too-hard book can end up being just right.

How we teachers use books in the classroom will also determine how "difficult" they are. If you assign all of your students to read *Fast Food Nation* for

October 15, some might drown in the facts and statistics. That's why, at BPHS, we built that book into a whole unit, with three teachers, five weeks, lots of support, and many concrete activities that brought the book's ideas alive. Students divided the book into five sections, used text coding (p. 115) and bookmarks (p. 116) to harvest their responses along the way, and met regularly in small discussion groups to compare notes. There were no factual recall quizzes, but plenty of on- and off-campus investigative activities that brought the book's biggest ideas alive. Supported by these activities, even our "low readers" became experts on the fast food industry and developed strong stands on the issues.

We think it's time to desegregate teenage readers, and invite them into the world of real, full-strength, adult books. And happily, the term "adult" applies to a very wide range of materials, from easy-reading page-turners (e.g., *Crispin*) to thick, highly technical tomes with teeny-weenie type (e.g. *The Mismeasure of Man*). There's plenty to choose from in genres, topics, and levels of reading challenge. We've tried to balance our list, indicating the degree of difficulty with the "read-o-meter" gauges beside each title.

And also remember: kids don't always have to read a whole book. Dipping in for a chapter or two works just fine with many nonfiction titles. Many of these books are promising candidates for jigsawing, where kids read just one section and then combine their learning in small groups (see page 149) As you build your classroom library, gradually read the books yourself, continue talking with kids and colleagues, and you'll become increasingly skillful at steering individual students toward interesting, readable books—or selections thereof.

Do you, the teacher, have to read each of these books before your students do? Absolutely not. First of all, if we limit kids to books we have read ourselves, we leave them an unnecessarily narrow choice, limited by our own reading habits or special interests. Besides, there are a million great books for kids, and no fulltime school teacher has time to read them all. So, no, you don't have to read a book before collecting it or using it. Just build your reading list from trustworthy sources: the suggestions of colleagues, friends, family, and former students; the scoop from magazine and newspaper book reviewers; the blurbs on book-related websites; the various award sponsors, like American Library Association; and even professional organizations like the National Council for Social Studies which recognize worthy books for young people each year.

A quick note on censorship. When we invite teenage students to graduate from controlled school books to real grownup books, we add challenge, rigor, and reality to the curriculum. We also incur some risks. Adult books, even when they are mainly about historical or scientific matters, sometimes contain adult themes or behavior. For example, in her powerful minimum-wage exposé, *Nickel and Dimed,* Barbara Ehrenreich admits to smoking marijuana and then facing a corporate drug test at the Wal-Mart, where she earns $6.50 per hour. *Stupid White Men* uses some bad words, *God's Fool* has brief but explicit sex scenes, and so forth. All three of these books are meritorious, thoughtful, and important—and none of their risqué words or deeds will shock the sensibilities of most contemporary teens.

But if book censorship is a big issue where you teach, then don't *assign* anything questionable. Rather, let kids choose the books they wish to read. If needed, send a copy of any chosen book home with a note to parents saying "Your child has chosen this book for chemistry class. Let me know if you have any questions." Most of our colleagues don't explicitly ask for a signature, feeling this notification process gives parents a fair chance to look the book over and object if they must. If a parent nixes the book (which happens about once a year, where we teach) you can call up the American Library Association, alert the ACLU, go to the mattresses and have a freedom of speech shoot-out— or you can let it be Mom's call. Parents have heartfelt reasons for protecting their kids from certain ideas. The kid could pick another book.

Here's the key to the format we have used to present our top-20 books:

1) Title and author
2) Difficulty level

- **challenging,** adult books
- **moderate** difficulty for teens
- **easier** books for younger readers, those who struggle, or kids who want to "go light"

3) A short blurb describing the content and flavor of the book
4) In capital letters, the SCHOOL SUBJECT AREAS covered by the book
5) In parentheses are thematic or integrated units the book could fit or anchor

For the rest of the list, we've just provided a sentence or two to highlight the subject matter or unique features. You can learn much more about each title, including reading sample pages in most cases, by searching Amazon.com, bn.com, or similar websites.

Finally, here are a couple of things we have *not* done. We have not listed familiar, classic works that are already widely used in public schools. We haven't reminded you that *Huckleberry Finn* can be used in U.S. history class or that *The Diary of Anne Frank* is useful in Holocaust studies. Often, these well-known books mainly appear in English classes, but are not being widely used by teachers of other subjects. If you're inspired now, you can find these oldies (with plenty of copies available, probably) for yourself. But in this special bibliography, we want to highlight new and different titles, books that most of us have never thought about using in school.

Another thing we haven't done is include all the publishers' names, their cities, or dates of publication as in a standard bibliography. Two reasons why: 1) you don't need this stuff to find a book these days; and 2) skipping this material gave us room for 20 more books. We've also violated protocol by putting the book title first (instead of the author's name), to make it easier for you to scan for content. The top-20 list is in alphabetical order; the longer "recommended" list is in some loose but hopefully useful categories. All recommended books are widely available in paperback editions.

Because we're trying to liven up kids' reading lives here, and give them some relief from their snooze-inducing diet of everything-is-hunky-dory textbooks, we have intentionally included a lot of thought-provoking, muckraking, even incendiary books. Yes, some of these authors are trouble-makers, malcontents, rebels, and iconoclasts. So were Mark Twain and Henry David Thoreau; it's an American tradition. But there are contrary books available on almost every topic. If you don't like Michael Moore's take on American politics, replace him with Anne Coulter, Bill O'Reilly, Pat Buchanan, or Rush Limbaugh—or pair a liberal and a conservative book and let kids determine who they think is right.

Every day, more books with great connections to secondary school subjects are being published—and thousands of others have been in print for years. Teachers like you, who are trying to broaden their students' reading diets, will be ever-vigilant for these new gems, and will gradually incorporate them into reading lists and classroom libraries.

Twenty Great Trade Books for Content-Area Reading

Echo of the Big Bang, Michael D. Lemonick

This lively and well-written account describes astronomers' struggle to confirm the Big Bang theory about how the universe began, and drastically alters our ideas about how the universe works. Lemonick shows real scientists at work designing satellite experiments to confirm this theory. PHYSICS, ASTRONOMY (origin theories, scientific methods, professionals' work lives)

E = MC²: A Biography of the World's Most Famous Equation, David Bodanis

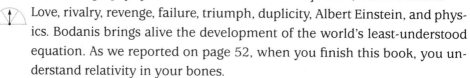 Love, rivalry, revenge, failure, triumph, duplicity, Albert Einstein, and physics. Bodanis brings alive the development of the world's least-understood equation. As we reported on page 52, when you finish this book, you understand relativity in your bones.

PHYSICS, CHEMISTRY, HISTORY (nuclear power, radiation, scientist biographies)

Family, J. California Cooper

Knowing that her children, particularly the girls, will face a life of endless abuse as slaves, Clora attempts to poison them and commit suicide herself. Though she dies, her children survive the ordeal. Rather than disappearing, Clora's spirit hovers over them and narrates the story as her children grow up as slaves. Haunting, riveting, and deeply disturbing; addresses many of the same issues as *Beloved* but much more accessibly.

HISTORY, ENGLISH (slavery, Civil War, African American history)

Fast Food Nation: The Dark Side of the All-American Meal, Eric Schlosser

A good, old-fashioned no-holds-barred muckraking exposé on every aspect of the fast food industry. Schlosser leaves no aspect of the business unscathed; there's bacteria in the meat, child exploitation behind the counter, family farms being destroyed, and animal cruelty in the slaughterhouses—all backed up with 63 pages of careful documentation.

SCIENCE, SOCIAL STUDIES (nutrition, food safety, industrial agriculture, labor law, advertising)

Feed, M.T. Anderson

This innovative novel creates a near-future dystopia where every citizen is fitted with a microchip that constantly feeds individualized commercial messages and trivial entertainment directly to the brain—a plausible extrapolation of current trends toward the commercialization of every aspect of human life, complete with junk-input from every direction. Like the characters in *A Clockwork Orange,* these teens speak a futuristic argot that chillingly reflects their distorted interior lives. A savage satire of what it means to be a teenager in America today.

ENGLISH, SOCIAL STUDIES, SCIENCE (the future, risks and benefits of technology, consumerism and consumption, adolescent development)

The Future of Life, Edward O. Wilson

A comprehensive look at the perils facing the planet by one of our leading scientists, the father of sociobiology. Wilson presents a deeply worrisome picture of the earth's current state, looking at resource depletion, pollution, global warming, and other assaults to our biosphere. But later, he turns hopeful and practical, endorsing the actions of NGOs (non-governmental organizations) that are already having significant impact worldwide. If you poll teenagers on the big topics they wonder about, the future always tops the list. This book directly, readably, and articulately addresses that concern.
SCIENCE, SOCIAL STUDIES (the future, ecology, global warming, natural resources, environmental politics)

Genome: Autobiography of a Species in 23 Chapters, Matt Ridley

Here's what good popular science writing sounds like: "Imagine that the genome is a book. There are twenty-three chapters, called Chromosomes. Each chapter contains several thousand stories, called Genes. Each story is made up of paragraphs, called Exons, which are interrupted by advertisements called Introns. Each paragraph is made up of words, called Codons. Each word is written in letters called Bases." Readable and utterly current, this topic appears in newspaper headlines every day.
SCIENCE, SOCIAL STUDIES (genetic engineering, bioethics, stem cell research)

Girls: A History of Growing Up Female in America, Penny Colman

An upbeat history of the roles of girls (and women) including native Americans, pioneers, former slaves, mill workers, children of farmers, and immigrants, told through excerpts from letters, diary entries, and published memoirs.
HISTORY, SOCIAL STUDIES (gender roles, history of childhood, women's issues)

The Hot Zone, Richard Preston

Novelization of a real outbreak of the Ebola virus, spread from infected apes in a Virginia lab. Shows how possible—perhaps likely—such an epidemic may be. When you hear the symptoms of Ebola ("crashing and bleeding out") you definitely will not be playing with any stray monkeys.
BIOLOGY, CHEMISTRY, SOCIAL STUDIES (plagues, emergency preparedness)

Left for Dead: A Young Man's Search for Justice for the U.S.S. Indianapolis, Peter Nelson

 The ultimate science fair and history project. The research of 11-year-old Hunter Scott, which was inspired by a passing reference in the movie *Jaws,* uncovered the truth behind a historic WWII naval disaster. The *Indianapolis* was torpedoed in 1944, and hundreds of sailors who survived the sinking were gradually killed by sharks as rescue came too late. Young Scott's research ultimately led to the reversal of the wrongful court martial of the ship's captain.
HISTORY, SCIENCE (World War II, naval warfare, military justice, sharks)

Material World, Peter Menzel

 Photographers spent one week living with a "statistically average" family in each of 30 countries, learning about their work, their attitudes toward their possessions, and their hopes for the future. Then, a "big picture" shot of the family was taken outside the dwelling, surrounded by their (many or few) material goods. Fascinating demographic, economic, and statistical details surround the photos.
SOCIAL STUDIES, GEOGRAPHY, ECONOMICS (families, cross-cultural studies, regional history, distribution of wealth, globalization)

A Mathematician Reads the Newspaper, John Allen Paulos

 Paulos looks at 52 different news stories, from sports to the stock market, politics to war to health, and finds fascinating puzzles and concepts that call on mathematical thinking. For example, how much stock in a company do you need to own in order to have an influence on its policy? Great for jigsawing—students can focus on topics they care most about. Challenging but lively.
MATHEMATICS, SOCIAL SCIENCE, ECONOMICS (mathematical persuasion, statistics, interpreting the news)

Maus: A Survivor's Tale, Art Siegelman

 The stunning, eloquent Pulitzer-Prize-winning depiction of Nazism in comic-book form. Using stories of his own father's survival, Spiegelman draws the Jews as mice, the Germans as cats, the Poles as pigs, the French as frogs, and the Americans as dogs. Incongruous? *Publishers Weekly* said: "The quasi-innocent simplification of the comic-book genre turns out to

be a surgical instrument baring the malignancy of adult evil."
HISTORY, ART, ENGLISH (World War II, fanaticism, Holocaust)

Nickel and Dimed: On Not Getting By in America, Barbara Ehrenreich
This celebrated *New Yorker* magazine reporter tries to make a living (and have a life) in several minimum wage jobs: waitress, house-cleaner, nursing home aide, and Wal-Mart clerk. It doesn't work. This look at the underside of capitalism profiles the millions of poor people in America who work full-time.
SOCIAL STUDIES, MATHEMATICS, ECONOMICS (labor, sociology, economic hierarchies, poverty)

Our America: Life and Death on the South Side of Chicago, LeAlan Jones and Lloyd Newman
After five-year-old Eric Morse was dropped from the 14th story of the Ida B. Wells housing project, a National Public Radio producer gave these two young men a tape recorder and asked them to investigate the story. The result is a documentary of contemporary life in a tough city neighborhood, where local residents experience violence and death as part of their everyday struggle for survival. A very personal and humanizing portrait of the authors' families and friends.
SOCIAL STUDIES, CURRENT EVENTS (poverty, urban issues, violence, welfare)

A Parrot in the Oven: Mi Vida, Victor Martinez
A lyrical, episodic, multiple award-winning Mexican American coming of age story. Manny wants to be *vato firme,* a guy to respect, and the year leading up to his initiation into a gang is filled with pain and tension. Meanwhile, his family struggles with violence, discrimination, and inner turmoil in the dusty California town where Manny is trying to grow up.
SPANISH, ENGLISH, HISTORY (Mexican American issues, ethnic studies, family history)

Postville: Culture Clash in the Heartland, Stephen Bloom
A look at what happens when members of a fundamentalist Jewish sect move to a small Iowa town and set up a kosher slaughterhouse that becomes the dominant economic force in the area. The mostly Lutheran farmers and townsfolk are deeply alienated by the behavior (or is it just the cultural differences?) of the newcomers, who make few efforts at

peacemaking. The book culminates in a hotly contested town election, basically a referendum on the Jews.

HISTORY, ECONOMICS, ENGLISH (culture clash, prejudice, ethnic studies)

Rethinking Columbus: The Next 500 Years, Bill Bigelow, ed.

 This book has changed the way that "the discovery of America" is taught in classrooms across the country. Bigelow uses mostly primary sources to show the inhumanity of the famous explorer; nothing is more damning or disturbing than Columbus' own journal. This book gives readers a sense of how Europeans came to dominate this hemisphere—and celebrates over 500 years of the courageous struggles and lasting wisdom of native peoples. Also contains a role-play trial of Columbus, materials on Thanksgiving Day, resources, historical documents, poetry, and more. Some critics say this book is too "politically correct" and that's another great discussion topic for kids.

HISTORY, GEOGRAPHY (Age of Exploration, colonialism, native peoples)

The Things They Carried, Tim O'Brien

 Widely acknowledged to be the greatest Vietnam novel, O'Brien's book unfolds as a loosely strung, graphic series of war memories evoked by specific objects carried by soldiers going into battle. "They carried all the emotional baggage of men who might die. Grief, terror, love, longing—these were intangibles, but the intangibles had their own mass and specific gravity, they had tangible weight." And it goes much deeper; this is a deeply structured meditation on war, humanity, writing, storytelling, and truth.

HISTORY, ENGLISH (war, Vietnam, Southeast Asian history, writing)

Zero: Biography of a Dangerous Idea, Charles Seife

One of the most interesting math books in recent years, this historical study of the development of zero covers everything from the number line to black holes. While some sections are challenging, kids can be guided to skip stuff that's too hard and still appreciate the book. Zero (and its companion, infinity) were such frightening concepts in many cultures that higher mathematics was impeded for centuries. We're in debt to Eastern cultures—it took the whole world to create nothing.

ALGEBRA, GEOMETRY, CALCULUS, PHYSICS (history of mathematics, world history, astronomy)

Also Recommended

Current Issues

Affluenza: The All-Consuming Epidemic, John De Graaf, David Wann, and Thomas H. Naylor

 How our relentless quest for stuff we don't need breeds sick individuals and despoils the world.

The Beauty Myth, Naomi Wolfe

 Cultural expectations about appearance still stalk and distort the lives of even the most powerful, accomplished women. One young woman commented: "I just wish I had read this book when I was an impressionable teenager."

The Bully, Paul Langan

 This is one of seven YA novels called the Bluford Series from Townsend Press, each one dealing with a pressing teen concern. We have seen whole classes of otherwise distractable city kids totally engrossed in these 100-page books (plus, they sell for a dollar each).

Confederates in the Attic, Tony Horwitz

 Glimpse into the unique subculture of Civil War re-enactors, or, as they prefer, "living historians."

The Cuckoo's Egg: Tracking a Spy Through the Maze of Computer Espionage, Clifford Stoll

 Hunt down some very clever international hackers in this page-turner.

The Culture of Fear: Why Americans Are Afraid of the Wrong Things, Barry Glassner

 How T.V. news keeps us frightened about highly unlikely perils.

Fasting Girls: A History of Anorexia Nervosa, Joan Jacobs Brumberg

This book blends history, religion, psychology, and sociology. It won the Watson Davis Prize for the best book translating ideas for the public, given by the History of Science Society.

Food Fight: The Inside Story of the Food Industry, America's Obesity Crisis, and What We Can Do About It, Kelly D. Brownell

We must build a mass movement against a food industry and a social order intent on fattening us, argues this fact-filled but ferocious manifesto.

Food Revolution, John Robbins

A very broad, very compelling explanation about why people should subsist on a plant-based diet.

Geeks: How Two Lost Boys Rode the Internet Out of Idaho, Jon Katz

Not all tech nerds are losers or Columbine perpetrators. Some just need to blow town.

Half and Half: Writers on Growing Up Biracial and Bicultural, Claudine C. O'Hearn

First-person accounts of 18 writers with biracial or bicultural backgrounds who grew up in the U.S. or emigrated here.

Ishmael: An Adventure of the Mind and Spirit, Daniel Quinn

The premise is a strange one. An all-knowing ape and his single human pupil engage in a telepathic semi-Socratic dialogue. The moral: mankind must cease living as "takers" and return to earth-loving ways.

Life and Def, Russell Simmons

Biography and opinion from the pioneer producer of rap, hip-hop, and "Def Poetry Jam."

Media Unlimited: How the Torrent of Images and Sounds Overwhelms Our Lives, Todd Gitlin

Far from being a glorious information age, ours may herald the death of intelligence, love, and democracy.

The Mismeasure of Man, Stephen Jay Gould

 The eminent scientist recounts the long series of "scientific" procedures developed to prove that white European males are the pinnacle of evolution, including phrenology, cranial measurement, and IQ testing.

One World, Ready or Not: The Manic Logic of Global Capitalism, William Greider

 Globalization and its effects.

Pigs at the Trough: How Corporate Greed and Political Corruption Are Undermining America, Ariana Huffington

 This conservative/liberal commentator bites some of the hands that feed her.

Punk: The Illustrated History of a Music Revolution, Adrian Boot and Chris Salewicz

 A visual history of the 1970s musical trend traces the rise of punk as both music and a worldwide sociocultural movement.

Savages, Joe Kane

 The uneasy relationship between a "primitive" tribe in Ecuador and an oil company that is bent on extracting the oil beneath this ancient culture.

Stupid White Men, Michael Moore

 America's scruffiest "left-wing nut" deconstructs the corporate-political establishment. A worthy companion is Moore's film on gun violence, *Bowling for Columbine.*

War Is a Force That Gives Us Meaning, Chris Hedges

 After two decades as a battlefield reporter in Yugoslavia, Africa, and the Middle East, Hedges writes about the eternal drug of war; how it intoxicates the combatants as it destroys the culture of both the attacker and the attacked.

Science and Technology

The Axemaker's Gift, James Burke

 Fascinating history of technology covering what we lose as well as what we gain from each new technological revolution.

Black Stars: African American Women Scientists and Inventors, Otha Sullivan and Jim Haskins

 Twenty-five mostly unsung women of color and their contributions.

Brainstorm: The Stories of Twenty Kid Inventors, Tom Tucker

 Ever eaten a Popsicle, kept your ears warm with earmuffs, or resealed your breakfast cereal with the built-in cardboard tab on the box top? Thank a kid inventor.

Complications: A Surgeon's Notes on an Imperfect Science, Atul Gawande

 Ruminations on surgery and fallible doctoring from the admired *New Yorker* columnist.

Dead Reckoning: The New Science of Catching Killers, Michal Baden and Marion Roach

 This delightfully creepy book tells how forensic investigation can bring murderers to justice or free an innocent on death row.

The Double Helix, James Watson

 The classic insiders' story of the race to describe the structure of DNA, including rampant professional pecadillos; a warts-and-all telling, not excluding the authors'.

The Encyclopedia of Preserved People: Pickled, Frozen, and Mummified Corpses from Around the World, Natalie Jane Prior

 Egyptian mummies, bog bodies, Einstein's brain, and the Ice Man can tell us things that skeletons can't.

The Evolution of Useful Things, Henry Petroski

 Learn the origins of the fork, scotch tape, and other tools of living.

Frames of Mind: The Theory of Multiple Intelligences, Howard Gardner

Arguing against the long-held notion that intelligence is a unitary trait, Gardner asserts that humans have several different types of intelligence including linguistic, logical-mathematical, kinesthetic, spatial, interpersonal, intrapersonal, and naturalistic.

Girls Think of Everything: Stories of Ingenious Inventions of Women, Catherine Thimmesh

 Collective biography of women and girls who changed the world with their inventions, including "white-out" and the "snugli" baby carrier.

Krakatoa: The Day the World Exploded: August 27, 1883, Simon Winchester

 Recounts the cataclysmic volcanic explosion heard round the world; 40,000 died in fire, ash, and tidal waves.

Lincoln's DNA and Other Adventures in Genetics, Phillip Reilly

 Thoughtful and fact-filled vignettes on the burgeoning applications of the genome: genetically engineered crops, DNA fingerprinting, cloning, gene therapy, and more. Highlights moral dilemmas, but mostly leaves them to the reader to wrestle.

Longitude: The True Story of a Lone Genius Who Solved the Greatest Scientific Problem of His Time, Dava Sobel

 In the early 1700s, sailors had no reliable way to determine their east-west position. A remarkable clockmaker found the solution.

The New Way Things Work, David Macaulay

 This grownup picture book by an architect/middle-school teacher de-mystifies zippers, windmills, parking meters, meat grinders, jumbo jets, jackhammers, electric guitars, egg beaters, and more.

The Periodic Table, Primo Levi

 Levi, an Italian chemist who survived Auschwicz, uses elements from the periodic table to open each chapter of this allegorical look at scientific thinking—and human nature.

Our Posthuman Future: Consequences of the Biotechnology Revolution, Francis Fukuyama

 The way genetic engineering is headed, we may not exactly be "human" anymore.

Raptor Red, Robert Bakker

 The biography of an individual female dinosaur growing up, mating, raising her young, engaging in battles.

A Short History of the Universe, Peter Silk

 Unlike most introductions to cosmology, this one uses beautiful illustrations to show what the big brains think is happening "out there."

Stephen Biesty's Incredible Cross Sections, Stephen Biesty

 One of a series of beautifully illustrated books explaining the inner structure and workings of everything from jumbo jets to plywood.

They All Laughed: From Light Bulbs to Lasers, The Fascinating Stories Behind the Great Inventions That Have Changed Our Lives, Ira Flatow

 NPR commentator tells how serendipity figured in many scientific discoveries and inventions, including teflon, lasers, xerography, and Velcro.

They Saw the Future: Oracles, Psychics, Scientists, Great Thinkers, and Pretty Good Guessers, Kathleen Krull

 A well-illustrated exploration of the lives of 12 visionaries, from 700 B.C. to the present, including Hildegard, Black Elk, Nostradamus, Jules Verne, and Jeane Dixon.

To Engineer Is Human: The Role of Failure in Successful Design, Henry Petroski

 Witty professor of engineering explains the positive aspects of failure.

Uncle Tungsten: Memories of a Chemical Boyhood, Oliver Sachs

Growing up in a warm and talented scientific family.

The Whole Shebang, Tim Ferris

 A plain language account of the various mechanisms believed to have contributed to the universe as we now know it, from the Big Bang to inflation to superstrings.

Why Buildings Fall Down, Matthys Levy and Mario Salvadori

Two engineers explain the most important and interesting structural failures in history, and especially in the 20th century.

Why Things Bite Back: Technology and the Revenge of Unintended Consequences, Edward Tenner

 Did you ever wonder why helmets make football more dangerous than rugby? Why the lines at ATMs are longer than they used to be at human-staffed teller windows? Why filter-tip cigarettes actually do not reduce nicotine intake?

Why Zebras Don't Get Ulcers: An Updated Guide to Stress, Stress-Related Diseases, and Coping, Robert M. Sapolsky

 It seems that humans are built to endure short-term stress, but not well adapted to the steady constant onslaught that modern life hands us.

Mathematics

The Adventures of Penrose, the Mathematical Cat, Theoni Pappas

 A humorous and approachable tour of mathematical concepts from fractals to infinity.

Aha! Gotcha: Paradoxes to Puzzle and Delight, Martin Gardner

 Exercises on logical thinking that introduce various mathematical concepts and statistics, without seeming like homework.

The Annotated Alice: The Definitive Edition, Lewis Carroll, annotated by Martin Gardner

 What would happen one of America's foremost mathematics writers were to annotate the world's most famous (and mathematical) Victorian children's book?

Celebrating Women in Mathematics and Science, Miriam Cooney, ed.

 Here are break-the-mold role models for girls, from the National Council of Teachers of Mathematics.

Damned Lies and Statistics: Untangling Numbers from the Media, Politicians, and Activists, Joel Best

 How good statistics go bad in the hands of dumb and/or nefarious people.

The Da Vinci Code, Dan Brown

 The big "beach book" of 2003 has been recommended by some math teachers for its symbology, ciphers, and code-breaking, as well as its historical and artistic content.

Does God Play Dice? The New Mathematics of Chaos, Ian Stewart

 Not quite a potboiler, but the best "non-technical" book on chaos theory.

e: The Story of a Number, Eli Maor

 In mathematics, *e* is the center of the natural logarithmic function and of calculus. Maor's book is a "popular" (but not simple) history of this universal constant.

Flatterland, Ian Stewart

 In this "sequel" to the weird 1885 book *Flatland,* Stewart offers a fictionalized tour of modern math and physics.

Fractals, Googols, and Other Mathematical Tales, Theoni Pappas

 Explores mathematical concepts and topics such as real numbers, exponents, dimensions, and geometry in both serious and humorous ways.

How to Lie with Statistics, Darrell Huff

 Huff warns: "The secret language of statistics, so appealing in a fact-minded culture, is employed to sensationalize, inflate, confuse, and oversimplify." Must reading for alert, self-protecting citizens.

An Imaginary Tale, Paul Nahin

 All about the square root of −1, the quintessential imaginary number.

The Joy of Pi, David Blatner

 Explores the many facets of pi and humankind's fascination with it—from the ancient Egyptians and Archimedes to Leonardo da Vinci and the modern-day pi-geeks.

Math Curse, John Scieska

 A sophisticated and funny picture book for all ages that addresses math phobias and misconceptions.

Mathemagics: How to Look Like a Genius Without Really Trying, Arthur Benjamin and Michael Shermer

 Shows you how to add, subtract, multiply, and divide faster in your head than with a calculator, let alone using pencil and paper.

My Best Mathematical and Logic Puzzles, Martin Gardner

 From the *Scientific American* columnist, a wide range of engaging math thumbsuckers.

The Number Devil: A Mathematical Adventure, Hans Magnus Enzenberger

 Illustrated fantasy starring a little red guy who calls prime numbers "prima donnas," irrational numbers "unreasonable," and roots "rutabagas."

Once Upon a Number: The Hidden Mathematical Logic of Stories, John Allen Paulos

 Mathematics can describe everything that happens: the Bible's codes, the stock market's ups and downs, even the Clinton sex scandal.

The Tipping Point: How Little Things Can Make a Big Difference, Malcom Gladwell

 How "social epidemics" work, from the transmission of measles to the sales of trendy shoes—and how they can sometimes be engineered. Also has social studies and business education connections.

To Infinity and Beyond, Eli Maor

 The world's most mind-blowing concept, aimed at the lay reader.

History

The American Revolution for Kids, Janis Herbert

One of a unique series that combines historical facts with hands-on activities, like making period clothing, brewing root beer, coding messages, doing battle re-enactments, and dancing the minuet. See also *The Civil War for Kids.*

Anne Frank: The Biography, Melissa Mueller

Not the novel, but everything that happened outside that attic. Follows the rest of the Frank family on through their deaths at concentration camps—or survival, in Mr. Frank's case.

At Her Majesty's Request: An African Princess in Victorian England, Walter
Dean Myers

 A true story of an orphaned African princess who narrowly escaped death
by human sacrifice in a West African village in 1850, was rescued by a
British sea captain, and given as a "gift" to Queen Victoria of England.

The Big Test, Nicholas Lehmann

 Did the introduction of the multiple-choice S.A.T. test advance true meri-
tocracy in America, as its makers claim, or simply sustain the privileges of
the same-old elite?

Black Stars of the Harlem Renaissance, Jim Haskins

 Meet Louis "Satchmo" Armstrong, Eubie Blake, W.E.B. Du Bois, Duke
Ellington, Marcus Garvey, Langston Hughes, Zora Neale Hurston, Paul
Robeson, Bessie Smith, and more.

Bury My Heart at Wounded Knee: An Indian History of the American West, Dee
Alexander Brown

 Beginning with the Long Walk of the Navajos in 1860 and ending 30 years
later with the massacre of Sioux men, women, and children at Wounded
Knee in South Dakota, Brown tells how the American Indians lost their
land and lives to a ruthlessly expanding white society.

Coal: A Human History, Barbara Freese

 An exquisite chronicle of the benefits and damage of the black mineral,
from ancient Rome to industrial England to modern-day China.

Days of Jubilee: The End of Slavery in the United States, Patricia and Fredrick
McKissick

 Chronicles the various stages of emancipation beginning with those slaves
who were freed for their service during the Revolutionary War, to those
who were freed by the Thirteenth Amendment to the Constitution, using
slave narratives, letters, diaries, military orders, and other documents.

A Different Mirror: A History of Multicultural America, Ronald Takaki

 This readable and passionate history covers many American ethnic
groups. A natural candidate for jigsawing.

Everything You Know Is Wrong: The Disinformation Guide to Secrets and Lies,
Russ Kick, ed.

 An infuriating and possibly accurate collection of muckraking articles. If you suspect that our government knew about the 9/11 attacks well in advance and did nothing, this is the book for you.

Fight On! Mary Church Terrell's Battle for Integration, Dennis and Judith Fradin

 Extraordinary life of "Mollie" Terrell, the first black woman appointed to the Washington, D.C., Board of Education, a cofounder of the NAACP, fighter against lynching, and colleague of Susan B. Anthony.

Flags of Our Fathers, James Bradley

 The story of the men pictured in the famous photo and statue of the U.S. flag being raised at Iwo Jima. Written by the son of one of the men in the sculpture.

Founding Brothers: The Revolutionary Generation, Joseph Ellis

 A fresh look at the founding fathers, in which Washington's stock rises. An Eritrean cab driver whom we met in Columbus, Ohio insisted we put this book on the list. "Your kids need to know how great the father of their country really was," he said.

Freedom's Children: Young Civil Rights Activists Tell Their Stories, Ellen Levine

 The author interviewed 30 adults who were among the participants, and in some cases the leaders, of numerous civil rights demonstrations in the 1960s, many with violent, tragic outcomes.

Ghost Soldiers: The Epic Account of World War II's Greatest Rescue Mission,
Hampton Sides

The fascinating story of the horrific Bataan death march in the Philippines.

Guns, Germs and Steel, Jared Diamond

Why have Caucasians dominated most of the world, over much of recent history? A long, tough book; a good jigsaw candidate; immensely provocative.

Hiroshima, John Hersey

Pulitzer prize-winning author John Hersey recorded the stories of six Hiroshima residents who survived the nuclear attack in 1946.

Kids at Work, Russell Freedman and Lewis Hine

 A photographer's crusade against child labor. Hine, a schoolteacher, felt so strongly about the use of children as industrial workers that he became an investigative reporter for the National Child Labor Committee.

Lies My Teacher Told Me: Everything Your American History Textbook Got Wrong, James Loewen

 Columbus was a bloodthirsty bum who was sent back to Spain in chains; Ponce de Leon was a slave-trader; and Woodrow Wilson was a white supremacist. And that's just for openers.

No Easy Answers: The Truth Behind Death at Columbine, Brooks Brown and Rob Merritt

 What really happened at Columbine High School, told by a friend of one of the shooters.

A People's History of the United States: 1492 to the Present, Howard Zinn

 Unabashedly left-wing history of America; starts with the eradication of native peoples and moves on from there.

The Rape of Nanking: The Forgotten Holocaust of World War II, Iris Chang and William Kirby

 Under Japanese occupation in 1937–38, Japanese soldiers raped and slaughtered thousands of unarmed, unresisting Chinese civilians in Nanking. Truly horrifying details open up questions about human nature, the prevalence of war, and the idea of reparations.

Remembering Slavery: African Americans Talk About Their Personal Experiences of Slavery and Freedom, Ira Berlin et al., eds.

 Stories of slavery survivors transcribed by the Federal Writers' Project in the 1930s.

Salt: A World History, Mark Kurlansky

 Salt, the only rock we eat, has influenced the development of trade routes, the founding of cities, and has even been used as currency. Nice chemistry connection; try jigsawing.

Seven Wonders of the Ancient World, Lynn Curlee

 Some of humankind's greatest feats and the timeless desire of cultures to leave a permanent mark on the Earth.

Six Days in October—The Stock Market Crash of 1929, Karen Blumenthal

 A chronicle of the six-day period that brought the country to its knees, from fascinating tales of key stock-market players, to the allure of stocks and the power of greed.

What If? and *What If? 2,* Robert Cowley, ed.

 Eminent historians imagine what might have been. What if Alexander the Great died in battle at age 21? What if Napoleon invaded America? What if Hitler went on trial? What if there had been no A-bomb to "end" World War II?

What Jane Austen Ate and What Charles Dickens Knew, Daniel Pool

 From fox-hunting to whist, the social history that sets the context for understanding 19th-century literature.

Who Built America? Vols. 1 & 2: Herbert Gutman, ed.

 United States history through the lens of regular, everyday working people instead of magnates, presidents, and aristocrats. Tons of primary sources.

The Year 1000: What Life Was Like at the Turn of the First Millennium, Robert Lacey and Danny Danziger

 A lively look at the Middle Ages, covering topics kids are really interested in: religious belief, superstition, medicine, cuisine, agriculture, politics, and bathroom arrangements; fascinating and humorous connections to our modern era.

Novels

Bodega Dreams, Ernesto Quinonez

 A brilliant, overlooked book about growing up and making it in the barrio, not escaping. *Publisher's Weekly* said Quinonez has "a poet's ear for the barrio's Spanglish rhythms and idioms, a brujo's gift for describing its alma, and an intense, unrelenting streetwise energy."

Crispin: The Cross of Lead, Avi

The horrors of feudalism are dramatized in this action-packed story; the frantic flight of a 13-year-old peasant boy across 14th-century England. 2003 Newberry winner.

Esperanza Rising, Pam Munoz Ryan

 This magical novel set in 1930 recounts a 13-year-old Mexican girl's fall from riches and her immigration to California.

The Eye of the Needle, Ken Follett

 British intelligence agents must catch German spy Die Nadel before he reveals the Allies' plans for the invasion of Normandy. Fast paced; never a dull moment. Plus, the details about World War II espionage are historically accurate.

Fail-Safe, Eugene Burdick and Harvey Wheeler

 When the United States accidentally destroys Moscow with an atomic bomb, the president must make the hard decision to either go to war with the Soviet Union or keep world peace by destroying New York City as restitution.

Fever 1793, Laurie Halse Anderson

 A 16-year-old girl and her family fight for survival in the yellow fever epidemic that swept Philadelphia (then the nation's capital) in 1793.

Foster's War, Carolyn Reeder

 When his older brother joins the army during World War II in order to escape the rages of an authoritarian father, 11-year-old Foster fights his battles on the homefront.

The Glory Field, Walter Dean Meyers

 A rich, well-researched novel telling the saga of an African African family, beginning in Africa in 1753, through slavery to freedom and up to the present day.

God's Fool, Mark Slouka

 This touching novel, based on the lives of Chang and Eng, the Siamese twins made famous by P.T. Barnum, vividly depicts life in Asia, Europe, and America in the middle- and late-19th century.

The Joy Luck Club, Amy Tan

 Four mothers, four daughters, and four family stories of Chinese immigration. All Tan novels are recommended.

The Last Lieutenant, John J. Gobbell

 As Corregidor falls to the Japanese and U.S. troops in the Philippines surrender, Lt. Ingram escapes capture with a handful of men. Their goal is to prevent a spy from communicating the U.S.'s knowledge of the upcoming attack on Midway.

A Lesson Before Dying, Ernest Gaines

 An unfairly condemned black youth becomes a man while awaiting execution.

The Middle Passage, Charles Johnson

 A newly freed slave accidentally hops aboard a square rigger bound for Africa to pick up slaves. Mutiny ensues. A National Book Award winner.

Morning Girl, Michael Dorris

 A 1492 encounter story; Carribean brother and sister meet the first European explorers.

Out of the Dust, Karen Hesse

 A short, powerful, and poetic story of the American dustbowl.

The Perks of Being a Wallflower, Stephen Chbosky

 If you don't think YA is real literature, try this one. A sweet, aching, full-strength growing-up novel.

Roll of Thunder, Hear My Cry, Mildred Taylor

 A black family in the Deep South stands up to the "night riders" in the 1930s.

A Single Shard, Linda Sue Park

 Newberry Award-winning story about Tree-ear, a 12th-century Korean orphan who finds his future through his intuitive interest in the potter's trade.

Snow Falling on Cedars, David Gutterson

 A love story set in the mid-50s in Washington state, against a backdrop of the Japanese internment during WWII and the long-term distrust it spawned.

Song of Solomon, Toni Morrison

 More accessible than Morrison's *Beloved,* and to many readers, just as powerful.

A Step from Heaven, An Na

 Na's dark tale of a family of Korean immigrants won the ALA's Printz Award for teenage literature.

Stones from the River, Ursula Hegi

 The rise of Nazism, seen through the eyes of a local librarian in a small German town.

Summer of My German Soldier, Bette Greene

 Already feeling isolated as the only Jewish child amongst her Baptist class-mates, Patty's problems multiply exponentially when she innocently helps a frightened young man who happens to be an escaped German prisoner of war.

Biography/Memoir

All Creatures Great and Small, James Herriot

 Classic collection of country veterinarian stories by the avuncular York-shire vet.

Always Running: La Vida Loca, Luis Rodriguez

 Growing up with gangs, guns, and drugs in the L.A. barrio. The book was written as a cautionary tale for Rodriguez' young son.

Angelhead: A Memoir, Greg Bottoms

 The harrowing account of a brother's descent into paranoid schizophrenia and the family's struggle.

Bastard Out of Carolina, Dorothy Allison

 A raw story of a young girl who bounces around a rural southern family.

A Heartbreaking Work of Staggering Genius, Dave Eggers

 In a suburban Chicago family, both parents die within months, leaving the author to raise his baby brother. Not just a touching story, but a book that's also stylistically adventurous.

Honky, Dalton Conely

 Tells of growing up white in a mostly minority New York neighborhood. "If the exception proves the rule," Conely declares, "I'm that exception."

A Hope in the Unseen, Ron Suskind

 The biography of an ambitious black boy who "escapes" from the inner city to attend Brown University—but at what cost?

A Hunger of Memory, Richard Rodriguez

 What happens when you exchange your language and ethnic identity for upward mobility?

Into the Wild, Jon Krakauer

 Heart-rending story of Christoper McCandless, a lost and lonely 20-year-old who decides to winter alone in Alaska and ends up frozen to death in an abandoned school bus.

Inventing the Future: A Photobiography of Thomas Alva Edison, Marfe Delano

The story of Edison's life, richly illustrated with period photographs; an inspiration to students interested in a career in science.

Mahalia: A Life in Gospel Music, Roxanne Orgil

The life of the great gospel singer Mahalia Jackson. Her story links music, faith, the northern migration of African Americans, and the struggle for civil rights.

Naked, David Sedaris

 A collection of loosely linked, semi-autobiographical stories about growing up fabulous.

On the Rez, Ian Frazier

 The tale of life among the Oglala Sioux in South Dakota; troubling, hopeful, and stereotype-shattering.

Red Scarf Girl: A Memoir of the Cultural Revolution, Ji-Li Jiang

 A memoir of growing up during Mao Tse-Tung's campaign of intimidation and terror.

Rocket Boys, Homer Hickam

 Dreaming of becoming NASA rocketeers, Hickam and his friends teach themselves trigonometry and physics. The excellent film *October Sky* was based on this book.

Ryan White: My Own Story, Ryan White with Ann Marie Cunningham

 Twelve-year-old Ryan White decided to be the "first kid with AIDS to speak out, fight back—and win." And he did. More than melodrama, though it is heartbreaking.

There Are No Children Here, Alex Kotlowitz

 The story of two young brothers growing up, which is no easy task in this tough Chicago neighborhood.

Warriors Don't Cry, Melba Beals Patillo

 The memoir of one of the Little Rock Nine, who integrated Central High in the 1950s.

When I Was Puerto Rican, Esmeralda Santiago

 Tells of her childhood years in tropical Puerto Rico and her later move to New York, with many struggles inside and outside the family.

A Winter's Season: A Dancer's Journal, Toni Bentley

 An inside picture of the incredibly tough, demanding, and creative world of professional ballet.

Woman Hollering Creek, Sandra Cisneros

The loosely connected collection of stories about growing up Mexican in Chicago. Also recommended: *The House of Mango Street.*

Personal Growth

Boys Know It All: Wise Thoughts and Wacky Ideas from Guys Just Like You,
Michelle Roehm and Marianne Monson-Burton, eds.

 More than 30 boys from around the country write on issues ranging from sibling problems and using computers to how to talk to girls.

Chicken Soup for the Teenage Soul: 101 Stories of Life, Love, and Learning (and many other similarly titled volumes) Jack Canfield et al., eds.

 Inspiration, platitudes, or banalities? One kid called this book "the tools for surviving high school." We can respect that.

Emotional Intelligence, Daniel Goleman

 Turns out that IQ is not enough—you also need EQ, which is what your grandmother called "people skills."

Food and Loathing: A Lament, Betsy Lerner

 The story of uncontrolled binging and dieting, a pattern plaguing too many American girls. When Lerner first read Descartes, she immediately made her own translation: "I weigh x, therefore I am shit."

Help! My Teacher Hates Me, Meg Schneider

 How to deal with the roller-coaster issues of middle school.

Men Are from Mars, Women Are from Venus: A Practical Guide for Improving Communication and Getting What You Want in Your Relationships, John Gray

 Debatable pop sociology on the purported differences between men and women.

Never Good Enough: How to Use Perfectionism to Your Advantage Without Letting It Ruin Your Life, Monica Ramirez

 Especially meaningful for "gifted" students.

Not Much, Just Chillin': The Hidden Lives of Middle Schoolers, Linda Perlstein

Chronicles a school year at a suburban Maryland middle school, exploring the changes in personalities and school performance of students caught between childhood and high school.

Real Boys, William Pollock

Aimed at parents, but readable for teens, this book attacks "gender straight-jacketing" and calls for "open-hearted, strong-hearted men with as much familiarity with love, joy, sorrow, and fear as they have with rage and dirty jokes."

Reviving Ophelia: Saving the Selves of Adolescent Girls, Mary Pipher

 Why do so many teenage girls suffer from anorexia, depression, and low self-esteem? Because they are living in a "looks-obsessed, media-saturated, 'girl poisoning' culture." Great to read alongside *Real Boys,* above.

Seven Habits of Highly Effective Teens, Sean Covey

 Be proactive, put first things first, give other people lots of compliments, etc. The very opposite of rocket science, but it does work.

You Just Don't Understand, Deborah Tannen

 The academic explanation of why men won't stop and ask for directions. The noted sociolinguist explains why men and women frequently miscommunicate.

Adventure/Sports

Baseball: The American Epic, Geoffrey C. Ward and Ken Burns

 The most exciting and memorable achievements in the history of America's national pastime.

Blue Latitudes: Boldly Going Where Captain Cook Has Gone Before, Tony Horwitz

 The always entertaining traveloguer follows the voyages of the famous explorer.

Coming into the Country, John McPhee

 A detailed, classic look at Alaska, America's last frontier, disguised as a canoe trip.

The Concrete Wave: The History of Skateboarding, Michael Brooke

 A colorful crash course featuring skateboarding's history, inventors, investors, stars, companies, media, and technological advances in a magazine-like layout.

Dogsong, Gary Paulsen

 Running the Iditarod dogsled race with America's most popular writer among pre-teen boys.

Fire, Sebastian Junger

 The opening piece on the nature of fire and the character of firefighters should be read by every chemistry student.

For Love of the Game, Michael Shaara

 Using baseball to sound the depth of human experience, this short novel about a troubled pitcher takes place during one baseball game.

Guts: The True Stories Behind Hatchet and the Brian Books, Gary Paulsen

 Paulsen writes top-rated adventure novels that appeal especially to boys. This one takes us fans behind the scenes.

Hoop Dreams, Ben Jarovsky

 The journeys of two inner-city kids from the playgrounds to high school competition to college recruitment; subject of a PBS documentary film.

The Hungry Ocean, Linda Greenlaw

 A woman breaks the gender barrier in dangerous offshore fishing. See also her *Lobster Chronicles.*

Into Thin Air, Jon Krakauer

 Tale of an ill-fated Mt. Everest expedition, told by a veteran mountaineer and outdoor writer.

It's Not About the Bike, Lance Armstrong

 The world champion bicycle racer details his recovery from cancer.

Little Girls in Pretty Boxes: The Making and Breaking of Elite Gymnasts and Figure Skaters, Joan Ryan

 Scathing critique of the parents, coaches, and judges who exploit young female athletes and endanger their lifelong health. A powerful plea for reform.

Seabiscuit, Laura Hillenbrand

 Some have called this saga of a runty horse and his rag-tag human crew the best sports book ever written.

CHAPTER FIVE
Tools for Thinking: Reading Strategies Across the Curriculum

W e've explained how kids need more engaging real-world reading in order to learn our school subjects. We just listed a hundred and fifty books that promise this kind of engaged reading experience. We've also explored the active mental work kids must do to make sense of all this rich material. Now, how can we make sure students actually *do* that mental work in our classrooms? And how can we do this within the time constraints we face and still teach the subjects we were hired to teach?

The strategies described in this chapter are simple, quick, easy-to-use tools and activities to help students engage in, grapple with, and remember concepts in chemistry, math, history, or any subject. The writing or jotting or sketching required for these activities need not be corrected and graded—though you may want to check briefly to see what the kids need help with or to confirm that they are actually using the strategies. The activities need not create more work for you as a teacher, but should make your job easier by helping students think as they read. If you decide to use them as starters for more extensive projects and writing activities, "upgrades," so to speak, that's fine—but it's not a requirement for their success.

Before we go further, however, let's make clear what we mean by "strategies." Reading experts often refer to **mental strategies that readers use** to understand what they are reading. But they also talk about **instructional strategies that teachers use** to help students learn those mental strategies. Or perhaps they talk about **whole-class or individual student activities** that combine both of the previous two. What follows is really a collection of the latter. These involve discussion, writing, drawing, and even having kids get up and move around the room—activities that help students engage with, understand, and apply the reading they do—and in the process, learn to use their minds more effectively as they read. Most activate a number of the mental strategies good readers use to understand a text.

The teaching strategies are organized in five categories, covering key aspects or stages in reading, as follows:

Showing kids how smart readers think

Before: activities that prepare students to read

During: helping students construct, process, and question ideas as they read

After: guiding students to reflect on, integrate, and share ideas after they're finished

Learning vocabulary

Let's think back to Chapter 2, on how good readers think, and consider what exactly these strategies achieve for us as teachers of various subjects.

☞ **Showing kids how smart readers think:** this category, though it includes just one strategy, is overarching, and goes to the very heart of good reading.

☞ **Before: activities that prepare students to read.** This includes 1) *getting students focused* on and excited about the reading, 2) *developing purposes* for reading, 3) *activating students' questions, beliefs, and predictions* about issues in the reading, and 4) *making connections with students' prior knowledge* to help make sense of the reading.

☞ **During: helping students construct, process, and question ideas as they read.** As effective readers work through text, they *visualize* what is happening in a story or historical situation or science experiment. They may notice they have *questions* about the topic. They make *connections* between various parts of the piece and with their own lives or the larger world around them. They make *inferences,* going beyond the information given to other implications it offers. They *distinguish important ideas* from minor elements or digressions. And they *monitor their comprehension,* noticing when they understand and when they've lost the thread. The mind of a good reader is extremely active, not a passive sponge.

☞ **After: guiding students to reflect on, integrate, and share the ideas when they're finished.** This is when readers *synthesize* ideas within their reading and between what they've read and what they already knew about a topic, to make larger *inferences* and *connections.* They *follow up on the questions and purposes* they had and consider whether they've learned answers, found surprises, or developed a new perspective on the topic. And they share their thoughts to help others with this process.

☞ **Learning vocabulary:** this overlaps with reading-for-thinking in all three stages, because effective vocabulary study goes well beyond looking up and memorizing definitions of words in a list.

In each of these big categories, we start with activities that are simple and easy to use, and advance to some that are more complex. There are a great many more such activities in the useful books on reading that we cite—but we've chosen the 24 below because they effectively cover a number of the mental strategies good readers use.

Here then are 24 essential strategies to promote the thinking students need for learning effectively from what they read. Since most of these have been developed over the years by many educators, we've tried to credit the progenitors where possible, as well as cite recent updates and variations.

101

TOOLS FOR

THINKING:

READING

STRATEGIES

ACROSS THE

CURRICULUM

Teaching Tips

To insure a reading strategy works and becomes an effective, regular part of students' repertoire, you must actively instruct them how to use it. Some key steps:

☞ Introduce just one strategy at a time. Then have students practice it repeatedly, during brief stretches of in-class reading time, using short articles or excerpts.

☞ Model the activity yourself, as you explain to students how to use it.

☞ Particularly for a strategy that will be used individually, practice the strategy first as a whole class, comparing various responses that students write (or draw, or talk through), so kids see the various ways it can work for them.

☞ As students make use of the strategy during in-class reading time, move around the room, observe what they are doing, and provide help when it's needed.

Showing Kids How Smart Readers Think

Think-Alouds: Actively Exploring Meaning as You Read

When to Use

✗ Before Reading

During Reading

After Reading

DESCRIPTION

The teacher reads a passage aloud and stops repeatedly along the way to explain her mental processing of the ideas being portrayed. She models the process first, and then students try it in pairs or in a whole-class discussion. When done together as a whole class, this strategy essentially becomes what is called a **Directed Reading Thinking Activity.** DRTA's, as they are dubbed by reading people, involve the same process of reading, stopping to reflect aloud at key points, and then moving on, except that the whole class participates.

WHY USE IT?

Many students are quite unaware of the mental activity that takes place during effective reading. Some simply search for answers to the questions at the end of the chapter or on the pop quiz. Others mechanically read words, hoping meaning will magically arrive. Think-alouds help students to really see how active their thinking needs to be for high comprehension. This is not an activity to use just once or twice. Repeated think-alouds will demonstrate a wide variety of mental strategies, showing students very concretely how to bring the material to life, manifesting the thinking strategies we've described in Chapter 2, or illustrating the kinds of thinking involved in your subject. After you demonstrate a think-aloud, students can practice orally, themselves, in whole-class discussion, small groups, or pairs. We want them to internalize the processes, to make them a natural part of reading.

HOW DOES IT WORK?

1. Before you begin, let students know you'll be stopping to think as you read, and indicate what they should notice in your thinking—e.g., *Watch how I use the information in the passage to figure out what's really going on. We call this "inferencing."*

2. Use a short passage, and provide students with copies so they can follow along. Stop after a couple of sentences to tell what you think is coming next, make a connection to your own experience, question what a statement might mean, or express confusion about some idea, etc.

3. When you stop to think, shift your voice to indicate that you've moved from reading the words to your own thinking.

4. After modeling, have students try it in pairs or taking turns in the whole class. If students have difficulty putting thoughts into words, point out a key spot or two where they can stop, and ask them if they have questions, are reminded of something in their own lives, etc.

FOR MORE INFORMATION

Beth Davey. 1983. "Think Aloud: Modeling the Cognitive Processes of Reading Comprehension," *Journal of Reading,* Vol. 27, pp. 44–47.

EXAMPLE

Kenya Sadler, of Foundations School in Chicago, uses a think-aloud to introduce students to the biography collection, *Black Stars of the Harlem Renaissance*.

Kenya reads aloud from the book's introduction and shares her thoughts as she goes:

> . . . The real estate speculators envisioned a new suburb of downtown Manhattan. They built beautiful town houses and apartment buildings abroad tree-lined avenues. Then the real estate market declined, and rather than pay huge mortgages on empty buildings, the speculators rented to Blacks for the first time.

Wow. So if the real estate market hadn't declined, then there may not have been a Harlem Renaissance, because they wouldn't have rented to Blacks. Okay, I need to make a note to myself about that, because that's something important.

> The Black population of New York grew fast, fueled by the large northern migration of Southerners. It could no longer be contained in the scattered Black enclaves downtown. Blacks were desperate for living space and willing to pay the high rent prices of Harlem.

But where would they get the money? Hm. If the market is declining, then that means that people don't have as much money. How is it that Blacks were able to afford to pay the high rent prices of Harlem? I also made a connection here. This reminds me of Bronzeville, the area in Chicago from 26th Street up to, like, 43rd Street, where you have the huge boulevards, King Drive Boulevard, with all of these mansions. And back in the 20s and 30s they were all owned by whites. And then somewhere in the 50s and 60s they started to turn them into apartment buildings for Blacks. So they went from the white mansions to these Black apartment buildings, and one house would end up holding maybe four families. And now they're actually being converted back to the mansions.

> Before long, Harlem became the largest residential center for Blacks in the United States.

That's a really big statement. There are a lot of Blacks in Chicago now. So there weren't that many at that time? Hm.

Kenya has modeled a number of important reading strategies: 1) noticing important ideas; 2) asking questions; 3) making connections with her prior knowledge; and 4) taking notes, which she had been previously teaching her students to do.

Before: Activities That Prepare Students to Read

When to Use

✗ Before Reading

During Reading

After Reading

Brainstorming

DESCRIPTION

Brainstorming—we all know what it is, but probably don't use it as much as we could. This is a classic group activity for helping students recall what they know or think might be involved in a topic, with just a few simple rules. The teacher gives a key word from the text or passage about to be read, and students call out their associations, ideas, and responses to that cue. They can toss out any sort of related idea, with no debating or criticism allowed, and all ideas are written on the board. Quantity is highly valued and the pace is brisk.

WHY USE IT?

This is a quick and simple way to help students realize what they already know about a topic, and to reveal to you, the teacher, their knowledge, conceptions, and misconceptions. You can discover which kids may already be experts on a topic, and others who may be feeling anxiety about the challenges ahead. You can identify ideas and issues to return to later. And you can help students see that they aren't starting completely cold, but have good ideas to contribute to the class, ideas they can build on as they learn. This signals that you believe they are active learners from the start, rather than just passive vessels entering the subject without a clue.

HOW DOES IT WORK?

While spontaneous brainstorming works just fine, it can also help for students to make a few notes privately, before the whole-group sharing begins. This especially helps if the class has just a few outspoken leaders amid ranks of passive or unconfident kids. Record the list of brainstormed ideas simply in the order that they come up. Use a sheet of newsprint or an overhead, so you can return to it later to emphasize major points in the reading and to notice what everyone has learned, after reading and processing the ideas in class. The more you can demonstrate that, "Hey, you guys already know something about this subject," and then, later, "Look at all we've learned," the better.

FOR MORE INFORMATION

We believe the earliest description of this strategy can be found in: Alex F. Osborn. 1953. *Applied Imagination: Principles and Procedures of Creative Thinking*. New York, NY: Scribner.

Clustering

When to Use

✘ Before Reading

During Reading

After Reading

DESCRIPTION

Gabriel Rico, who first popularized clustering as an aid to students' writing, describes it as "a nonlinear brainstorming process akin to free association." Clustering is simply a kind of brainstorming that links ideas in a two-dimensional map, with connections based simply on students' mental associations as they think about a new topic. It's similar to **Mind Mapping,** except that the latter activity is a more extensive representation of ideas after students have completed their reading.

WHY USE IT?

Like brainstorming, clustering helps students discover things they already know about the topic they will be studying. However, in her book, *Writing the Natural Way,* Gabrielle Rico describes how clustering not only helps access ideas, but reduces the anxiety people feel as they wrack their brains about a topic. As a person thinks and perhaps gets stuck, "This relaxed receptivity to ideas usually generates another spurt of associations." In other words, it is meant to open students up to connections and possibilities they might not have realized when they started. This is why the activity requires, like brainstorming, that all ideas be accepted, and that the students toss them out as quickly as possible without censoring or questioning the connections they make.

HOW DOES IT WORK?

1. Identify a key "nucleus" word—e.g., *infinity, erosion, manifest destiny*—and write it on the board.

2. The rules: Everyone works separately at first, writing the nucleus word and circling it, in the center of a piece of paper. They think of words and ideas that connect with this word and write them around it, drawing circles around the words and connecting these with lines to the nucleus word. As more connections occur, students jot them down, drawing lines to show which words they connect to. Work quickly. Don't reject anything.

3. Allow sharing and discussion between students in pairs or among small groups, and then construct a group cluster on the board, following the same pattern of associative thinking, as students offer words from their individual clusters.

4. As with brainstorming, be sure to refer back to the clustering later, to point out which ideas emerged as important in the reading and what the class has learned.

FOR MORE INFORMATION

Gabriele Rico. 1983. *Writing the Natural Way.* Los Angeles, CA: Tarcher; Joseph Vaughan and Thomas Estes. 1986. *Reading and Reasoning Beyond the Primary Grades.* Boston, MA: Allyn & Bacon.

KWL

When to Use

✗ Before Reading

During Reading

After Reading

DESCRIPTION

The teacher leads students, usually as a whole class, to list first what they think they already **Know** about a topic, then what they **Want** to know, and later, after reading, what they've **Learned.**

WHY USE IT?

This is a widely-used strategy, helpful for students of all ages and achievement levels. First, the **K** step asks students to access their prior knowledge about a topic. And again, why is "prior knowledge," so crucial? Because when knowledge is surfaced, students have an easier time making connections between new information they are learning and something familiar, which in turn helps make sense of the new stuff.

The **W** stage, generating questions about the topic, develops purposes for reading. The return to **L,** "what we've learned," tells students how and whether they've achieved the goals they set. And often they realize misconceptions which the reading clears up.

HOW DOES IT WORK?

1. As students brainstorm what they already know, list the items on chart paper or an overhead so they can look back as the unit progresses. Take time to reflect back repeatedly—KWL is not just an exercise to rush through at the start, but a tool to support thinking as you go.

2. While the **K** step usually goes smoothly, students often need help getting started on the **W** questions— perhaps not wanting to show their lack of knowledge, or because they're too infrequently asked. To help with this, use items in the **K** column to tease out the questions—*"I notice that you said Iraq was a desert. So what do you wonder about how people live in such a place?"*

3. After completing the **K** and **W** columns, students can group and label the items in categories they decide on, to give shape to the reading. This step is very similar to the **List–Group–Label** vocabulary strategy described later.

4. When completing the **L** list at the end of the project, be sure to compare it to the **K** and **W** columns. Students should not only become more aware of what they've learned but also how, as is often the case in learning, some questions didn't get answered, while unexpected ideas turned up instead.

FOR MORE INFORMATION

Donna Ogle. 1986. "The K-W-L: A Teaching Model That Develops Active Reading of Expository Text," *The Reading Teacher,* Vol. 39, pp. 564–570.

Taxes

What we know	What we want to find out	Brian M — What we learned
TAXES - issued by government • pays for things government needs • on all goods bought by people - income tax, property taxes, Federal Tax, State Tax, Mortage Tax, Luxury Tax Tax evasion Main Income for government Tax deductables Increase Yearly! APRIL 15th Accountants	- What are they? - Who pays them? - Do they pay salaries? - Whose salaries? - What does the government do with taxes? - % of income paid? - What are write offs + tax deductions? - How could tax money be better managed? - How does the IRS operate? - What are different types of taxes? - Why are there taxes?	- Taxes pay for a great deal of things like police, fire dep, teachers, gas, electricity, etc. - Money collected by government is revenue. - Some places you have to pay money to the government and the state out of your paycheck! - When the money-maker of the family is covered by social security + he dies, the family can receive his benefits. - Some states have no sales tax - Some states have up to 8% sale tax! - When someone works hard for the things they have + doesn't want to throw them away when they die, but instead give them to a loved one they have to pay a stupid tax! Defense — 40.2% Income security — 27.3%

Anticipation Guide

When to Use

✗ Before Reading

During Reading

After Reading

DESCRIPTION

Too bad the name is kind of clunky, because it doesn't really communicate the power of this strategy. Anticipation guides are brief sets of questions (3-to-5 items) that help kids activate their prior knowledge (including misconceptions), make predictions, engage important issues that will surface in the reading, and enter a text thinking. Students simply circle their answers or jot brief responses, and may talk them over with classmates before reading. The most powerful anticipation questions aren't factual recall, but invite students to take a stand on a controversy or a big idea in the reading.

WHY USE IT?

Getting students to think about key concepts *before they read about them* provides a tangible purpose for reading: namely, to compare what I believe with what actually turns up in the text. This process is sometimes called "frontloading" (Wilhelm and Smith), a great term for investing class time in activities that launch kids into the text with their brains switched on. Reading becomes a support for, or a challenge to, the positions students have taken. The questions guide students to focus on the big ideas in the reading. Instead of simply an assignment, reading becomes part of an ongoing conversation students have joined—maybe partly accidentally. Of course, some topics, like "kinetic molecular theory," will call just for simple prediction about the content. Others, like "the discovery of radioactivity" more readily invite controversy and expression of important beliefs. But even the simpler prediction questions still help students think as they read.

Anticipation guides are easy to prepare and take little class time—they are a great way to dip your toe into pre-reading activities. A five-item guide might take two minutes for students to respond, two minutes to compare answers in pairs, and another two minutes to hear what one volunteer per question says about his or her answer.

HOW DOES IT WORK?

1. Create a few (3–5) short questions or statements related to the text, using true/false, yes/no, or agree/disagree formats. The best questions pose big, open-ended issues, rather than previewing micro-details from the text. If your students are reading Orwell's *Animal Farm,* you might ask: "It's never O.K. to have just a few people in charge of a government or organization—true or false?" Studying earth's biosphere, you might offer "Human pollution of the atmosphere is always wrong—agree or disagree." For a Civil War unit: "Suppose you were in Lincoln's cabinet deciding whether to issue the Emancipation Proclamation, and a poll showed he would lose the next election if he signed it. Would you vote to: a) sign it anyway; b) not sign it; c) wait a few months and decide later?"

2. Kids can go right into the selection after completing the anticipation guide. This is meant to be a brief get-ready activity—correct answers are not what it's about. The questions you pose should not have single correct answers. All we are trying to do is activate prior knowledge, beliefs, and ideas, and send students into the text thinking.

Variation: With a little more time, you can deepen this strategy by having kids discuss their answers with a partner or small group. Then call the class back from these conversations to make some consensus predictions or surface a core disagreement, before reading. If kids are slow to talk, have them jot down their justifications first.

Variation: After reading, come back to the anticipation guide and compare the original responses with the students' deepened or changed thinking.

FOR MORE INFORMATION

H. Herber. 1978. *Teaching Reading in Content Areas* (2nd ed.). Englewood Cliffs, NJ: Prentice Hall; Michael Smith and Jeff Wilhelm. 2002. *Reading Don't Fix No Chevys.* Portsmouth, NH: Heinemann, pp. 84–87; Kylene Beers. 2003. *When Kids Can't Read: What Teachers Can Do.* Portsmouth, NH: Heinemann, pp. 74–80.

EXAMPLE

In the South Shore Small School for the Arts, Terrence Simmons prepared his freshmen to read LeAlan Jones and Lloyd Newman's *Our America: Life and Death on the South Side of Chicago,* with the following questionnaire. While this went beyond our "agree/disagree" format, it was extremely effective, drawing students into the issues explored in the book. Keep in mind that while there are some grammar errors in this example, it was written as a first draft for discussion, and not as an essay to be turned in or published.

1st period Literature
4/8/03 div.691

1. Do you know anyone that lives in the projects? yes

2. If yes, do they have a temper. No, believe it or not shes a very sweet person.

3. Does living in a poor neighborhood cause people to be violent? ~~Not in my opinion~~ I think so because when you're poor that causes people to steal money and material things.

4. What do you think happens in the projects? I don't really know. All I know is what I see on tv, which is stealing, ~~And~~ a lot of killing, and selling drugs.

5. Why do you think people live in the projects? Some people just like the life style, but for the most part its because thats all they can afford.

6. Do you view negatively of people that live in the projects? No, because I know someone in the projects that is nice. I think that you can have all the money in the world and be worst that someone poor.

Reading Aloud

When to Use

✘ Before Reading

During Reading

After Reading

DESCRIPTION

The teacher reads aloud short articles, brief passages of interesting material, or successive installments of a story, biography, or high-interest book in her subject area. Individual students, pairs, or small groups may also read passages aloud.

WHY USE IT?

The aim of this activity is not to test students' reading or listening ability, but to let the whole class experience powerful language about important ideas. Reading aloud evokes the time-honored human experience of listening to stories, telling family and cultural histories, trading "war stories," hearing lessons from elders—around a fire, at the dinner table, in family gatherings, at business conferences, wherever people meet in groups. People of all ages enjoy hearing stories, ideas, and beliefs told aloud. It helps students grasp the big ideas, fascinations, and questions that make our subjects meaningful to us as thoughtful adults. Good teachers have learned that reading strong writing aloud draws in students who would otherwise resist engaging in school topics. If students are to read aloud themselves, repeated practice and preparation is as much a teaching tool as the performance, because it helps improve reading fluency.

HOW DOES IT WORK?

Choosing the Text: This activity is not the same as orally reading from a textbook. To achieve the preceding aims, the reading must explore important issues, surprising facts or experiences, or fascinating, funny, or thought-provoking problems. It must be well-written, in clear, vivid language. And whether the teacher or students do the performing, it must be read with expression and understanding.

If Students Do the Reading: Provide time for individuals or small groups to practice. Groups can use "Readers' Theater," in which they divide up the reading, reciting some sentences individually, some as pairs, and some as a choral group. Reading into a tape recorder helps students hear themselves and improve with practice.

FOR MORE INFORMATION

Teri Lesesne. 1998. "Reading Aloud to Build Success in Reading," in Kylene Beers and Barbara Samuels, *Into Focus: Understanding and Creating Middle School Readers*. Norwood, MA: Christopher Gordon.

Dramatic Role Play

When to Use

✗ Before Reading

During Reading

✗ After Reading

DESCRIPTION

Choose a situation or event that will be described in the reading students are about to do and prepare a very brief description of it. Students work in pairs or small groups (depending on the number of characters involved) and rehearse role plays to represent the event. One or more groups present their role play for the class.

WHY USE IT?

In his research comparing competent and struggling eighth-grade readers, Jeff Wilhelm found that successful students consistently visualize what they are reading about, while struggling ones do not. As he searched for ways to help students visualize, he found that just telling them to do so was generally ineffective, while short, simple role plays were quite powerful, sometimes when nothing else would work. While many teachers use drama as a means for re-expressing ideas **after** reading, role plays that are carried out **before** reading are especially effective because they help kids build pictures of the action in their heads, to be accessed as they get into the content.

HOW DOES IT WORK?

1. When designing a role play, keep the scene simple, focused on a single problem or challenge. Leave it open for the students to improvise. For example, before reading the illustrated book, *Pink and Say* by Patricia Polacco, a true account of an African American and a white soldier in the Civil War, Steve had the students count off by two's. He instructed, "One's, each of you is a Union soldier who has been wounded. You're lying on the ground, barely conscious. The battle is over, but you can't walk. Two's, each of you is a Union soldier who has gotten lost from his company. You're frightened, and occasional bullets whiz by. You discover the wounded man lying on the ground. What do you say to each other?" For science or math, the roles can represent objects, such as chemicals, viruses, or electrons and nuclei, numbers or variables. One of our favorite science teachers recently invited her students to create a "Dance of Mitosis."

2. After the groups have rehearsed their role-plays, two or three can present to the whole class, particularly if they have developed differing takes on the same situation. However, as long as everyone has experienced the scene in their small groups, the main purpose of the activity—helping students create mental visualizations of the events described in the reading—will be achieved even if time for sharing is not available.

FOR MORE INFORMATION

Jeff Wilhelm. 1997. *You Gotta BE the Book*. New York, NY: Teachers College Press, pp. 87–112.

Probable Passage

When to Use

✗ Before Reading

During Reading

After Reading

DESCRIPTION

The teacher selects a set of 8-to-15 key terms from the piece to be read. Working in small groups, students place the terms in categories the teacher has established. Each group creates a "gist statement," which they predict will summarize the reading. Finally, they list things they *hope to discover* as a result of words they didn't understand or questions that were inspired by the process.

WHY USE IT?

This activity takes some time, but addresses a number of important mental strategies for good reading. It leads students to use their **prior knowledge,** focuses on important vocabulary, and uses **prediction** to build active thinking about a topic before reading. Predicting helps readers become conscious of their expectations and how the reading either fulfills or surprises them—an important aspect of learning. The activity gets students talking in small groups in a carefully organized way. It helps them become conscious of the structure of a story, argument, or explanation. And finally, the "to discover" step helps set **purposes** for students' reading.

HOW DOES IT WORK?

1. Choose 8-to-15 key words, so they invoke main elements or ideas in the reading. Similarly, the categories for labeling these words depend on the subject and kind of writing to be studied. Categories for a news article on the spread of the disease, SARS, could be: *Problem, Setting, Causes, People, Solutions, Unknown Words.* The word list might include: *Hong Kong, SARS, respiratory, epidemic, coronavirus, genetic shift, travelers, virulence, Center for Disease Control and Prevention, quarantine, death rate, co-evolution.*

2. Model the strategy first, with a group of words on a topic in your subject, thinking aloud so the students will understand what is involved.

3. Provide a few key directions: The "unknown words" category is only for terms the group does not know. Tell students whether you want them to use all the words in their gist statement, or only a certain proportion. Explain that if their gist statement doesn't completely match the reading, there's nothing wrong—but it does show that their expectations and the reading differed, and that's important to realize.

4. When the reading is completed, return to the "to discover" lists to see which questions got answered and which did not.

FOR MORE INFORMATION

Kylene Beers. 2003. *When Kids Can't Read: What Teachers Can Do.* Portsmouth, NH: Heinemann; K. Wood, 1984. "Probable Passages: A Writing Strategy," *The Reading Teacher,* Vol. 37, pp. 496–499.

EXAMPLE

When Brenda Dukes of Foundations School used Probable Passage to introduce a unit on "number concepts" in eighth-grade math, here's how one student team grouped their words in the categories she provided:

Ways of representing numbers
    40
    VI
    decimal

Types of numbers
    even or odd
    whole numbers
    integer

How they work
    hundreds, thousands
    place value
    addition, subtraction,
    multiplication

How they're used
    clocks
    age
    calendar
    counting

Unknown words
    rational
    exponential
    abundant number
    deficient

Write a sentence telling one important thing you think you'll learn about numbers based on these words and categories:

    We think we'll learn about how you can multiply with different kinds of numbers, like Roman
    numerals or decimals.

During: Helping Students Construct, Process, and Question Ideas as They Read

When to Use

Before Reading

✗ During Reading

✗ After Reading

Post-It Response Notes

DESCRIPTION

Students use small sticky notes to mark spots in the text, jotting responses, flagging important passages, noticing aspects of the topic, or showing thinking strategies they're trying out. They then refer to these notes in discussions or while doing other work after they've read.

WHY USE IT?

Occasionally, most of us have looked back after half an hour of reading to realize we have no idea what we just read. Tracking and returning to important spots in our reading is something that all competent readers do, particularly with material for a course or other practical purpose. So this strategy helps students become aware of information or elements in the text, and their responses to it, without lengthy note-taking. And when the notes mark particular concepts, facts, or thinking strategies that you, the teacher, wish to emphasize, they help students actively watch for them. Sticky notes are thus a great tool for supporting many of the during-reading strategies that follow.

HOW DOES IT WORK?

1. When students first try this thinking tool, give a few simple directions about what they should watch for as they read, and what to write on their sticky notes. Example: *As you read the article from the Internet on "Radiation and Risk"* [www.physics.isu.edu/radinf/risk.htm], *place sticky notes at any spots where you were confused and write a few words or phrases on them to explain your confusion or question. Also place sticky notes at points where the information surprised you and explain on them how your thinking was changed.*

2. Students like using multiple colors of notes to distinguish between various kinds of responses. The small $1\frac{1}{2} \times 2$-inch notes don't take up lots of space. A supply of larger notes is also great for occasions when students have more to say about some question or idea.

3. If you need to assess this work, ask students to place the page number where they'd attached it on each note, and to then transfer the notes to a separate sheet of paper with their name on it.

FOR MORE INFORMATION

Stephanie Harvey and Anne Goudvis. 2000. *Strategies That Work*. Portland, ME: Stenhouse, pp. 67–80.

Coding Text

When to Use

Before Reading

✘ During Reading

After Reading

DESCRIPTION

A quick way for students to become conscious of and to record mental responses to their reading is to use a simple coding system. For example, if a student, while reading, notices a connection to another unit in your course, to another subject, or to something in her life, she jots a **C** in the margin; if she's confused, she writes **"Huh?"** Students may add brief phrases or comments explaining their thinking. If the book belongs to the school, or if the teacher wishes students to be able to spot their notations quickly during class discussion, the codes can be placed on the post-it notes we described in the previous strategy.

WHY USE IT?

If students are not accustomed to thinking actively as they read, they need to make conscious efforts to do so, but not so intrusively as to totally interrupt the flow of their reading. Symbols help students remember a strategy, notice when their thinking has followed it, and then very briefly note the spot in the text where that thinking occurred. If we want students to think more deeply as they read, we need to provide explicit mechanisms for them to do this, rather than just exhort them to "really think about this material."

HOW DOES IT WORK?

Here is a set of codes, called INSERT (Interactive Notation System for Effective Reading and Thinking), that teachers have found very useful:

✓	Confirms what you thought	??	Confuses you
✘	Contradicts what you thought	✱	Strikes you as very important
?	Puzzles you	→	Is new or interesting to you

Be sure to introduce just one or two symbols at a time and demonstrate for students when and how they might use them. Then ask kids to share their coded responses later, when they discuss or work with the reading.

You can invent your own coding system that matches the subject matter at hand. Stephanie Harvey and Ann Goudvis use codes widely to teach each of the seven thinking strategies that they describe in their book, *Strategies That Work* (Stenhouse 2000). A sampling of their codes:

R	Reminds me of. . .	A	Questions answered in the text
T-S	Text-to-self connections	D	Questions that could be answered
T-T	Text-to-other-text connections		through discussion

FOR MORE INFORMATION

Stephanie Harvey and Anne Goudvis. 2000. *Strategies That Work*. Portland, ME: Stenhouse; Joseph Vaughan and Thomas Estes. 1986. *Reading and Reasoning Beyond the Primary Grades*. Boston, MA: Allyn and Bacon (for the INSERT system).

Bookmarks

When to Use

Before Reading

✗ During Reading

After Reading

DESCRIPTION

By folding a piece of paper in thirds, each student makes a bookmark for keeping her place in the reading. On this bookmark, students write briefly and perhaps also illustrate their thoughts about key concepts or pieces of information as they encounter them in the text. Bookmarks can promote any of the thinking strategies good readers use—connecting, questioning, visualizing, inferring, summarizing. And they can be used after reading, in discussion groups, and as products to be reviewed by the teacher or by the students.

WHY USE IT?

While bookmarks can depict many kinds of thinking, a typical one is to connect the material with students' experiences or other things they've read. Personal connections bring a concept to life. Links with other materials the students know help them to organize knowledge into larger, more meaningful categories, and to notice related information that illuminates the topic. Connections in the larger world highlight the significance of the material. Bookmarks not only invite students to stop and reflect in the midst of reading, but also help recall important ideas as they read further.

HOW DOES IT WORK?

1. Model on an overhead transparency what a bookmark might look like for a particular concept. Provide specific directions for what to place on the bookmarks. For example, suppose your eighth-grade math students are reading *The Number Devil* by Hans Magnus Enzensberger, in which the young hero dreams that a devil constantly taunts him with math puzzles. The bookmark could include a) a description of one math puzzle that the Number Devil poses but doesn't completely solve; b) a diagram illustrating a puzzle; and c) on the second side a connection that one puzzle might have with some problem or situation in real life. In the sample on the facing page, the teacher has asked students to use a bookmark to jot down four kinds of notes: personal responses, important passages, questions, and importatnt statistics from the assigned section of the book *Fast Food Nation*.

2. For practice, have everyone in the class read a page of material, complete a bookmark using the directions you modeled, and compare the results.

3. After reading, students should use their bookmarks to discuss in small groups or the whole class the material you assigned.

Variation: As they read the assignment, students can complete multiple bookmarks that identify and expand on particular spots in the text. The bookmarks should focus on passages that seem especially important, confusing, or helpful.

FOR MORE INFORMATION

Carol Porter and Janell Cleland. 1995. *The Portfolio as a Learning Strategy.* Portsmouth, NH: Heinemann.

EXAMPLE

Front

Back

"Fast Food Nation"

English 7th pd.
11·22·02

Response

While I was reading how they killed the cattle in these huge slaughterhouses it made me very sad. I also can't believe that they feed the cattle a lot of meat waste. Thats very unsanitary. It was also sad to read about how thousands of workers get injured & even killed on this dangerous job. It's scary to know about E. Coli and other food-poisoning viruses out there.

Important passage

"Getting rid of them makes a good deal of financial sense, especially when new workers are readily available & inexpensive to train"

Questions

Why do people work under these dangerous conditions?

Why don't they just close down F.F. restaurants that have cases of food poisoning?

Will they come up with a vaccine to help figh against food poisoning?

Important Statistics

- Injury rate in a slaughterhouse is about 3x's higher than the rate in a typical American factory. pg. 172

- 1,300 inspectors were responsible for the safety of more than 5 million work places across the country for OSHA pg. 179

Double-Entry Journals

DESCRIPTION

Good old traditional notetaking worked well enough for many of us in college. But not all our students are as prepared to handle their reading as we were. So we can help them fill their notes with more real thinking as they read. In this strategy, also called the Cornell system, students take notes on their reading in two columns with a line drawn vertically down the middle of each page. In one column, they summarize important ideas from the text. In the other, they write their own thoughts and responses—questions, confusions, personal reactions, or reflections on what the information means.

WHY USE IT?

Many students need to learn how to take effective notes when they read and to identify important concepts and facts they will need later, rather than view everything as equally significant. They also need opportunities to reflect on the topic, to wonder about its significance, or ask themselves what might be implied by the ideas presented. This is a more continuous, self-directed response tool, compared to sticky notes and bookmarks.

HOW DOES IT WORK?

1. Read aloud through a short selection on the overhead (or photocopy for all to follow). Model for students how to distinguish between important and minor ideas in their reading, re-stating ideas in your own words in column one, thinking aloud about why you chose those items and then jotting down this thinking, along with other responses, in column two.

2. Give students a chance to practice this kind of thinking and note-making with another short piece of reading and share the results together.

3. For a specific assignment, have students do some double-entry notetaking as they read on their own, and again compare the results in class together—thus gradually turning more responsibility over to them.

4. If you require students to take these notes regularly, you'll probably want to check their notebooks periodically. Stagger the due dates for various classes so you aren't overloaded with paperwork. Skim over and check off the entries quickly and, if you have time, comment on just one or two for each student, perhaps with sticky notes of your own.

FOR MORE INFORMATION

Descriptions of the double-entry notetaking approach are published by many colleges and universities. The original source: Walter Pauk. 1962. *How to Study in College*. Boston, MA: Houghton Mifflin.

EXAMPLE

My Comments

My notes on
TEXT "the abnormal present"

A 30-year period
is defined as "normal"
for climate, in the
context of the last
thousand years.
But not in context
of a million years.
Past known climate
patterns aren't
particularly
regular yet,
it is said,
climate is not
random.

I wonder ———
if this is true?
Prove that climate
is not random,

Note that 90% of
the past millions
years has been
colder than
now.
Now is a
"warm interglacial
period"
which only lasts
8,000 - 12,000 yrs &
has already lasted
10,800 yrs.

! ———

→ then
we will
have the
Nobel Prize

119

Sketching My Way Through the Text

DESCRIPTION

Drawing simple pictures or diagrams can help students conceptualize ideas from their reading. In this strategy, students create a sequence of sketches to illustrate thoughts, steps, or stages of a process described in their reading. The sketches may show linear changes over time, a cyclical process, or a group of related elements such as the various parts of a plant or elements in its ecosystem. These are not highly refined drawings, but quick and simple representations, so you must reiterate that artistic ability is not the point of the exercise.

WHY USE IT?

We don't all think in the same way. As researchers on multiple intelligence explain it, words and numbers are just two of the many modes by which people may understand an idea. Drawing is especially powerful because it helps students visualize what they are reading about, and that's one of the most effective thinking strategies that good readers employ. A sequence of drawings expands thinking, further revealing processes of change and development or multiple perspectives around a topic.

HOW DOES IT WORK?

1. Demonstrate a series of sketches for your students, illustrating material the class is studying. Even if you were good in art, don't get carried away. Make sure the drawings are rough diagrams and stick figures, so the kids understand they are not meant to reflect artistic merit. If you're teaching history, the sketches can show a series of important events—but they might also represent the attitudes or concerns of various groups of people: perspectives of various states at the Constitutional Convention, government vs. settlers vs. Native Americans, etc. In math, the drawings can represent steps in the process of solving a complex problem.

2. When you first have the students practice, their sketches should be large so that the class can easily compare and see the many ways that an idea might be represented.

Variation: After reading, students make sketch sequences on newsprint and tape them up around the room. Then, in a "gallery walk," small groups move from one set of drawings to the next, noticing how people pick up on various aspects of the reading. Or make transparencies, if money is no object, and have the class discuss them one at a time.

FOR MORE INFORMATION

Linda Hoyt. 2002. *Make It Real: Strategies for Success with Informational Texts*. Portsmouth, NH: Heinemann, pp. 139–141.

EXAMPLE

In the *Interactive Mathematics Program* the "Chef's Hot and Cold Cubes" activity ingeniously uses the concept of unmeltable ice cubes to represent negative numbers and ever-burning charcoal briquets to represent positive numbers. As the chef adds or removes cubes from the cooking pot, its temperature goes up or down. The temperature of the pot can be increased one degree by either adding a hot cube (adding a positive number) or removing a cold one (subtracting a negative number). Thus, students can envision a very understandable representation of adding and subtracting positive and negative numbers. Multiplication of positive and negative numbers simply means adding or taking out multiple "bunches" of cubes. Here is one student's set of drawings for several of the chef's actions.

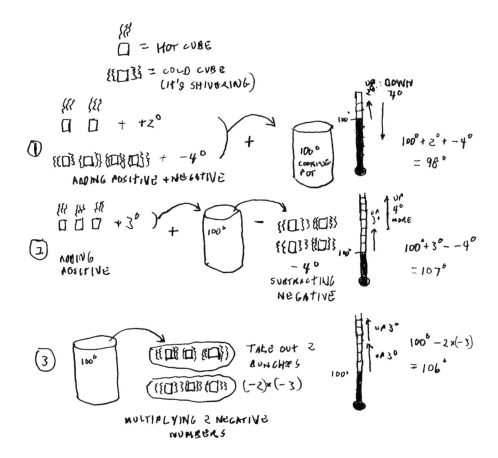

Cold cubes and hot cubes
Adding and subtracting postive and negative numbers

It Says/I Say

When to Use

Before Reading

✗ During Reading

✗ After Reading

DESCRIPTION

The teacher poses three or four questions that require students to draw inferences rather than just find information in the text they are reading. Students jot notes in three columns:

It says   *I say*   *And so*

For each question, students respond by a) finding and summarizing one or more spots in the reading that relate to the question; b) writing out their own thinking that builds on the portion summarized; and c) drawing a conclusion that proposes an answer to the question.

WHY USE IT?

Struggling readers often see reading as simply taking in words, hoping they "receive" the "correct" meaning from the text. They aren't aware that good reading requires a lot of inferring—going beyond the literal information presented and using inference to tease out its implications. This strategy is happily designed to address this need, explicitly leading students through the process. But also, at the opposite extreme, students often draw conclusions that appear unjustified or surprising to a more experienced reader. "It says/I say" helps students identify words in the text that inspired their interpretations, thus either substantiating them or leading these struggling readers to revise and improve their thinking.

HOW DOES IT WORK?

Once again, modeling by the teacher is key to getting this strategy started. When modeling "It says/I say," use a short piece of text that contains some ambiguity or invites interpretation. For example, after everyone reads a couple of pages on the attitudes of restaurant managers from *Nickel and Dimed: On (Not) Getting By in America,* by Barbara Ehrenreich (pp. 22–23), you might ask "Why do you think managers treat the waitresses so badly?"

On an overhead under *"It says,"* you might jot, "The managers have to make sure the company makes money." Under *"I say,"* "They probably feel pressure to show they're doing a good job and getting the most from the salaries being paid. Maybe they even worry that some customers are spies for the corporate office." For *"And so,"* you might conclude, "So they stop caring about treating people considerately and just get on their case."

This strategy especially benefits from discussion. Once students complete their charts, talking together about what they've written will help their thinking expand.

FOR MORE INFORMATION

Kylene Beers. 2003. *When Kids Can't Read: What Teachers Can Do.* Portsmouth, NH: Heinemann, pp. 165–171.

Say Something

When to Use

Before Reading

✗ During Reading

✗ After Reading

DESCRIPTION

This is a super-quick strategy to help students think as they read by enabling frequent, brief conversations between partners. Students pair up to read and, following a plan they've agreed on (or that you have assigned), stop after every couple of paragraphs or pages so they can each comment briefly on what they've read.

WHY USE IT?

While reading is usually a silent, solitary activity, adult readers are generally eager to talk with friends about what they're reading. Yes, reading is internal and reflective, but for most of us, it also feeds the flow of conversation we live by. Conversely, our conversations often influence our understanding as we listen to other people's points of view. Adolescents are social beings, and we should capitalize on that energy to support learning, rather than try to suppress it. Talking over what they've read in small chunks helps students clear up confusions. It also helps them internalize the material, instead of just skimming thoughtlessly over it.

HOW DOES IT WORK?

1. This activity is handy when you've taught a number of strategies and need variety after lots of sticky notes, bookmarks, and other paper-and-pencil efforts. The keys to making it work are a) modeling—as usual—so that students understand the kinds of comments you want them to try out; b) practicing repeatedly as a whole class, so that students become accustomed to using the thinking strategies you've taught and go beyond just a cursory word or two; and c) moving around the classroom to listen in and encourage students to expand on their ideas. Help students realize that it's O.K. to talk about their confusions, ask questions, and respond to one another's ideas.

2. If kids disagree strongly in their discussion, you've got a wonderful problem on your hands—they're hotly engaged in your subject. But now you may need to teach a minilesson about taking another person's thoughts seriously and asking follow-up questions, rather than just playing "I'm right/No, I'm right." And particularly when discussion grows heated, students need to conduct their discussions quietly since other pairs may reach stopping points at different times.

FOR MORE INFORMATION

Kathy Short, Jerome Harste, and Carolyn Burke. 1996. *Creating Classrooms for Authors and Inquirers* (2nd ed.). Portsmouth, NH: Heinemann, pp. 512–515.

After: Guiding Students to Reflect on, Integrate, and Share Ideas

When to Use

Before Reading

During Reading

✘ After Reading

Exit Slips and Admit Slips

DESCRIPTION

At the end of class, students write on note cards or slips of paper stating one important idea they learned, a question they have, a prediction about what will come next, or a thought about a character, event, or other element in the reading. Alternatively, have students turn in such a response at the start of the next class— or provide three minutes for them to jot one when they arrive. Without grading these in detail, skim through them to observe what kids do or don't get, what they've noticed in their reading, and what ideas may need to be clarified or reinforced.

WHY USE IT?

Kids in middle schools and high schools rush from one class to the next, math to P.E. to social studies. In all but a few innovative programs, the day splinters into 45- or 55-minute pieces, followed by sports and after-school activities, plus the socializing that matters more than anything else for many teenagers. This activity helps connect one day's learning to the next, and last night's reading to this morning's discussion, across everything in between. It helps kids focus as they enter our classrooms, or solidifies learning just before they leave. And it provides a snapshot of where the kids are so we and they aren't taken by surprise at test time some days later.

HOW DOES IT WORK?

1. Administering this strategy is pretty simple. For 2–3 minutes at the end of class (or the start of the next one), students jot responses to their reading on note cards. Base directions on what you want to learn about their thinking. Keep it simple—"One thing I learned and one question I have," for example. If you've taught particular thinking strategies—connecting, summarizing, inferencing—you can ask students to use them.

2. Don't let the cards become a grading burden or you'll just tire of assigning them. Instead, glance them over for a quick view of how students are doing and whether you can move on or need to further explain a concept. Don't worry about spelling and grammar—these aren't senior theses, but just quick notes to you. If you absolutely need to give credit, use quick check marks on the cards and in your grade book.

3. After you've studied the deck and picked out a few typical/unique/incendiary cards, use these (without identifying their authors) to spark class discussion about various views of the reading.

FOR MORE INFORMATION

Kathy Short, Jerome Harste, and Carolyn Burke. 1996. *Creating Classrooms for Authors and Inquirers* (2nd ed.). Portsmouth, NH: Heinemann, pp. 466–471.

EXAMPLE

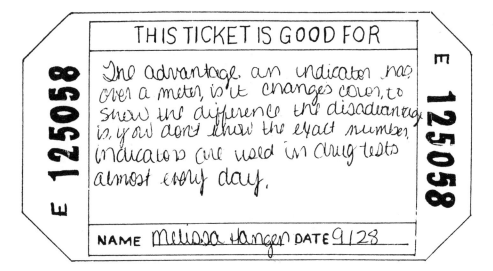

THIS TICKET IS GOOD FOR

E 125058

The advantage an indicator has over a meter, is it changes color, to show the difference the disadvantage is, you don't know the exact number, indicators are used in drug tests almost every day.

NAME Melissa Hangen DATE 9/28

Admit Slip—
Indicators Vs. Meters

I would have voted "~~Not~~ Guilty"
because the law that Congress passed
was purposely against Johnson because
he was favoring the south. The rule
was unconstitional to the president.
The republicans wanted to have one person
from there group as president so they
could punished the south. Most of the
Congress was part of the Radical Republicans
so they really got anything they wanted.
In a big way they were criminal.

Exit Slip—
Impeachment of Andrew Johnson

Mapping

DESCRIPTION

The idea of graphically displaying ideas has many variants: mind mapping, concept mapping, semantic mapping, and graphic organizers. The ever-popular Venn diagrams and timelines (shown below) also belong to this family of visual thinking aids. Students use two-dimensional diagrams to show how various ideas and pieces of information are connected in their reading. The teacher may provide a template or have students create their own, individually or in small groups. Our student samples illustrate these two options. One, called "concept attainment," uses a pre-set diagram that students fill in, to think about a key concept in the selection—explaining it, distinguishing it from others that are different, illustrating it, providing examples and applications for it, or exploring other aspects that the teacher may propose. Venn diagrams fit this pre-set category because they specifically ask students to divide a set of terms into three groups: two that are different from one another in some way and a third that shares the characteristics of both groups. The other example we provide represents a student's own graphic structure to represent her thinking.

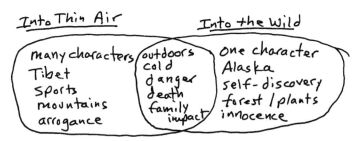

Venn Diagram

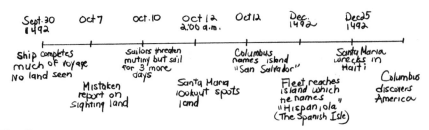

Timeline

WHY USE IT?

Mapping helps students get beyond the linearity of writing to perceive multiple relationships among ideas in their reading. It helps students understand and remember elements in the material by connecting them into a larger system, rather than leaving them as discrete items. Cognitive researchers tell us that our minds, particularly in short-term memory, can deal with only limited numbers of items at once. But batching together a jumble of items in some logical way makes them one larger mental unit—your friend's phone number is easier to remember than a separate string of 10 numbers, particularly if part of it reminds you of a famous historical date. Mapping groups and arranges ideas into larger units that are easier to remember. Understandably, as we work through a unit of study we often break it down in smaller pieces so that students can grasp one aspect at a time. The downside of this is that they might never add up the pieces into something larger that connects with big ideas and issues in their lives. So we need to make sure that the bigger picture doesn't get lost as we teach. This activity invites students to synthesize many aspects of an idea, rather than simply march dutifully and mindlessly through a series of tasks.

HOW DOES IT WORK?

1. As with many of our strategies, we urge you to model the activity, have the class practice and compare results, observing as students use the activity in order to help them and inform yourself about how they are doing.

2. Like the double-entry journal, this strategy specifically asks students to identify larger concepts in their reading, and then to group lesser elements under them. So mapping presents a great opportunity to teach a minilesson or two on this important thinking strategy. Use short samples of text to show students how you do this, as a competent adult reader, and to give them plenty of practice at it.

3. If you are going to use a pre-designed map, provide students with copies before they begin reading. Use ours or, if you prefer, adjust it to fit with the thinking required in your field. Ask them to place in the top rectangle an important word or phrase from the text (assigned by you or chosen by them) and to gradually fill in the spaces as they encounter the information they need. If students are to create their own kind of map, be sure they understand that there are a wide variety of ways to represent their thoughts. Use the completed sheets to help students review at the end of the unit of study.

FOR MORE INFORMATION

Dale D. Johnson and P. David Pearson. 1984. *Teaching Reading Vocabulary* (2nd ed.). New York, NY: Holt, Rinehart and Winston; R. Schwartz. 1988. "Learning to Learn Vocabulary in Content Area Textbooks," *Journal of Reading,* Vol. 32, pp. 108–117; Joyce Wycoff. 1991. *Mindmapping: Your Personal Guide to Exploring Creativity and Problem-Solving.* New York, NY: Berkeley Books; Rachel Billmeyer and Mary Lee Barton. 2002. *Teaching Reading in the Content Areas.* Aurora, CO: McREL.

EXAMPLE

Instructions: Draw a map to show the reasons the French considered aiding the American Revolution either openly or secretly.

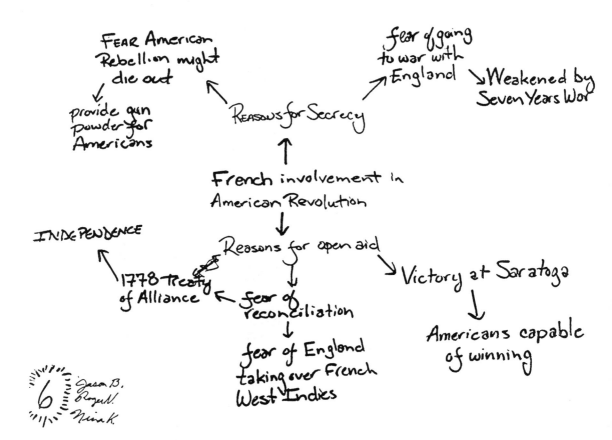

Mapping: Pre-set Structure

EXAMPLE

Map showing student's knowledge of the American Revolution

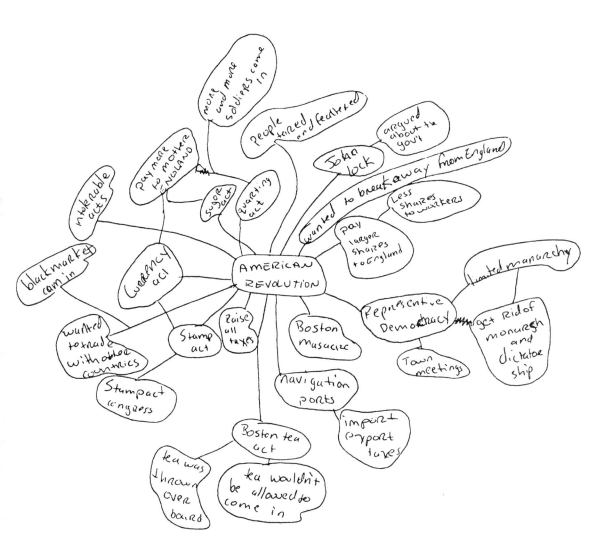

Mapping: Open-ended Structure

Written Conversation

DESCRIPTION

We all know that kids love to write notes to each other in school, but those notes rarely have anything to do with what we are trying to teach. The Written Conversation strategy harnesses the universal urge to share, but brings it into the curriculum. After reading (or hearing a lecture, or watching a video, or doing an experiment), pairs of students write short notes back and forth to each other about the experience. Also called **Dialogue Journals** or **Partner Journals,** you can think of Written Conversation as legalized note-passing in your content area.

WHY USE IT?

We often use "class discussion" as a key after-reading activity. But when you think about it, what is a class discussion? It is usually one person talking and 29 others sitting, pretending to listen, and hoping that their turn never comes. This ain't exactly what the standards documents call "engaged learning." In fact, whole-class discussion may be routine, but it is a pretty passive form of instruction, since most kids at any given moment are not actively engaged in the material. With Written Conversation, you can have a "discussion" where everyone is actively talking at once—though silently, in writing. Sure, you may have a few kids drift off the topic or say they can't think of anything—but you'll also have a solid majority of the class actually thinking about your subject.

HOW DOES IT WORK?

1. After the reading is completed, have students identify partners for a written conversation. If necessary, the teacher pairs up students.

2. Explain the activity first, if this is new to them, so kids understand that they will be writing simultaneous notes to one another about the reading selection, swapping them every two or three minutes at the teacher's command, for a total of three exchanges (or two or four, depending on your time constraints), and keeping quiet along the way. They are to write for the whole time allotted for each note, putting down words, phrases, questions, connections, ideas, wonderings—anything related to the passage, or responding to what their partner has said, just as they would in an out-loud conversation. Spelling and grammar do not count—after all, these are just notes.

3. The teacher can leave the topic open ("What struck you about this reading?") or can give an appropriate open-ended prompt: "What do you understand and not understand in this selection?" "What are the most important ideas here?" "Do you agree or disagree with the author, and why?"

4. Both students in each pair start writing a note (e.g., "Dear Bobby, When I read this chapter, I was amazed that Abraham Lincoln actually said . . ."). Meanwhile, the teacher watches the time, and after two or three minutes, asks students to exchange notes. The teacher reminds: "Read what your partner said, and then take two minutes to answer, just as if you were talking out loud. You can write

responses, feelings, stories, make connections of your own, or ask your partner questions—anything you would do in a face-to-face conversation."

5. After the planned two- or three-note exchange is complete, the payoff comes when you say: "O.K., now you can talk out loud with your partner for a couple of minutes." You should notice a rising buzz in the room, showing that kids have plenty to talk about.

6. Next, a short whole-class discussion can be much more engaged and productive, because everyone will have fresh ideas about the topic. Ask a few pairs to share one highlight or thread of their written conversations as a way of starting the discussion.

7. Some predictable problems. The first time you try this, the kids will tend to shift into oral conversation when papers are passed (adults also do this—it's a normal human response when you are bonding with a partner). Be ready to remind them to "keep it in writing" during the transitions. Then, even with the best instructions, some kids will write two words and put their pens down, wasting two good minutes of writing time with each pass. You have to keep stressing that "We write for the whole time." If necessary, provide additional prompts to the class or individuals to help them keep going. Finally, after you call kids back to order at the end, when they are talking out loud with their partners, you may find it very hard to get them back. This happy little "management problem" shows you that kids are connecting to each other and the material.

FOR MORE INFORMATION

Harvey Daniels and Marilyn Bizar. 1998. *Methods That Matter: Six Structures for Best Practice Classrooms.* Portland, ME: Stenhouse, p. 118.

EXAMPLE

Nelly, Did Mr. Gridley say that microwaves gave off ionizing radiation? I thought that kind was dangerous, and I don't understand why they'd let us have something in our homes that's dangerous. Did I just hear him wrong?

—Rose

Yea, microwaves do give off ionizing radiation which is dangerous. But microwaves give off such small amounts so they're not dangerous. Mr. Gridley said that we can only have under 5,000 mREMs a year. Microwaves give off such small amounts that we won't come close to ~~having~~ reaching 5,000 mREMs.

Nelly

That still kinda creeps me out though. I don't want to grow a third ear just cause I wanted to make some oatmeal in my microwave. Jeez

—Rose

Save the Last Word for Me

When to Use

Before Reading

✗ During Reading

✗ After Reading

DESCRIPTION

This is another discussion strategy to develop thinking. However, it uses groups instead of pairs, and helps each student compare his or her interpretation to others'. While reading, each student selects several statements or passages of particular interest to him, and writes each one (or a summary) on a note card. On the back of each card, the student jots his reaction to the selected passage. Then, in small groups or as a whole class, students take turns sharing one of their selected passages. After a student reads or re-states a passage, others offer their thoughts and responses. The author of the card gets the last word by reading his own reaction from the back of his card—or stating a fresh view, if hearing the others has altered his interpretation.

WHY USE IT?

This is a structured form of group discussion that helps students see how the meaning of any piece of reading is recreated by the reader, and not just funneled into her head from off the page. As students share their passages and hear various people's responses, they hear similarities and differences in one another's thinking. But instead of being drawn into a defensive debate, each card-reader gets the face-saving protection adolescents often need, as he listens and decides for himself whether to stick with his interpretation or, free of others' criticism and judgment, to revise it.

HOW DOES IT WORK?

1. To help everyone quickly locate the passage being discussed, students should indicate on each card the page number for their selection. Be sure students understand that when they write a comment on the back of a card, it can take the form of a question, a connection with something in their own lives, an explanation of why the statement is important, or why they disagree with it—any of the kinds of thinking that good readers employ.

2. Have students complete three or four cards as they read. When they're finished with the reading assignment and the cards, they should organize them according to which seem most important, or most worth sharing. That way, if someone else chooses to read the same statement, each student has several back-up choices.

3. Be sure to circulate among the groups as they share, to see how they're doing and what ideas they're focusing on.

FOR MORE INFORMATION

Kathy Short, Jerome Harste, and Carolyn Burke. 1996. *Creating Classrooms for Authors and Inquirers* (2nd ed.). Portsmouth, NH: Heinemann, pp. 506–511.

RAFT—Retelling in Various Perspectives and Genres

DESCRIPTION

RAFT stands for Role/Audience/Format/Topic. This is a more extended writing activity that expands on topics in students' reading. Instead of simply giving an assignment, however, the teacher provides some options for each of four aspects of the writing, and each student designs her own personal "assignment" by choosing off the four lists. The aspects are:

The **Role** the writer takes

The **Audience**—the person or group to whom the writer is speaking

The **Format** of the writing—letter, news article, poem, etc.

The **Topic** within the reading

The following chart shows some possible choices for a chemistry writing assignment on a collection of articles about radioactivity. One student might choose Marie Curie for her **Role** and decide to write a letter (the **Format**) arguing to a university department chairman (her **Audience**) about why it's important to let her research this just-discovered force of nature (her **Topic**). Another student might choose to write as Albert Einstein, sending a letter to President Truman about how the U.S. could build a new, very powerful weapon—an atomic bomb.

WHY USE IT?

This is a more time-consuming activity than most in our collection. However, as the reading research tells us (see Chapter 12, pp. 251–253), students highly appreciate choice in their learning, but rarely get any. The choices in this activity are especially meaningful, strongly affecting the vocabulary, style, and focus of the writing. So the assignment brings out your students' creativity. And reformulating the ideas in a different voice helps students internalize them.

HOW DOES IT WORK?

1. First, you need a list of choices in each area, for your topic. Develop the lists yourself, brainstorm lists with the class, or, if the kids are ready for it, ask them to create the options on their own.

2. Provide class time for the work so you can conference with individuals and keep track of their progress. You can insure that they've made their RAFT choices, marshaled the information they need, started their drafts, etc. by using the "Classroom Workshop" structure described in Chapter 8 of this book to keep students working as you circulate and conference with individuals.

3. Sharing the writing is important. Students can read to the whole class, but it's also fine to use smaller groups so more papers get heard in a limited time span.

FOR MORE INFORMATION

C. M. Santa. 1988. *Content Reading Including Study Systems.* Dubuque, IA: Kendall-Hunt; L. M. Feathers. 1993. *Infotext: Reading and Learning.* Markham, ON: Pippin.

EXAMPLE

RAFT options chart based on Internet articles about radioactivity. *Directions to students:* Choose one option from each column to create your own writing topic. Some choices can be mix-and-match. Others pretty much go together.

RAFT Chart for Radioactivity Unit

ROLE	AUDIENCE	FORMAT	TOPIC
Antoine Henri Becquerel	Pierre and Marie Curie	Personal letter	The mysteriously ruined film in his desk drawer, and what it might be caused by
Marie Curie	Director of Paris Industrial Physics School	Written request	Explaining why it's important to use a lab in the school for experiments on radioactivity
Albert Einstein	President Truman	Formal letter	How a new, more powerful bomb could be built
Mother of a U.S. soldier in 1945	Newspaper readers	Op-ed piece	Why an A-bomb should/should not have been used on Japan
Nuclear medicine doctor	Medical patients	Brochure	How lung and heart problems can be diagnosed using radioactive chemicals
Home repair company owner	Home owners— potential customers	Advertisement mailed to homes	Why home owners should use the company to have their basements radon-proofed
Head of Atomic Energy Commission	Members of environmental organization	Speech at organization conference	Why it's a good idea to build new nuclear-powered electric generators
Head of environmental protection organization	U.S. Senators	Testimony for Senate hearing	Why it's not a good idea to build new nuclear-powered electric generators

Extended Projects

DESCRIPTION

We've emphasized that the thinking activities in this section will usually be short and informal, and needn't require loads of class time or extensive grading. However, it still makes for a tremendous learning experience if you decide to expand a reading-and-thinking activity into a larger, more formal project for your students. This can take many forms, a number of which are described in Chapter 10 on Inquiry Units—a subtopic investigated by small teams of students, or a study around a big theme such as "plagues and epidemics over the centuries," or a simulation activity in which students take roles within a family, a community, or a government.

WHY USE IT?

It's essential for our students, at least some of the time, to dig deeply into a topic, to reflect, live with, and let important ideas really sink in, rather than always rush from one item to the next on our mandated standards list. The National Science Standards, for example, urge that serious learning in science requires that we cover fewer topics in greater depth, rather than skim lightly through all the possible elements of chemistry or biology or physics. Our students need to learn how to pursue information and ideas, to connect pieces of knowledge together, and to apply what they're learning in new situations. Kids tend to remember these big projects long after they've left our classes, when the many facts and details that they learned for the tests have faded from memory. Sure, you may not be able to pursue such projects all of the time (though some innovative schools do just that, for almost their entire curriculum). But if you do trade some of your coverage for a big project or two or three over the course of the year, you needn't feel one bit guilty.

HOW DOES IT WORK?—AN EXAMPLE

Since there are so many ways to design large inquiry projects, and we devote all of Chapter 10 to them, we'll simply describe one brief example here, with comments by several students who participated in it.

When Terrence Simmons at South Shore High School decided to assign *Our America: Life and Death on the South Side of Chicago,* by LeAlan Jones and Lloyd Newman, he built it into a project that engaged his students very deeply. He started off with an anticipation guide to survey their attitudes toward people living in the public housing developments nearby (see preceding **Anticipation Guide** strategy). A main focus of the book is on residents' responses to the death of a child who was dropped from the 14th story of one of the buildings. Terrence instructed his students to take notes on the many interviews of residents conducted by the authors, and to list at least three relevant facts or arguments from each "witness." Then, after about three class periods reading through the interviews, students divided into groups of three, each consisting of a judge, prosecuting attorney, and defense attorney. For part of a class period they reviewed their evidence, categorizing whether entries supported either the guilt or innocence of the children accused of the crime. After Terrence's prep session for the students in each role, the trials were conducted and decisions reported from each group. The following is a typical moment in one group's trial:

Prosecutor: This really hurt Eric's [the victim's] momma. She's suffering.

Defense: I object! It doesn't matter what his momma feels. That doesn't mean the boys are guilty or not guilty.

Judge: He's right. It's not an argument. That doesn't prove nothing.

Tatiana commented later on the notetaking: "It was very helpful. If the other side questioned you, you could go to the page in the book where you got your evidence."

Kelly, on the trials: "We should do these activities because they give kids a chance to comprehend more details and do better. It also teaches them other skills, life skills. You have to do a lot of work behind the trial, but you feel good when it's done."

Tatiana had just one complaint about the book itself: "This version cut off half the story! Give us the original! They sugar-coated it." Naturally, we love it when kids want to read more.

FOR MORE INFORMATION

Harvey Daniels, Marilyn Bizar, and Steve Zemelman. 2000. *Rethinking High School.* Portsmouth, NH: Heinemann, pp. 119–122; Harvey Daniels and Marilyn Bizar. 1998. *Methods That Matter.* Portland, ME: Stenhouse, pp. 20–56.

Learning Vocabulary

Word Meaning Graphic Organizer

When to Use

Before Reading

✗ During Reading

✗ After Reading

DESCRIPTION

There are dozens of graphic organizers for vocabulary study, but we offer this one because it clearly shows how to embed vocabulary learning into the wider process of reading. It asks students to think about a word in a variety of ways, to notice when and how it's being used, and why it's important to know. Students complete the organizer in small groups as they read and discover the various pieces of information about it.

WHY USE IT?

Remember those long lists of words you studied in preparation for the S.A.T. exam, once upon a time? How many do you remember and use now? Vocabulary is not learned effectively by memorizing lists and definitions, but by seeing words in use, in their customary contexts. In return, good vocabulary study supports and deepens students' thinking about the material they are reading. An effective vocabulary graphic organizer allows students to gather their contextualized experiences of a word in one place, where they can put the pieces of their knowledge together and solidify it.

HOW DOES IT WORK?

1. The more complex graphic organizers work best as whole-class or small-group activities, rather than individually. As Janet Allen explains,

   If you truly don't know a word, it is virtually impossible to complete the form. If you do know the word well enough to complete the form, you don't need to complete it. Students learn extended meanings of the target word here by virtue of their *joint* knowledge. (1999, p. 57)

   So place the students into groups to do this work.

2. Choose three to six words from the material the students are studying that you believe will be challenging for them. Avoid longer lists—even adults find they lose focus rather than learn more when trying to digest too much vocabulary all at once.

3. The groups can have a number of organizer sheets going for each of the key words in a study unit, and add various entries as they encounter information that expands their understanding of each word.

4. As students read, they meet periodically in their groups to discuss which aspects of the words they think they've learned about, and then decide together how to fill in the boxes on the sheet. Explain that they shouldn't expect to fill in every box right away; the idea is to discover more about the words as they go along.

FOR MORE INFORMATION

Janet Allen. 1999. *Words, Words, Words.* Portland, ME: Stenhouse, p. 57; Camille Blachowicz and Peter Fisher. 1996. *Teaching Vocabulary in All Classrooms.* Englewood Cliffs, NJ: Prentice-Hall.

EXAMPLE

Target word:
Exothermic

Topic where word is found:
Whether an overall reaction is exothermic or endothermic depends on the quantity of energy added (endothermic) compared to the amount of energy given off (exothermic) in the bond-making steps.

Parts of the word we recognize:
Thermic— like thermal underwear. So it's about being warm

Examples:
*Gasoline burning in a car engine
Explosions*

So the word means:
If heat is released overall when the steps of a chemical reacton are all added up

Why it's important:
If you are trying to combine two chemicals, you need to know whether to heat them or provide cooling because it's going to give off heat.

Where is the word used?
*Our chemistry book — chapters on energy
Web article on making your own hotpack for muscle injuries
Chemistry sites on the web*

How it connects with other words:
Types of chemical reactions— maybe combination reactions are often exothermic ones.

Vocabulary Tree

When to Use

Before Reading

✗ During Reading

✗ After Reading

DESCRIPTION

This graphic tool is focused on linking groups of related words or ideas, and allows for plenty of flexibility in the number and placement of branches (and roots, if the student so desires) to illustrate the relationships among the various words or sub-topics. The trunk is of course the core word or concept, and the branches show the connected elements, along with examples for them.

WHY USE IT?

Each of these vocabulary graphics focuses on a somewhat different aspect of the words and their relationships. The previous one takes a single word and asks the student to go deeper with it. The one that follows next helps students see relationships among a set of words from their reading. This one can work either way, allowing the student to expand on a single idea or topic or to link a word to others related to it.

HOW DOES IT WORK?

1. Ask students to choose several words from among a list of important words in the reading they are doing. Two to five words are plenty—the aim is to explore them in depth and pick up additional vocabulary along the way.

2. For each word, the student can draw a tree trunk on a sheet of paper and write the word near the bottom of the trunk.

3. As students read, they are to add related words, information, and/or examples, one to each branch. The branches, of course, may have branches of their own.

Variation: Have the whole class or small groups work together on vocabulary trees that are drawn on newsprint, hung on the walls, and added to as a study project proceeds.

FOR MORE INFORMATION

Dan Kirby and Carol Kuykendall. 1991. *Mind Matters: Teaching for Thinking*. Portsmouth, NH: Heinemann.

EXAMPLE

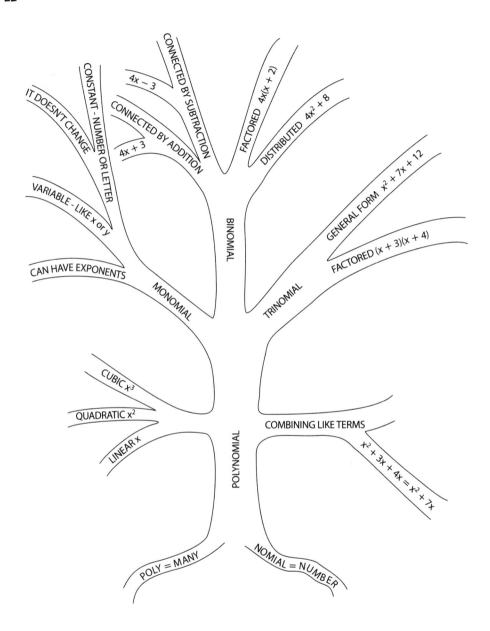

IT DOESN'T CHANGE

CONSTANT - NUMBER OR LETTER

4x − 3

CONNECTED BY SUBTRACTION

FACTORED 4x(x + 2)

DISTRIBUTED 4x² + 8

CONNECTED BY ADDITION

4x + 3

VARIABLE - LIKE x or y

BINOMIAL

GENERAL FORM x² + 7x + 12

FACTORED (x + 3)(x + 4)

CAN HAVE EXPONENTS

MONOMIAL

TRINOMIAL

CUBIC x³

QUADRATIC x²

LINEAR x

COMBINING LIKE TERMS

x² + 3x + 4x = x² + 7x

POLYNOMIAL

POLY = MANY

NOMIAL = NUMBER

List-Group-Label

When to Use

✗ Before Reading

✗ During Reading

✗ After Reading

DESCRIPTION

The name tells the story. The class develops—or the teacher may provide—a list of 20 to 25 key vocabulary words from the assigned reading. In small groups, students arrange the words in clusters based on something the words have in common. A cluster must contain at least three words in order to count, but words can be used more than once. The students then decide on labels for each cluster.

WHY USE IT?

Effective vocabulary learning requires that students work with words, think about them, and see them in a context. Working together, students pool their knowledge and learn from one another. This activity can help either before or after students read. Even though a student may not yet know everything he needs to know about a particular word, the clusterings help make sense of it, connecting it with other words he knows more fully, and suggesting where he might look to find out more about it. And providing labels from the clusters helps students think about both the words and the larger topic in more organized ways.

HOW DOES IT WORK?

1. Before students read, or after they have completed a reading selection, organize them in small groups for this vocabulary work. Balance membership in the groups, so each includes students of varying achievement levels. That way, the students can help one another, and no one group is left completely at sea.

2. If many of the words are unfamiliar to the students, provide time to look them up or find them in context—after all, if the group knows nothing about the words, the activity can't really go forward—though some guessing at the start can be productive, too. Then the groups can pool their knowledge to place the words in clusters, however they think the words might fit together. When all the words are arranged, the students decide on a label for each cluster.

3. Students can look back through the reading to see how their increased understanding of the words helps them comprehend the text better—and vice versa.

Variation: Have the groups record their lists on newsprint so they can be hung around the room for ongoing reference. Then kids can watch for the words as they read further. They can also add more words to the lists as they continue to read and learn about the topic. This is one way to create a word wall, which many teachers have adopted as a vocabulary-building activity.

A list for a set of U.S. history readings on African American soldiers in the Civil War might look like this, including some of the military terms and latinate words favored by mid-nineteenth century writers and leaders:

chattel	serfdom	amenability
edifice	fatigue duty	auspices
escalating	sagacity	quartermaster
permeated	contrabands	commissary
reprisal	philanthropic	mustered out
retroactive	avocation	parapet
frock coats	remuneration	

Categories that students choose for the words might include "military," "actions," "conditions and relations between people."

FOR MORE INFORMATION

Camille Blachowicz and Peter Fisher. 1996. *Teaching Vocabulary in All Classrooms,* Englewood Cliffs, NJ: Prentice-Hall. J. E. Readence and L. W. Searfoss. 1980. "Teaching Strategies for Vocabulary Development," *English Journal.* Vol. 69, pp. 43–46.

CHAPTER SIX
How to Use a Textbook

We talked earlier about what makes textbooks hard. Now let's talk about what can make them easier, more accessible, and more useful for young readers. In Chapter 5, we described 24 specific, Into-Through-and-Beyond strategies that can help students better understand what they read, including textbooks. In this chapter, we are going to add six more structures and strategies that work especially well with textbooks. But before we get to those activities, we need to look at the number one question we always face in determining the role of textbooks in our teaching: how much is enough?

The Curse of Coverage

Too often, we just divide the number of pages in our textbook by the number of days in the school year (e.g., $\frac{1200}{180}$) and then assign those six or seven pages every day to "get it done." But in our hearts, we know that this kind of "coverage" doesn't really work. Sure, we can make students read daily sections of the textbook as a matter of compliance and obedience. And then we can claim that we "covered" all 1200 pages of Western Civilization. But how many of those names, dates, places, and big concepts will the kids remember one week after the final exam? By the Fourth of July, most of those ideas will probably be, sadly, history.

When we use a textbook in this traditional and mechanical way, we aren't doing it out of cussedness. Maybe we believe that kids *need* to read the whole book to understand the main ideas in our subject. Or maybe our department or district requires that we assign the entire text. Perhaps our state's high-stakes test covers a vast inventory of details that matches the index of our textbook to a 'T.' Each of these seems like a good reason to assign the whole textbook, page by page. But still, as professionals, we have to interrogate our decisions bravely and honestly. Inertia affects teachers, not just objects in space. We, too, have continuing comfortable habits, and the textbook may be one of them. After all, the simplicity of a single-book curriculum, especially one we have practiced for many years, has its own siren-like attractions.

American schools have embraced the coverage model of curriculum, as embodied in our giant-sized textbooks, for most of the last century. This commitment has not, to put it kindly, served us well. If all the worrisome test scores and ranting pundits mean anything, they say that we have not yet maximized kids' learning in any of the traditional school subjects. Indeed, as the NAEP tells us, while a reasonable number of U.S. students have basic factual and operational knowledge in most subject areas, only a fraction (17% in mathematics, for example) understand a field well enough to do higher-level operations or performances. (2000)

It's simply not enough to mention ideas, either in a textbook or in a lecture. No matter what learning theory you subscribe to (constructivism, information processing, behaviorism, cognitivism) all agree on one thing: to remember ideas, learners must *act upon on them.* Period. You can have students move their noses above any number of pages, left to right, top to bottom, but that is neither teaching nor learning.

The harder the text—meaning the more content loaded or the more "inconsiderate"—the more help young readers need. They need you, the teacher, to break the work into steps and stages, and to give them tools and activities and work habits that help. But all this helping takes *time, time, time.* And, as far as we know, schools aren't handing teachers any more of that commodity to use. So you have to prioritize; you have to decide to teach a few things well and fully—and let some other stuff slide. Like the social studies teachers at Stagg High School, you could try to identify the 12 or 16 absolutely key, "fencepost" concepts in every course you teach. You might agree in principle that kids would do better to understand a dozen key ideas deeply, than to hear 1,000 ideas mentioned in passing. But what are the right fenceposts for *your* subject, *your* course?

In *Understanding by Design,* Grant Wiggins and Jay McTighe (2000) remind us that the content of any subject field has different levels of importance. There are some anchor ideas we want students to understand in a deep and enduring way, others that are important to know about, and finally, some aspects where a passing familiarity is sufficient. In other words, as we look at our textbook, we need to be asking: what are the really big ideas here, where are the places to slow down, dig in, and "uncover" ideas, not just cover them? What are the ideas or procedures that we want kids to really remember and deeply understand, long after the course is over? Wiggins and McTighe say we can identify these core ideas by using four filters:

1. Does the idea, topic, or process represent a big idea having enduring value beyond the classroom?
2. Does the big idea, topic, or process reside at the heart of the discipline?
3. To what extent does the idea, topic, or process require uncoverage?
4. To what extent does the idea, topic, or process have the potential for engaging students? (pp. 10–11)

What a healthy exercise to filter our textbooks through these questions! We recently heard some mathematics teachers vigorously arguing whether the long division of polynomials constitutes an "enduring" idea or not. And down the hall, the English teachers were debating whether one Shakespeare sonnet was too many—or not enough. These are vital conversations to have, among colleagues and within ourselves, not just to determine what sections of our textbook to use, but to be sure we are planning the most powerful and memorable learning experiences for all our students.

What's Really on the State Test?

Whatever our subject, we may believe that "the state requires us" to cover everything in the textbook, however thinly. Sounds plausible, given the current fervor of politicians to supervise us, but we'd better be sure it is the reality. For example, on our recent Illinois exam, the U.S. history test strongly stressed World War I to the present. Teachers who went too slowly, carefully covering everything from pre-colonial times forward, never got there. Thus, the kids who got "too much" early American history (including a full and respectful treatment of the native peoples) were "wasting their time" as far as the state assessment went. This has happened to teachers across the curriculum who make assumptions about what's on a standardized test but never check to be sure. We still hear English teachers saying that they are doing grammar drills to "get the kids ready for the S.A.T.," in spite of the fact that the S.A.T. has no grammar questions (the ACT does).

In fact, the 50 states differ widely in the sort of high-stakes tests they actually administer. While some do sponsor old-style factual recall and multiple-choice testing, more and more are using constructed responses, items that present some data (a chart, article, or problem) and then ask students to work with it. This newer kind of test tries to determine not just whether students retain factual information, but whether, given an authentic problem, they can reason effectively. If these are the kinds of tests used in your state, you can breathe a little more easily about skipping the occasional textbook chapter, and focus on making sure your kids can think like a scientist, a mathematician, a historian, or a writer.

Ways to Use Textbooks More Effectively

This chapter is where we get extra pragmatic. In a minute, we'll launch into a half-dozen strategies that can help kids get the most out of their textbooks, while sustaining engagement and keeping the classroom reasonably lively. By way of introduction, let us preview some key themes from all the activities that are coming up:

- Have empathy. Remember, not only are you a grownup and a subject matter expert, you have also read this textbook five or 10 times before. The material may seem easy to you, but it may really be Greek to the kids.

- Help kids get started. In the old days, the teacher's main role was to assign reading and then check for understanding later. Now we *front-load* our teaching, giving students support before and during reading, not just handing out quiz grades afterwards. That's what all the pre-reading activities in Chapter 5 are for, along with a few new ones coming up here.

- Don't leave kids alone with their textbooks. We can harness the social power of collaboration, having kids work in pairs, groups, and teams at all stages of reading to discuss, debate, and sort-out ideas in the book.

- Choose wisely. Make more selective assignments; instead of plowing through the whole book, make strategic choices about what is most important, assigning fewer pages and helping students study them much more carefully.

- Supplement richly. Our textbooks are no longer the sole source, "the Bible" for our courses, but are one important resource, coordinated with magazine articles, newspapers, websites, trade books, primary sources, and more.

ACTIVITY 1 ⟶ CHECKING OUT THE TEXTBOOK

If you look in the very front of your textbook's teacher's edition, you will probably find a section advising you to teach kids about the design of the textbook, to actually review its features and organizing principles, at the start of the course. But how many of us really do that? Between getting to know kids' names, handing out all the materials, and filling out all the paperwork, we often end that first day of class by saying "Read Chapter One for tomorrow." Mistake! A little time invested introducing the textbook now can pay big dividends down the road.

Sometimes the publisher's suggested "introducing the textbook" lesson is a combination of genuine orientation and PR flak—hardly what the kids need at the beginning of the course. Our colleague Jim Burke has developed a generic "meet your textbook" model that's both teacher- and kid-friendly, and it follows on the next page with Jim's kind permission. This is a pretty extensive process; you may decide to do several, but not all, of the activities listed here, depending upon the nature of the textbook and the experiences of your students. Sure, it would be ideal to do the whole activity at the beginning of the year, but if your kids are struggling with the textbook *anytime,* it is a wise decision to stop and take a couple of class periods to carefully uncover the text's structure.

ACTIVITY 2 ⚒ JIGSAWING

Even if you are laboring under tough requirements to "cover" material, having every student read every page in the textbook may not be the only alternative. There are some cases where we can divide up the text, letting the kids specialize in a smaller number of topics (and pages). Instead of reading everything in the textbook (recognizing that reading doesn't necessarily guarantee remembering) they can hear oral summaries of some sections.

Our friend Donna Stupple certainly risked her colleagues' disapproval when she jigsawed *A Tale of Two Cities* in her English classes. While some colleagues tut-tutted this insult to a sacred text, Donna figured the language was just too hard for her kids to plow through. But she did want them to sample Dickens' voice and pick up some cultural background from the era. So instead of having every kid read the whole novel, Donna created five "leapfrogging" jigsaw groups. For the first assignment, Group A reads Chapter 1, Group B reads Chapter 2, etc. Then, in the next round, Group A reads Chapter 6, Group B reads Chapter 7, and so on. This way, each kid reads every fifth chapter, all the way through the book.

In class, it worked like this: The kids would first meet in their "expert groups"—the students who had read the same chapter met to review the content and make sure they had a common understanding of the main

Your Name: _____ Date _____ Period _____

ACCESS: Textbook Feature Analysis

Directions: Use this activity to better understand the textbook in this class. Its purpose is to teach you how the textbook works by showing you what it is made of and how these elements are organized.

Types of Text 1. Skim through the book and make a list of all the different types of documents or types of text you will have to read (include graphic texts like graphs, maps).	
Sidebars and Pull Boxes 2. Find examples of pull out boxes or sidebars. What kind of information appears in these? Are they standardized throughout the book (e.g., "Profiles in History," "Science in the Workplace")?	
Feature: Typography 3. Find examples of different type faces and styles. Write down the examples and where they appear (e.g., large, bold type for chapter titles [e.g., 24 point font], 18 point font for subheadings throughout the chapter). How does this book use **bold-faced type**? What does it mean when they use *italicized words*?	
Feature: Color 4. Does the textbook use color to convey information (e.g., what does it mean when you see words in red ink on the page?)	
Feature: Symbols and Icons 5. Does the textbook use symbols or icons to convey information? (e.g., if you see an icon with a question mark in it, what does that mean? Are you supposed to do something, like ask a question? Does it mean this is a potential test question? Or is it a link to a theme running throughout the book?)	

Features: Images and Graphics 6. What kind of information accompanies illustrations or images? Find examples of a map, chart, and a photograph and then look for captions or sidebars that explain or discuss the image. How is the image identified (e.g., Figure 2.6)?	
Organization 7. How are chapters organized? Make a brief but accurate outline.	
Navigation: Headers and Footers 8. Look at the top and bottom of the pages of the book. These are called the header and footer. What kind of information is contained in this space? What do you notice as you flip through 50 consecutive pages (e.g., does the content of the header or footer change? If so, in what way, for what purpose?)	
Testing! Testing! 9. Imagine you must now prepare for a big test. What features of this book would help you to prepare for that test? (Hint: Do not limit your answer to the practice or study questions.)	
Reading Speed 10. While your teacher times you, read one page of the book, taking notes as you normally would while reading it for homework. How long did that take you? Now do the math: If your teacher tells you to read the opening section for tomorrow and this section is 10 pages long, how much time do you need to allot for your homework in this class?	
Concerns 11. After familiarizing yourself with this textbook, you may have concerns or questions. Getting these answered up front might help you read the textbook with greater success and confidence. Take this time to list any concerns you might have (e.g., reading speed, vocabulary).	

characters, key events, and big ideas in the text. Then kids reformed into heterogeneous "base groups" composed of one expert on each chapter, 1 through 5. Next, in chronological order, the expert for each chapter recounted the key elements of the chapter to the rest of the kids, who hadn't read it. After this round of highlights from each chapter, the groups transitioned into general discussion about the five-chapter segment of the novel.

Many books couldn't be studied this way because information in earlier chapters is crucial for understanding later ones. But textbooks frequently *can* be easily subdivided. Let's see how this might work. Chapter 8 in MacDougal-Littel's *The Americans* covers the reform movements between 1820–1850. There are four distinct strands which emerged during this period—religious renewal, abolitionism, the early women's rights efforts, and workplace reform—each of which receives several pages of coverage in the textbook. Since these movements are part of a wider trend in society (and because the page-number totals are about the same), this period presents a fine opportunity to jigsaw. Instead of reading the whole chapter, each student specializes in one of the four topics by: 1) studying just that section of the chapter; 2) meeting in an expert group to review key elements of their chosen reform movement; and 3) joining a heterogeneous group to brief classmates and to hear from them about the three other reform movements. When students set off to do their chosen reading, it is important, as always, to use some good pre-reading activities (chosen from Chapter 5) to activate their prior knowledge and send them into the text thinking. Or you can use the following Textbook Jigsaw Sheet, which gives support for students both during reading and at each of the meetings.

We know that jigsawing can be controversial—or simply out of the question—for teachers who are required to be on the same page with colleagues throughout the year. Or for teachers who worry, sincerely, whether hearing an oral summary from other students is as good as reading an expert's version in print. However, as we weigh the "risks" of jigsawing, it is important not to overestimate the impact of standard, read-the-chapter work. We need to always wonder: is covering material the same as understanding it? Are kids actually working, thinking, and engaged with the text we assign—or are they just imitating a sentient life form while remaining functionally unconscious? With jigsawing activities, when kids sit down to find the links between movements like abolitionism and worker's rights, they are coming pretty close to "doing history," not just dutifully accepting what the textbook says. Plus, this kind of genuine historical work can create the curiosity and motivation to read a whole book, like *Uncle Tom's Cabin,* that connects the movements of the period in a vivid, powerful way. And in other subjects it's the same; when you

History

Textbook Jigsaw Sheet

Step #1—Reading

To prepare for your Expert Group and Base Group meetings, please respond to the following items, either while you are reading or after you have read.

Passages: Please mark any words, lines, or sections of the text that "stick out" for you. These passages might be important, puzzling, curious, provocative, or surprising—whatever strikes you. You may use post-it notes or our standard coding system if you wish.

Big Ideas: Jot down two or three of the main points, big ideas, or key terms in this section.

_____

_____

_____

_____

_____

Reactions/Connections: What were your feelings and responses to this reading? What personal connections did you make with the text? Did it remind you of past experiences, people, or events in your life? Did it make you think of anything happening in the news, around school, or in other material you have read?

_____

_____

_____

_____

Step #2—Expert Group Meeting

In just a few minutes, each of you will explain your section of the chapter to classmates who have not read it. So now, meeting with other experts on this section, you need to review the key points, confirm your understanding, answer any questions you may have about the reading, and make sure you're all "on the same page."

Step #3—Base Group Meeting

*When the group meets, the discussion will have two stages. **First,** each person should take about one minute (no more!) to give the group the big ideas, the highlights, of their chapter section. **Next,** everyone joins in a general conversation about the readings as a set. Try to find connections, similarities, and differences, or themes in the different readings. We'll have a whole-class discussion when we get back together.*

Math Textbooks Are Different

We have been talking here as though textbooks in all subject fields are basically alike, which clearly they are not—and in mathematics, the differences are greatest. Can we take a moment to empathize with our math colleagues? All of us who teach school must cope with grownups who say "Oh, I hated X (your subject) in school." But math? It seems like everyone's got it in for math. As our colleague Arthur Hyde points out, math is the only school subject in which virtually every American citizen can tell you exactly when they "hit the wall" and gave up—whether it was long division, right triangles, or quadratic equations. Singer Jimmy Buffet has even penned a crude little tune called "Math Sucks" that evokes a hearty sing-along at his Margarita-soaked summer concerts.

Actually, math does not suck at all. But mathematics textbooks are typically the hardest of all to read. They have the highest content load per sentence of all the secondary textbooks (Barton and Hiedema 2002), are full of abstract ideas, and use symbolic signs and signals that are specialized and different from other kinds of text. Further, the explanations of concepts are quite typically short, compared to the amount of the book given over to problems and applications. You can't safely skim through a math textbook just to "get the gist of it," because every single word, letter, or symbol may be critical to understanding.

There are two main approaches used in current math textbooks. In one style, the authors present a concept and then provide problems that allow students to practice the idea that was introduced. In the other approach, the authors lead students through a more step-by-step process, where they set up experiences so students can "discover" concepts for themselves. There is plenty of controversy in the math world about which approach is best; the more inductive approach seems to have a potential advantage in student engagement. But both types of texts are still filled with abstract ideas, symbolic language, and very high concept density. When you compare this genre of text to a novel or a historical report, you might even question whether "reading" is the right term for what goes on when students use some math textbooks. Still, math teachers tell us (and the National Council of Teachers of Mathematics standards confirm) that Before-During-and-After reading strategies (like the ones here and in Chapter 5) are one key to helping students think mathematically. And as Vanessa Brechling's story on page 178 showed us, these activities really do work, "even in math."

have to read, write, talk, and listen, it is much harder to "fake it" than it is to slide through a textbook assignment without understanding.

ACTIVITY 3 ⚊ GUIDE-O-RAMA STUDY GUIDES

Sometimes teachers will prepare a written guide, a handout that shows students the way through a textbook chapter. This strategy does more than activate prior knowledge and set purposes for reading—it actually leads kids through the thicket of text, terms, charts, diagrams, and pictures step by step, *while they are reading.* Unfortunately, we too often create reading guides that are more like an outline of the textbook chapter, or a checklist of items we might include on the test later on. Sure, it is worthwhile to tell kids what counts, but that kind of list-guide misses the opportunity to coach, to model, and to have a mentoring conversation with young readers as they work.

That's why we like the "Guide-O-Rama," a funny name for a special kind of tool that combines a genial reading roadmap with a think-aloud written down. Sounds weird, we know, but here's a sample. This one was designed to accompany the opening chapter of an Astronomy text.

Star Search Guide-O-Rama—Chapter One

Page # *Tip*

111–113 Read this introductory section slowly and carefully. It sets up the big ideas you'll need later.

112 When I was a kid I always wondered where all those goofy constellation names came from. And why so many of them don't actually look like the crab or the spider or whatever they are named for. I mean, Big Dipper, I can see it, but Ursa Major (Big Bear)?

Have you ever tried to spot Betelgeuse before? Do you think you could find it now, using the Orion's belt key?

113 The diagram on the lower left is really helpful.

The sidebar on the tilt in earth's axis is a good reminder of how the seasons work, if you don't remember.

114 So, will any of us live to see any perceptible change in the heavens during our lifetimes? How do you know?

115–119 Since this is October and we will be studying the Fall sky, you can skim the pages covering Northern Hemisphere Winter, Spring, and Summer.

SUBJECTS	*Page #*	*Tip*
MATTER	120	The "Looking West" diagram sure confused me, how about you? I just relied on the whole-sky map instead. Anyone who can explain Fig. 5 to the class gets extra credit.
		There are 39 Fall constellations listed, too many to find them all. I started with the most familiar ones, and found about ten before I moved on.
	121	When we go out stargazing Thursday night, we will be following the instructions in the box on the right to orient ourselves to the star map. Read the steps now and see if you "get it."
	122–129	You can skip the whole Southern Hemisphere section, but do this one experiment as you flip through: what big or general differences do you see in the "look" of the southern sky year-around from the northern sky? (Hint: check the Milky Way)
	132–135	Lots of tough vocab here. The three big ones to understand are *celestial sphere, celestial time,* and *celestial latitude.*
		Don't sweat the *planisphere* stuff for now. We'll get to that next week.

Get the drift? The Guide-O-Rama lets you informally coach, support, and chat with kids as you steer them along. It also invites you, as the most experienced reader in the room, to open up your head and show students how you "thought your way through" the same text they are reading. On the practical side, now that we are using textbooks more selectively and strategically, the Guide-O-Rama is a handy place to embed written directions about where to dig deep, what to skim, and when to skip ahead.

Of course, creating a really useful guide takes significant preparation time on the teacher's part. But the tool really helps kids—and once created, it can be reused, as long as you stick with the same book. You definitely do not have to make a guide for every chapter; after all, we are looking for kids to develop their own textbook comprehension strategies from all these good structures we are modeling. But once you have created your first Guide-O-Rama, you may find that this is a pretty fun way to infuse even dull textbook chapters with a bit of your own spin, personality, and humor.

ACTIVITY 4 ✐ VOCABULARY WORD SORTS

One thing that makes textbooks so tough for kids is all the new vocabulary and the high rate at which it is typically introduced. Without some advance guidance, students have no idea where, mentally, to hang all those new words. That's why it is so important for teachers to conduct effective pre-reading activities focused on vocabulary, so kids enter the text thinking, on the lookout for words, and actively making meaning right from the start. In Chapter 5 we shared three vocabulary strategies that work well with textbooks. Here's another that's a special favorite.

Social Studies

Science

In her eighth-grade class at Baker Demonstration School, Kathleen McKenna is preparing for a unit on soil conservation. But before she assigns the chapter in the textbook, she wants to introduce her students to some of the key words they will be encountering. So Kathleen has brought to class several sets of key words, each one hand-printed on a little 1″ × 3″ piece of paper. Among the terms included:

Carbon Dioxide	Topsoil
Subsoil	Contour Plowing
Abrasion	Decay
Conservation Plowing	Mechanical Weathering
Decomposers	Acid Rain
Sod	Ice Wedging
Erosion	Chemical Weathering
Mites	Conservation
Earthworms	

Kathleen has carefully included some terms that kids already know *(earthworms, sod);* some familiar words that are used in an unfamiliar way *(ice wedging);* and others that are brand-new *(contour plowing)*. She gets kids into groups of four or five and hands each a full set of word strips to work on. Her instructions are simple: "Using the best thinking you can, put these words into categories that you can agree on as a group. What goes with what? If you have no idea what a word means, then guess. Choose someone to be the official 'spotter' in your group who can report on what you did. O.K.? In about five minutes, spotters be ready to explain how your group sorted the words."

The students take a few minutes to scan the whole set, confirming some meanings and guessing at others. Then individual kids start suggesting groupings ("Let's put the plowing ones together"); trying out different hypotheses

Substituting for the Textbook

Jeff Janes teaches Introduction to Physical Science to freshmen at Andrew High School in suburban Chicago. "Honestly, I hate textbooks," he says. "They're full of mistakes. They're boring to the kids, and they're too simplistic. They don't go deep enough, and they include a lot of stuff that 95% of my students will never need to know, even if they go into a science career. I mean, quantum physics for ninth graders?" Jeff is also concerned because the textbook adopted by his department doesn't even match well with the Illinois state assessment, which changes every year as let's-get-tough legislators pile mandates on the schools.

So now Jeff teaches without a textbook—almost. The first time he tried it, he forgot to tell the parents in advance. "A political mistake," Jeff admits, ruefully recounting the barrage of questions he fielded at that Fall's go-to-school night. "The parents think the textbook is the subject, I realized. So what I do now is tell them in advance how I teach, and when they hear the rationale, they have no problem with it. They remember they didn't like the textbook when they were in school either. But now I do issue the textbooks to the kids. I say, 'Use this as a reference, use the glossary if you need it.'" But Jeff makes no regular reading assignments in the textbook. Doesn't he use the textbook for anything else? "Well, I'm a really awful artist, so I do make overhead transparencies of some of the drawings and diagrams in the book."

So what do the kids read instead? For the backbone, Jeff writes his own text, far shorter than the textbook, focusing on a much smaller number of topics. And he delivers this text to kids in the form of a PowerPoint presentation, both computer-based and in paper print-out form. Why is this better than a textbook? "Well for one thing," Jeff laughs, "the author is there to answer questions and talk to the students."

What does the mini-text include? What does it leave out? Jeff says there are two criteria for including a topic in his home-made baseline text, one of which he's proud of and one not. "First, as the science expert in the room, I've got to ask, what are the ideas that are fundamental to science, things kids have got to understand so they can continue their study of science in the future, and be able to consider a career in the field?" For Jeff, the gotta-haves include things like Newton's laws of motion, the kinetic theory of matter, the origin and history of the universe. The second criterion that Jeff's not so proud of? "What's on the Prairie State exam."

The rest of students' reading includes a wide variety of articles on physical science, chemistry, and earth science (all of which are covered in the state's physical

continued

science exam, taken after the fifth semester of high school). Jeff makes extensive use of the *Chicago Tribune* and the neighborhood's own daily newspaper for real-life examples. When Chicago Cubs home-run king Sammy Sosa was suspended from baseball for using a cork-filled bat, the class read about it avidly. Using their knowledge of physics, they determined that "corking" a bat is a bad idea, scientifically—increasing bat speed but decreasing the force that helps you hit home runs. Jeff also directs students to the Internet for science information and stories; his favorite is the NASA website. But he is adamant about teachers checking Web sources before sending kids their way: "You've got to screen the Web stuff first—it's even less reliable than the textbook."

Finally, Jeff's students read science magazines *(Science News, Discover, Nature, Scientific American)* and trade nonfiction books. Last year, some favorite books for students were *A Short History of the Universe* and *E = MC²: A Biography of the World's Most Famous Equation* (see pages 51–53). Kids also read selections from more challenging science trade books, with coaching and conversation from Jeff, including *Genome: Autobiography of a Species in 23 Chapters* and Stephen Hawking's *A Brief History of Time.*

So how well does this textbook-free physics course work? Pretty well, judging by the kids' grades and test scores, which Jeff reports are higher than under the old textbook-based model. "I call this 'No Secrets Education.' I tell the kids what we are going to study, we study it, and that's what I assess. And they do great. Plus, I know I'm sending a few young scientists into the world, which makes me really happy."

("I think these are different kinds of erosion"); and dealing with anomalies ("Do earthworms erode the soil or help it?"). There's still plenty of buzz in the room when Kathleen calls kids back together, and asks the spotters to briefly share their group's categorization scheme. As reports are shared, there's lots of overlap in the categories, and some good questions are posed along the way ("Isn't soil erosion a natural process too? Is it something we humans should always be trying to prevent?")

By now it's only 10 minutes into the class, with plenty of energy present and lots of ideas left to be shared. But Kathleen just says: "Well, I guess you guys are ready to read the chapter now." While the kids don't quite storm the pile of textbooks, they don't waste any time either. Within one minute, the classroom is hushed, as kids read about soil erosion and conservation. Some kids silently nod or smile as now-familiar terms pop up, and categories, some predicted and some surprising, emerge.

The magic of this activity is in its process. Word sorts are pretty fun, they are social and collaborative, and if you set them up right, they go very quickly. In Chapter 5, the similar "List-Group-Label" strategy is structured for learning vocabulary during or after reading. But the goal in this case is not for kids to correctly classify all the vocabulary or even know what all the words mean before they read the selection. In fact, a wrong guess is just about as useful as a right one because it still prepares the kid to meet the word in the textbook. Once there, he can confirm or disconfirm his prediction; either way, that's an active process and a big help in remembering. So word sorts, even when kids don't know the definitions, set a purpose for reading: they get students watching for key vocabulary and prime them to stop and think when those words appear in the text.

ACTIVITY 5 ⟶ TEXTBOOK CIRCLES

In Chapter 9, we will introduce a small-group reading activity called Book Clubs or Literature Circles. This structure is simply a school adaptation of the adult reading groups you sometimes see meeting in bookstores, libraries, or maybe your own living room. Basically, this is just people picking books they want to read and talking about them with their friends. In school, we often use this structure with trade books connected to a teaching field—like historical novels set during the Civil War or biographies of famous scientists. But some teachers have also successfully applied the Book Club structure to textbooks. There are a few challenges. Most textbooks don't provide the narrative structure or emotional engagement that novels or trade nonfiction books typically do. Still, even if textbooks are dry and overpacked, the social power of working and talking together can enhance students' understanding of them.

In Peru, New York, Jodie Bonville uses Textbook Circles with her middle school social studies class, and here's how she describes it:

> Our social studies curriculum deals with the history of the eastern hemisphere (the development of civilizations of Mesopotamia, Egypt, China, India, Greece, and Rome). The textbook we use is the Prentice Hall *World Explorers,* which is a multi-volume set. The title from the series that we used for our "Textbook Circles" was *The Ancient World.* Before we started reading the text, I had students fill out a KWL chart on what they **Knew** about the Romans and **Wanted to Know** about these people. The kids showed a high interest in the aspects of

everyday life in Rome, which was good because this volume had lots of information on the daily life of the Romans

I formed the Textbook Clubs myself, balancing student strengths and weaknesses in reading. As always in my classroom, I wanted to keep a balanced, mixed-ability model. It wasn't too hard to get our Roman Textbook Clubs going, because earlier in the year I had taught students the basic procedures for Book Clubs with literature. Back then, I trained students with short pieces of text and introduced them to various tools for notetaking, including role sheets (see pages 206–209). All these tools were explained, practiced and reinforced. So peer-led small-group discussions were already a part of our classroom culture.

When adapting Book Clubs to the Social Studies textbook, I needed to redesign some of the role sheets which students use while they are reading—and which they bring to the group to feed the discussion. I used some of the regular roles, like Connector, Illustrator, and Researcher. I also made up some new ones, including the "Amazing Reenactor," whose job was to dramatize aspects of Roman daily life, based on what they read in the text (I supplied them with a chest of props, like sheets for togas, etc). I also gathered some other materials for different group members and their roles, including reference books about Rome and websites about ancient civilizations bookmarked on the computer.

The Textbook Circles met on a simple schedule. Groups first met for one class period to read a selection from the textbook and make notes with their assigned role in mind. Mostly kids read silently and jotted notes, but some groups read certain passages out loud to each other, and talked about them as they went. The next class period the students had another 40 minutes to work on the tasks associated with their roles. Because we teach Social Studies every other day due to block scheduling, the students also had an extra day outside of class to continue working on their roles, so they would come to class really prepared and ready to share the following day.

During the Textbook Circle meetings, my own job was to facilitate and guide. I circulated around the room, listening as students discussed each section of the book. At first I just wanted to make sure that students were all engaged in the discussion, but after a while I could also sit in a group and take notes on the various interactions between students. After each Textbook Circle session, we gathered as a whole class to debrief, to discuss positives and negatives of their interactions and discussions, so that the next meetings could be even more productive.

As far as assessment was concerned, I created an informal "Textbook Circles Self-Assessment" sheet for kids to rate themselves as group members and as emerging experts on the content. I also kept the anecdotal notes from my visits to the individual groups. And, oh yes, I did give a unit test over the textbook, and the kids did very well on it. The students reported that they really enjoyed using Textbook Circles in Social Studies. They felt that being able to discuss the reading in a group helped them to remember information better. And they really enjoyed the different roles, because they helped bring the text to life for them—something I just love to do in my classroom.

～

For more information about Book Clubs, including many of the classroom tools and forms that Jodie used, as well as some further assessment ideas especially adaptable to Textbook Circles, see Chapter 9.

ACTIVITY 6 ～ SQ3R: REMEMBERING FACTS FROM LONG TEXTS

Back in 1941, Francis Robinson came up with a comprehensive model to help students remember big chunks of nonfiction text, such as textbook chapters. He called it SQ3R, standing for Survey, Question, Read, Recite, and Review. Today, if you look at any study skills website, homework center, or college help desk, you'll find a version of SQ3R. It is still the number one, most famous, most widely used comprehensive model for textbook study. It is old as the hills—but maybe it is old for a reason, like because it works. It ain't exactly what you'd call "a really fun activity," but when kids simply must retain large quantities of content-packed text, SQ3R can help.

The underlying assumption of SQ3R is: if you really want to remember big textbook chapters, you cannot simply read straight through them like a novel—you need to attack the text in a whole different way. You need to slow down, break the work into stages, and take multiple, conscious steps to retain information. In this model, the stages are: Survey, Question, Read, Recite, Review. Here's how it lays out.

Survey

☞ Preview the structure, organization, or plan of the chapter

☞ Think about the title

☞ Read the introduction and/or summary

☞ Read the headings and subheadings (boldface, color text, etc.)

☞ Look at any pictures, charts, or graphs

Why do this? By predicting what will be included in the chapter, you will remember more details.

(Do the next three steps for each subsection of the chapter.)

Question

☞ For the section of the chapter at hand, pose some questions you would like to have answered

☞ There may already be some questions supplied in the book, either at the beginning or end of the chapter

☞ You can formulate other questions by changing subheads into questions (for example, a subhead title "Causes of the Civil War" could be turned into the question: "What were the causes of the Civil War?"

Why do this? Having questions in mind results in (1) a spontaneous attempt to answer with information already at hand; (2) curiosity until the question is answered; (3) a criterion against which the details can be inspected to determine relevance and importance; (4) a focal point for crystallizing a series of ideas (the answer).

Read

☞ Read to answer the questions you have developed

☞ Mark or highlight the answers as you find them

☞ Adjust your speed—if content does not relate to a question, move on

Why do this? Reading the text in light of your own questions makes you a more active reader, helps you understand, evaluate, and determine the relative importance of material.

Recite

☞ After reading the section, stop and take a minute to paraphrase or summarize the information

☞ Jot down the question you were pursuing

☞ Answer the question in your own words; use only key words needed to recall the whole idea

☞ Test your comprehension of the section by asking: what were the main points here?

Why do this? It's important to solidify your understanding before moving on—there's lots more content coming!

Review

☞ Review your notes within 24 hours of making them, and again within a week

☞ First, read your written question(s)

☞ Try to recite your answer. If you can't, look at your notes. Five to 10 minutes should suffice for a chapter

Why do this? You can significantly increase retention if you use both immediate and later review.

━

Obviously, getting students fluent with the SQ3R program will require some training and experience. Smart teachers provide lessons early in the year when they demonstrate, and kids practice, each of these steps, with immediate guidance and feedback from the teacher. You can also make it sociable, putting kids into small groups to compare the predictions they have made after surveying, the questions they are developing for a subsection, and so forth.

SQ3R has proven quite popular with teachers and effective for kids in terms of content retention, but as we warned, this is not the kind of experience that turns kids on to a subject or galvanizes a lifelong interest. It can be a grind, chapter after chapter, and becomes laborious and mechanical if overdone. So while we certainly think this strategy should be in the repertoire of every teacher with a textbook to teach, it is not the whole package. Combining SQ3R with other approaches in this chapter, and in the rest of the book, will provide a deeper, more balanced, and more engaging experience.

One Final Suggestion: Get a Better Textbook!

One day, a group of math teachers from California came to visit our school in Chicago. An hour after the initial orientation had concluded, when everyone was supposed to be sitting in classrooms, we were surprised to see one of the visitors trotting down the hall with something clasped to her chest. "This is amazing!" she shouted, pointing at the textbook she was clutching. "It's fabulous! Where did you get this? Can I buy this copy from you? I've gotta show this to my colleagues back home!" The woman literally would not let go of the textbook, which she was holding like a drowning person with a life ring. In the end, we did get the book away from her, but only after sitting down at the computer and ordering an examination copy sent to her home.

The textbook happened to be *Interactive Mathematics Program* published by the Key Curriculum Press. The math teachers at BPHS had decided a few years earlier that IMP's hands-on, real-life-applied, NCTM-standards-based program was the best fit for our kids and our school. But the moral of this story is not that all you math teachers should go out and adopt IMP or any other competing math series.

We're just pointing out that it's possible to be using the wrong textbook and not even know it. It's important to be vigilant, to be on the lookout for new materials that might suit our students better. It is so easy to take the path of least resistance and keep re-adopting the same text over and over, without carefully scanning what else is available. Sure, doing systematic review of the alternative textbooks in any subject area can be a time-consuming process. Once you request the examination copies, the sales rep is always leaving you voice mail and you never find a series that pleases everybody in the department. But, even if you don't end up changing textbooks at all or budgets make it impractical, the conversations with colleagues that emerge while you are evaluating materials will be some of the best staff development you'll ever get, guaranteed.

Notes

Barton, Mary Lee and Clare Hiedema. 2002. *Teaching Reading in Mathematics.* St. Louis: MCREL.

McTighe, Jay and Grant Wiggins. 2000. *Understanding by Design.* New York, NY: Prentice-Hall.

National Assessment of Educational Progress. 2000. The Nation's Report Card: National Achievement-Level Results. http://nces.ed.gov/nationsreportcard/about/trend.asp. Accessed August 25, 2003.

Robinson, Francis Pleasant. 1970. *Effective Study* (4th ed.). New York, NY: Harper & Row.

CHAPTER SEVEN
Building a Community of Learners

Forgive us for starting a chapter by quoting research, but here's a report that really hits home. In a study of over 28,000 sixth and eighth grade students by the Consortium on Chicago School Research at the University of Chicago, classes providing high "social support" achieved one-year gains on standardized math tests of 1.67 grade equivalents, versus only .93 grade equivalents for those given low support. Gains for reading were 1.42 grade equivalents in classes with high support, versus .56 for those with low support. By "social support" the study observed whether teachers:

relate the subject to students' personal interests
listen to what students say
know them very well
believe they can do well in school

And in relating to peers, students receiving high support:

treat each other with respect
work together to solve problems
help each other learn

Social support includes measures of parent and community involvement as well (Lee, Smith, Perry, and Smylie 1999).

We've advocated in this book that we need to expand *what* kids read, and show them *how* to read it. But even though these things are crucial, they're still not the whole story. Good teachers know instinctively that the work of teaching runs even deeper than that. We need to make the classroom a community, a place where students feel safe to take the risks involved in learning, where they see it connected with their lives, and where they help and learn from one another instead of working only as isolated individuals. And we do this not just to make students feel good, but to give reading in our subjects the full meaning it deserves.

Teachers have many ways to build community, but we know that students respond strongly when they sense that the teacher knows something about them as individuals. Humor helps break a lot of the ice. Surveys of students show that giving them choices, even in small things, helps students feel respected and viewed as people who are maturing and worthy of trust. While some might think this means a loose or disorganized classroom, it's really quite the opposite. A class where students work well together and respect one another needs to be an orderly group. And the results are not just a better climate, but greater learning. Students who know each other well and have been taught to listen to one another, are more likely to take risks and stretch beyond their comfort level as they learn. The importance of climate and community in teaching is reflected deeply in the core propositions of the National Board for Professional Teaching Standards:

> Accomplished teachers understand how students develop and learn. They . . . are aware of the influence of context and culture on behavior. They develop students' cognitive capacity and their respect for learning. Equally important, they foster students' self-esteem, motivation, character, civic responsibility and their respect for individual, cultural, religious and racial differences. (1989, p. 3)

It may seem like the simplest truism to say that all learning takes place in a context that colors everything taking place. But it's a major issue that must be factored into every teaching activity we plan: whatever strategies we try to teach, they won't work if kids are turned off to school, or are just passively waiting for the teacher to give them the answers. School needs to be a place where kids feel some ownership and control (see Glasser, *Control Theory in the Classroom*), where they have the confidence to recognize and work on their confusions, where they take responsibility and learn how to help one another and why it's important to do so, and where they inquire into the big questions that matter for them. Otherwise, even when we teach strategies to help students deepen their understanding, they will only learn them mechanically, not recognizing when or why such strategies are needed.

Another insight into the context of reading is revealed by Jeff Wilhelm's research in *You Gotta BE the Book*. In his interviews of resistant eighth graders, Jeff found that to them, reading was simply "finding the answers to the questions at the end of the chapter," or sounding out the words on the page, whether these made any sense or not. Their struggles, in other words, reflected not just a lack of skills, but an unproductive conception of their role as readers in the classroom. Wilhelm's more recent inquiry, *Reading Don't Fix No Chevys* with Michael Smith, reveals that boys particularly are more engaged when reading and learning provide perceived benefits within the experience itself, rather than serving only a vague future goal like getting into college or joining the job world.

So unless the classroom is a place where kids see learning as useful and meaningful to them—connected to their individual interests, or shared with their friends, or focused on large issues they care about—teaching content reading "skills" or comprehension strategies or anything else simply doesn't stick for a great many of our students. In this chapter, we'll share some of the ways that effective teachers actively shape their classrooms so that the message is consistent and repeated and enacted: This school is a place where we all help each other learn, where the learning is for students, not just to keep the teacher off your backs, and where the experience of learning is engaging in itself and not just a set of skills you'll need "later."

There are five main ways that teachers build community as they go about teaching their subjects and using reading to do so, and we'll describe each one in more detail in this chapter. They:

- Make the classroom a place where students trust the teacher and believe it's safe to take risks.
- Provide students with choices and opportunities to take responsibility in the classroom.
- Connect learning with students' lives and the larger issues around them.
- Organize learning so that students work together and help one another.
- Read aloud from engaging and powerful writing in their fields.

Taking Action in All Subjects

The standards documents of all our professional organizations across subject areas urge many community-building strategies, not as feel-good frills but as powerful ways to teach content so that students really do learn. Of course, in lab science courses the role of group work has long been recognized and made an essential ingredient of students' learning process. And in any classroom where collaborative work in pairs or small groups is employed, and where the task involves discussing and thinking through ideas rather than just filling in blanks, a supportive community is being created. But there are additional strategies we can use to address the categories listed above:

Strategies for Building Community in the Classroom

☞ Make the classroom a place where students trust the teacher and believe it's safe to take risks, a place where it's okay to ask questions when they don't understand something, and where they'll receive the support they need to handle challenges.

- Share with your students your own passion for reading about your subject, as well as your struggles as a student and a reader.
- Value students' questions, both those that express confusion about the material being studied and those about larger implications or related topics.
- While students are doing in-class work, hold conferences with individuals to discuss their questions and set individual learning goals, to help make vulnerabilities less public, and to learn what support each student needs.

☞ Provide students with choices and opportunities to take responsibility in the classroom.

- Hold class meetings to set rules for the class. Then follow up with periodic meetings to address needs or issues as they come up.
- Create as many jobs and responsibilities for students as you can possibly think of, and rotate these periodically.
- Schedule in-class reading time with choices of articles and books about your subject.
- Use jigsaw activities in which small groups give presentations to help the rest of the class learn about various parts of a topic.

☞ Connect learning with students' lives and the larger issues around them.

- Conduct surveys of students' interests and past experiences, related to the course subject.
- Conduct inquiry projects within the course subject area, or connecting several subjects.

☞ Organize learning so that students help one another and learn from each other.

- Provide class time for book clubs, on books from a classroom library.
- Orchestrate small-group activities in which students help one another to understand course material.

☞ Read aloud from engaging and powerful writing in your field. Reading aloud evokes the sense of a group gathered around the fire to hear the stories that hold them together as a community.

Of course, no classroom is likely to embody all of these characteristics all the time. However, it's clear that they need to be present often enough to insure that students truly believe their teachers care intensely about them and their learning.

Following are some specific strategies to promote community in the classroom, defined by the preceding characteristics. There are few surprises here; all are approaches that good teachers have employed for years, and that education experts and teacher-authors have described in books on pedagogy and reading. These most definitely are not fluffy "team-building" exercises, but well-structured and thoughtful approaches for teaching important subject matter. Several of the key strategies are described in greater detail later in this book—see Chapter 8 for more on Classroom Workshop, and Chapter 9 for more on Book Clubs.

Make the Classroom a Place Where Students Trust the Teacher and Believe It's Safe to Take Risks

☞ **Share with your students your own passion for reading and for your subject, as well as your struggles as a student and a reader.** When Sarah Lieberman's eighth-grade humanities class at Perspectives Charter School complained about the length of a paper she'd asked them to write, she brought in her own college senior thesis on school integration policies. The kids were curious about the topic itself, and fascinated that their teacher would take on such an extensive project. Sarah also shares stories about her father, an accomplished English teacher and story teller, when the class works on family histories.

Humanities

It's important to help students understand that along with our passion, we adults also experience confusion and uncertainty, especially with new ideas or new skills. At Best Practice High School, Theresa Hernandez encourages her students in French to risk the inevitable mistakes they'll make as they try to speak the language, by describing the many *faux pas* she uttered while living in France. The following is one story she tells them: Complaining to a French friend that her eye hurt, she kept repeating "Mon Oeil!" The friend thought she was saying "Moneil," which is slang for "I'm just kidding." She grew increasingly frustrated at the ensuing lack of help, while the friend couldn't understand why she seemed upset when she insisted she was only kidding. Not knowing the slang, Theresa could make no sense of the growing conflict. Theresa adds that for practicing a foreign language, pairing kids with friends helps reduce their timidity as they try to speak.

Foreign Language

Teachers can find comfortable ways to take risks themselves, thus signaling to students that they value and support this behavior. Chris Tovani, in *I Read It But I Don't Get It,* tells kids about her own difficulties with reading when she was a high schooler, and the techniques for faking book reports that she resorted to as a result. Other teachers enjoy including occasional mistakes in their calculations or information as they work out a problem on the chalkboard, and kids gleefully point these out.

☞ **Value students' questions, both those that seek to clarify confusion about the material being studied and those about larger implications or related topics.** This requires more than just a quick "Any questions?" at the end of a lecture. Actively initiate the process by having groups confer briefly and jot their questions down, followed by reports of one or more questions from each group. Then be open about the fact that you don't always have the answers, and that there's nothing wrong with that—though of course if you come back the next day with some new information on the topic, it's especially good. And telling kids where and how you looked up the answer is even better. Following a digression and loosening up on your set lesson shows that you value students' curiosity. If we complain about students' lack of engagement in our subject matter, we must be ready to respond positively when they do show interest. And of course national standards such as those for science and social studies urge us to strongly emphasize the value of questioning.

When Best Practice chemistry teacher Mike Cannon conducts demo experiments, he asks his students to write down at least five questions afterward, in their notebooks. When he looks over the notebooks, he notices the most frequent questions and addresses the immediately relevant ones in class. Others may relate to an upcoming unit, so he lets students know the answers are coming soon. When he reaches the later item, he again refers back to their questions, and asks students to flip back to their earlier queries to jot down the answer they've now uncovered. Now that's spiralling.

Chemistry

Sometimes it's okay to lecture! At Perspectives School, Sarah Lieberman's eighth graders' questions often call for deeper inquiry as they study American history. One student recently wondered why slave traders focused on Africa, rather than some other part of the world. While not every student was as engaged as this, Sarah's own intense interest drew her to stop and share some of her knowledge, rather than maintain her usual facilitative get-the-kids-to-do-the-thinking approach. Indeed, the factors were complex—previously established European trade routes along the African coast, the spread of disease among enslaved Caribbean and South American indigenous people, and the

History

need for labor on the plantations in those areas. While Sarah herself was hesitant to use too much lecture-oriented teaching, a modest amount is obviously valuable if it dramatizes the enthusiasm and deep knowledge that the teacher brings to her work.

☞ **Hold quick in-class conferences with individual students to discuss their questions and to set individual learning goals, to help make their vulnerabilities less public, and to enable you to discover what support each student needs.** Here's how it looks in Kelly Vaughan's junior British literature class in the Small School for the Arts at Chicago's South Shore High School. Kelly's kids keep their work in portfolios which they review at the end of each unit. They write "Portfolio Reflections," identifying what they consider their best piece of work and why, the most challenging work and why, and the work that most interested them. Then each student lists two or three specific skills or abilities she has improved, and two or three to focus on for the next unit or quarter.

Kelly organizes a lot of the class work around half a dozen "stations," at which the students engage in a variety of activities, such as creating "mind maps," doing quick writes on various questions, making vocabulary cards, and creating their own poems related to those they're studying. Since kids work mostly independently at the stations for three or four days during the week, there is plenty of class time for Kelly to meet with individuals, look over their portfolios, and discuss how to pursue their goals.

Kelly wanted to give more support as students work on these goals, and so she's added several strategies to the process. One is an exercise to help students identify actions they can take to work toward a goal, including outcomes that would show they are achieving it. Otherwise, many of the goals tend to remain nebulous, and specific efforts are hard to initiate or acknowledge. Another refinement: she has typed up sheets listing all the students in each class, with short phrases outlining their goals—so that as she circulates around the room or checks in with individual students, she can easily get a focus on the particular support each one needs.

Best Practice High School Geometry teacher Amy Lubelchek regularly combines textbook reading, questioning, and conferencing organically. Students read an explanation of a math process and write down their understanding of how they think it's supposed to work, along with any questions about it. After a few responses are read aloud, kids go to work in small groups on sample problems, while Amy circulates around the room. "That's when 80% of the questions get asked," she explains. "Kids will be constructing a triangle, say, and realize it's not working—'So do I set my protractor like this?'

Later, when they present their work to the class [see below], which we do as often as possible, they've usually anticipated the questions that other students ask them."

Provide Students with Choices and Opportunities to Take Responsibility in the Classroom

☞ **Hold class meetings to set rules for the class. Then follow up with periodic meetings to address needs or issues as they come up.** At Foundations School in Chicago, the teachers addressed a conflict that kept flaring up between eighth-grade boys and girls by holding separate meetings with each gender group to talk over how to settle it, and what rules should be established to keep it from recurring. Everyone wanted to avoid the imposition of strict and narrow behavior rules, but the teachers made clear that they could not accept the disruptions that were occurring, and would need to impose such rules if the kids couldn't find a way to solve their problem. While the discussion swirled at some length before the issue was settled, the larger message was clear: this was a community in which the students and teachers all needed to listen to one another.

☞ **Develop as many jobs and responsibilities for students as you can possibly think of, and then rotate these periodically.** Many teachers ask the good writers in class to serve at an "editor's table" as students work on essays and other written outcomes of study projects. Book Club groups can feature roles such as illustrator, fact checker, and group observer, to facilitate the work of the groups. In the Small School for the Arts at South Shore High School, Karon Stewart varies the jobs in her math classes according to students' interests and the natural situations that present themselves. In fourth period Algebra/Trig, the two strongest students frequently serve as tutors, and the two most immersed in computers handle her tech needs. Meanwhile, it's a general rule that if a student receives help from her on a problem, then any other student having difficulty with that problem should consult the person she helped. She finds that four to six students acquire this role just about every day—and of course these aren't always the highest achieving kids. In a more ad-hoc vein, when Karon wondered how to help two French-speaking kids from Africa, one with decent English skills but the other lacking them, she decided to ask the stronger of these students to help two non-ESL kids who are taking French. In order to include a math focus, their job was to help the American kids write out word problems in French. Those two, in turn, were to help the African student who was struggling with English. Karon reports that all of these students

Math

are completing more of their homework assignments than before she initiated this activity.

☞ **Schedule in-class reading time with choices of articles and books about your subject**—a strategy we'll explore in depth in Chapters 8 and 9, on Independent Reading Workshop and Book Clubs. To give students wide options for reading you'll need to build up a classroom library and collection of interesting articles on your subject. Teachers who use Reading Workshop regularly often begin with a short minilesson on some aspect of their subject, or on the process of reading thoughtfully, before the reading time begins. They conduct conferences with individuals during the reading session, as described previously.

Finally, students write responses, exchange "dialogue journals," create posters, or otherwise process and share what they've learned with their classmates. Emphasize students' respect for one another and commitment to listen to, learn from, and question one another as this sharing proceeds. **Enact** this with explicit requirements for audience participation—oral performances should be aimed at informing and helping the whole group, not just obtaining a grade for the presenter. The class as audience should take notes on the presentations and respond to each presenter with questions and reflections.

☞ **Use "jigsaw" activities in which small groups of students give presentations to help the rest of the class learn about various parts of a topic.** This is one way for students to share with one another what they've learned from the more independent reading they are doing. In Melissa Bryant-Neal's senior Anatomy class at Best Practice High School, students are frequently asked to divide up readings and then present their portion of the topic to others in the class, either in small groups where each has read a different piece, or in presentations to the whole class. In their study of the digestive system, for example, Melissa provided brief cases of a number of digestive diseases, and kids chose which they'd like to investigate, ranging from acid reflux to neonatal jaundice to lactose intolerance. The students worked in small groups to investigate their particular disease on the Web for one double "block" period. They then presented the information they'd gathered to the rest of the class. To help groups organize their material, Melissa provided a structure for reviewing medical cases—patient profile, patient's medical history, a narrative of how the illness presented itself, symptoms, etc.

Then to insure that the rest of the students learn from the presenters, Melissa required that they write a journal entry for each presentation, choosing from a variety of possible modes—an illustration of the main idea, a list of three new vocabulary words learned and their definitions, a personal reflection related to the disease, a question the student asked and its answer, an idea that upset or moved the student, a song title and line connected with a main idea presented. A natural outcome of this activity was that class members asked numerous questions of each group. Several presentations had to be postponed when the class simply ran out of time. Obviously this project, like many we describe in this chapter, combined multiple characteristics that make the classroom a learning community.

Connect Learning with Students' Lives and the Larger Issues Around Them

☞ **Conduct surveys of students' interests and past experiences, related to the course subject.** Donald Graves says that if you don't know 10 specific things about a student, you don't know him or her well enough. He keeps a journal page for each kid to keep track of what he's discovering about their lives and interests. So as you learn about your students, bring in articles, magazines, books, etc. that appeal to their interests. Janet Allen in *It's Never Too Late: Leading Adolescents to Lifelong Literacy,* explains how she uses surveys repeatedly during the year to learn about students' attitudes toward her subject, their prior experience with it, the subjects and issues they are interested in, their attitudes toward school in general, their life experiences, their preferences as to various classroom activities—all to learn what particular strategies might make the difference for students who are struggling.

At Best Practice High School, the teachers organized a system for collecting and sharing a wide variety of articles on topics of interest to their students without creating a heavy burden for any one teacher. They first surveyed students to identify the dozen most widely shared topics—such as careers, sports, and violence—and then set up box-top collection trays, each labeled with one of the topics, in the teachers' work room. As staff run across articles on these subjects in newspapers and magazines, or on the Web, they cut them out and drop them in the trays. Teachers make copies of articles from the trays to provide students with readings on their preferred subjects. And they retain the surveys to keep track of individual kids' interests.

☞ **Conduct inquiry projects within the course subject area, or connecting several subjects** (described in more depth in Chapter 10). These projects generally start with a large question or controversial issue—such as energy consumption and renewable sources of energy, or types of social discrimination and how to reduce their occurrence. Individuals or teams of students choose to focus on particular aspects of the problem, based on their interests. Skills and information related to the subject area of the course are then introduced at times when students need these for their inquiry.

Sarah Lieberman's eighth-grade American History/English class spends several weeks reading biographies of famous abolitionists, concluding with projects in which each student profiles his or her chosen person. Sarah helps the kids make thoughtful choices about which abolitionist to study by first giving them one-page bios of half a dozen pre-Civil War activists, and then helping them develop their own definition of what it means to be an "abolitionist." The kids also write in response to questions she poses about the actions and influence of each one—e.g., "How do you think Helen Craft's story could have helped other enslaved people?" The kids swap papers, and Sarah asks if anyone has read an answer that changed his mind about his own argument. Several students realize this has happened and explain how their thinking changed.

Sarah, in other words, has smoothly integrated a lesson on persuasive writing into her activity to build the kids' interest and background knowledge of abolitionist writings. She does this for vocabulary as well, as the students read together excerpts from Frederick Douglass' fiery Fourth of July oration that asks, "What to the American slave is your Fourth of July?" The flowery 19th-century style is peppered with unfamiliar words such as *impudence, bombast,* and *impiety,* so the kids work in groups of three or four to define as many as they can from context and inference. She provides definitions only for those they still haven't figured out—so that she has both encouraged self-sufficiency and directly taught whenever it was needed. Finally, the kids are ready to create definitions of "abolitionist," so that as they begin their more extended reading, they're oriented to identify important issues, events, and themes. The project is not only an exploration in depth with a focus on the larger issue of social responsibility, but brings students to work communally, to learn from one another, and to consider issues they find important.

Organize Activities for Students to Help One Another and Learn from Each Other:

☞ **Provide class time for Book Clubs, using books from your classroom library—** another strategy so important that it has its own chapter later on. Book Clubs are explored more thoroughly still in Harvey's *Literature Circles: Voice and Choice in Book Clubs and Reading Groups* (2001). Book Clubs represent the next step beyond simply allowing students to read independently, and feature student-led discussions in small groups that share an interest in a particular topic

177

BUILDING A

COMMUNITY

OF

LEARNERS

History

English

or piece of writing. While the popular term *book clubs* may seem to imply that it's meant for reading long novels in English classes, this structure works equally well for short readings in any subject area.

When a group tackles a whole book, the students decide on the number of pages to be read by their next meeting. Especially when students are first getting accustomed to this work, everyone in the group will have specific roles or tasks to accomplish while doing the reading and during group discussions. However, teachers who frequently employ Book Clubs usually find that it's best to do away with assigned roles as the students become accustomed to this work. The jobs can easily make students' participation artificial and mechanical, compared to simply having engaged discussions on the reading, like those grownups engage in. Many teachers use self-evaluation forms to help group members self-monitor and improve their participation in the group.

Math

☞ **Orchestrate small-group activities in which students help one another to understand course material.** More and more, middle-school and high-school teachers are re-arranging their rooms so that students sit and work in small groups and teams, rather than in rows. Students confer as they work on assigned problems, and discuss issues in their groups before responding to a teacher's question. That's just how it looks most days in Vanessa Brechling's freshman Algebra class. Using the high-quality *IMP* (Interactive Mathematics Program) text, Vanessa's kids work in groups of four, using the following roles: reader, co-ordinator, recorder, and quality controller (borrowed from another good math program, Core Plus). We can watch as the kids explore the mathematical issues involved with a game called "Pig." One person rolls a six-sided die and adds to her score whatever number comes up on top, until a "one" is rolled, or until the person chooses to stop. A "one" means the person's turn is over and she loses all prior points for that turn. It's not unlike "twenty-one," if you're into that sort of thing. The math question, then, is: what is an optimum number of rolls to try before quitting? The larger math issue, Vanessa explains, is to learn what constitutes a mathematical approach to solving a problem. The reader in each group reads the text section on "Pig" to the group and helps them understand it. The co-ordinator then helps the group figure out a process for conducting an experiment to find an answer. The recorder writes down and summarizes what the group has determined and reads it back to the group. And the quality controller monitors the process to insure a quality result. What adds power to this structure is that when students ask Vanessa questions, she first checks to see if they've used the expertise in the group: "Did you ask the reader to explain the problem again?" Or, "Did you ask the co-ordinator what the next step is?" Vanessa's students gradually learn to depend more on one another and less on the teacher. Vanessa is teaching math as she builds community in the classroom.

Read Aloud from Engaging Material in Your Field

Isn't reading aloud just for little kids? you might ask. But the truth is, we all love a good story, and hearing it together opens up a lot of opportunities to reflect and relate as a group. Biology teacher Melissa Bryant-Neal sees it this way:

> I can't see why you *wouldn't* want to read aloud. A lot of my students don't get it if I assign reading and we don't read some of it aloud. It may be an article from the news, or even a section of the textbook or an introduction to a lab. The kids definitely sit up when an article connects what we're studying with some big current event or issue. Reading aloud engages the kids and gives us a chance to interact with the text. We'll stop and talk about vocabulary, or analyze a really dense paragraph. I start the reading, but I rarely read the whole selection myself. That would get boring fast. So we take turns, and whoever is reading calls on the next person to read. The kids help each other out when they stumble. I don't embarrass the students who are really insecure, but I do encourage those who are on the edge. Come to think of it, this is the one time during class when everyone is quiet.

Middle-school teacher Kenya Sadler reads picture books to her students at the beginning of the year. She chooses books to introduce issues of community and climate, and she likes picture books because they are brief and to the point. Students quickly get past the idea that these books are only for their younger brothers and sisters. Two favorites are *The Other Side,* by Jacqueline Woodson and Earl B. Lewis, and *The Empty Pot,* by Demi (who uses one name only). The first focuses on racial divisions and the second on being honest under pressure. While neither of these is far from her social studies subject matter, she's especially happy to take the time for them because she needs to have the kids working together smoothly in order to accomplish everything else she has planned for them.

When we review all of the steps and strategies that we've described in this chapter, they clearly reflect what group dynamics experts tell us make for well-developed groups. A classroom becomes an effective learning group when it features:

- high positive expectations on the part of both students and teacher
- leadership that is shared and diffused throughout the class
- a strong sense of friendship and cohesiveness within the classroom
- norms that are clear but flexibly adapted to the activities in which the class is involved
- communication that flows easily in all directions, among students and between students and teacher
- and ways of handling conflict that allow differences to be addressed constructively. (Schmuck and Schmuck 2000)

If these features are present in effective human groups of all sorts, we can certainly be sure that they are essential in any effort to improve students' reading and learning in our subjects.

A Look into One Classroom

How does community-building look in a classroom when kids are reading real-world material and getting help with their comprehension of it? In Seth Patner's freshman World Studies class, groups of students bend over their copies of a two-page biography of Iraq's former leader, Saddam Hussein, which Seth has printed off the Internet. He has asked each group to summarize a couple of paragraphs and present their summaries to the class—a relevant task for these mostly struggling readers. Observing one group of three students, he asks if they recognize the word *"coup,"* in the sentences describing some of the despot's early exploits. No one does, though they have not considered the effect on their understanding. How might they figure out the meaning? he asks, and all three students chorus, "Context clues!"—which they then use to solve the puzzle. Lacking an awareness of self-monitoring, they hadn't called on the comprehension strategy *they'd obviously been taught*. Nor had it occurred to them that they'd need to understand this concept in order to explain their paragraphs to the other kids in the class.

Seth is working hard at changing these kids' mindsets. He wants them to realize that this reading matters in their own lives, that some of the school's alumni and some of their older brothers and sisters went off to a war in a place with a complicated and troubled history that might well affect whether they live or die there. And he wants his students to begin supporting one another, figuring out together what it all means.

So Seth patiently circulates among the groups, asking how they interpret the reading, giving hints and suggestions as they prepare their summaries, and then encouraging them as they give their reports. The cooperative work and shared teaching responsibility that Seth has introduced are new to these students, but by the end of the period, kids are urgently asking questions, debating the implications, and dialoging with him and one another.

Notes

Allen, Janet. 1995. *It's Never Too Late: Leading Adolescents to Lifelong Literacy*. Portsmouth, NH: Heinemann.

Daniels, Harvey. 2001. *Literature Circles: Voice and Choice in Book Clubs and Reading Groups*. Portland, ME: Stenhouse.

Fendel, Dan, and Diane Resek. 1997. *Interactive Mathematics Program: Integrated High School Mathematics, Year 1*. Emeryville, CA: Key Curriculum Press.

Glasser, William. 1986. *Control Theory in the Classroom*. New York, NY: Perennial Library.

Lee, Valerie, Julie Smith, Tamara Perry, and Mark Smylie. 1999. *Social Support, Academic Press, and Student Achievement: A View from the Middle Grades in Chicago*. Chicago, IL: Consortium on Chicago School Research.

National Board for Professional Teaching Standards. 1989. *What Teachers Should Know and Be Able to Do*. Detroit, MI: NBPTS.

Schmuck, Richard, and Patricia Schmuck. 2000. *Group Processes in the Classroom*. 8th edition. Boston, MA: McGraw Hill.

Smith, Michael, and Jeffrey Wilhelm. 2002. *Reading Don't Fix No Chevys: Literacy in the Lives of Young Men*. Portsmouth, NH: Heinemann.

Tovani, Chris. 2000. *I Read It But I Don't Get It*. Portland, ME: Stenhouse.

Wilhelm, Jeffrey. 1997. *You Gotta BE the Book: Teaching Engaged and Reflective Reading with Adolescents*. New York, NY: Teachers College Press.

CHAPTER EIGHT
Independent Reading Workshop in Content Areas

Once in a while, when we hit a lull in the maelstrom that is teaching, when the storm of paperwork and accountability calms for a moment, we can slip back into our idealistic mode and reflect on the big goals that brought us into this work. For many of us, the now-overused term "lifelong learner" figures prominently in our hopes for students. Sure, we want them all to pass the state exam and get into a nice college. But we hope for more. We want our students to leave us with an enduring curiosity about our field, plus the motivation and the tools to continue learning.

So looking out at the adult community around our school, how do we recognize our "success stories," the alumni who are living the kind of thoughtful life we wished for them? Well, one thing they have in common is, they read—newspapers, magazines, and books—and they scan the Web with skill and purpose. They read not only what's required by their jobs, but also for recreation, for information, for citizenship. For these lifelong learners, being informed, having a book going, exploring a new field, making time for reading, are normal parts of life. And sometimes, these lifelong learners don't just read by themselves. They join book clubs or reading groups. They gather in each others' living rooms, in the back rooms of bookstores, community centers, or church basements, and talk about books. They read and discuss old-time classics and hot bestsellers, novels and biographies, books about people and history and science, about investing and dieting, politics and economics. And when they finish talking over each book, they pick another and set a date for the next meeting.

We've just described the main two kinds of independent reading that real, lifelong readers engage in: *individual* and *small-group* independent reading. The common feature is choice. Readers select their own material while in their easy chairs at home or as members of a discussion group. Typically, the chosen materials are interesting and accessible, written at a level people can fluently digest. There are no assignments, study questions, quizzes, grades, or tracking. Reading flows from intrinsic motivation (curiosity, wonder, pleasure, etc.), and is not driven by external rewards or punishments.

So if we want this future to become reality, to grow the community of life-long learners around our schools, part of every school day must be devoted to independent reading. Period. This means students are picking reading material and talking about it with their friends, kids acting like lifelong learners while they are *still in school*. It's too risky to wait until they graduate and hope they'll develop good habits someday, maybe. In this chapter and the next, we argue that some time should be set aside for independent reading *in every school subject*—and we'll offer specific classroom structures to organize it. How much time you allocate depends on how much you agree with our arguments—and on the very real constraints you live with. Yes, English teachers may be in a somewhat better position to employ this kind of activity. Indeed, language arts teachers in your school, if they follow the guidelines of the National Council of Teachers of English or the National Board for Professional Teaching Standards, already sponsor independent reading in their classrooms, perhaps dividing time between teacher-directed activities and student-driven "workshop" or "literature circle" time. But independent reading within content fields is for everyone. Remember our dream? Passing the state exam is not enough—we're trying to raise enthusiasts here!

What Reading Workshop Looks Like

Best Practice High School Chemistry teacher Mike Cannon has built up a healthy collection of articles related to chemistry topics, especially with the help of the Internet. Recently, he's started a unit on body chemistry, and he wants his students to inquire well beyond the textbook on this topic. Along with some sections from *ChemCom: Chemistry in the Community* (American Chemical Society 1998), he has identified a number of articles on teens' diet from various websites. Some are more general, but several focus on fats, sugars, and the various chemicals in soda pop (it took less than an hour to locate these on the Internet). The most popular articles turn out to be one titled "Oreo Cookies—Inedible?" found on the "C-Health" website, http://chealth.canoe.ca/health_news and another headed "Why Soda Pop Drains You Dry," at www.unhinderedliving.com/soda.html. The Oreo piece describes a recent lawsuit about the presence of trans-fatty acids in the cookies; and the soda pop article explains how, among other things, the phosphoric acid and caffeine in carbonated drinks both leach calcium from our bones, leading to osteoporosis. (Yikes—we didn't know this ourselves, until now!)

Under Mike's regular requirement, his students have posed many questions in their journals reflecting their concerns about their own health, so the kids are well primed. Throughout the spring, he's devoted about 45 minutes each week to Reading Workshop. The challenge is how to organize the classroom to allow for wide student choice among the readings, while the teacher supports and monitors the students as they work.

First, Mike needs to provide the whole class with some guidance that he knows they'll need, based on his familiarity with his students. They may need help with the technical vocabulary. Mike may decide that they especially need to better monitor when they've grown confused with unclear explanations. Or, he may be concerned that they've tended to choose topics they aren't really interested in.

So Mike's 45-minute Reading Workshop period begins with a short five-minute minilesson—in this case, a quick review of some basics he's already taught, on acids, fatty acids, and sugar molecules, since so much of body chemistry is built around these. Earlier in the year, Mike might have used the minilesson to explain to the students how he expects them to use their workshop reading time, but they're well-acquainted with it now, and so he focuses on the content he's helping them to understand.

For another five minutes, Mike quickly summarizes the focus of the various articles. And finally, he explains the written responses he wants each student to complete after they've read, and before brief student reports and discussion begin. Students are to write in their journals one thing they've learned from their article, their thoughts and feelings in response to the article, and one thing they may do differently as a result of reading the articles. The journal writing works well to focus students' ideas in preparation for their later discussion. Each student then chooses which article he or she will read, and Mike calls on students around the room for a quick verbal commitment to confirm the choices. Those who still have questions about the topic or the assignment also indicate this so he knows who will need individual help during the reading period.

During the 20-minute reading and writing time, Mike circulates among the students, holding short conferences with those who earlier asked for help, stopping to check on students who he knows are struggling, or responding to anyone else who has a question. Mike stops for a second to make a few brief notes on a small sticky note after each conference and places it on a sheet on his clipboard that lists all of his students next to Post-It sized little rectangles.

When they're finished reading, Mike wants the students to share what they've learned in a way that effectively informs others in the classroom about this material. So for the last 15 minutes of Workshop time, kids give brief reports on their reading. Not surprisingly, everyone demands to hear about the Oreo Cookies and the soda pop. Intense discussions ensue. In the fourth period class, Julie asserts, "We need to end the 'Barbie' syndrome, people

185

INDEPENDENT

READING

WORKSHOP IN

CONTENT

AREAS

Reading Workshop Schedule in Mike Cannon's Chemistry Class

05 min.	Minilesson
05 min.	Summary of article topics
20 min.	Reading and journal-writing time
15 min.	Reports and discussion

wanting diet drinks all the time so they don't get fat. We shouldn't all try to look the same." James asks, "Is it true that they used to put cocaine in Coca-Cola?" and their teacher responds that this did indeed happen, though it was back in the 19th century when people thought cocaine was good for their health. Stormy wonders, "Will they ever start taking the bad things out of these foods?"

The sixth period class is more doubtful. As Brittany puts it, "Oreos contain inedible ingredients, but people will still eat them because they taste good. Nobody will stop because of the articles." When many classmates agree with her, Mr. Cannon urges the students to consider trying gradual changes, rather than the all-or-nothing thinking typical of teenagers.

Afterward, Julie comments on the activity: "Some people have low comprehension. When we talk about the articles in class, or if another person has the same article, they get to hear someone else's opinion, and then they understand better. For me personally, the textbook is hard. I have to read it over several times to understand. It helps to hear about things in different ways."

Johnathan's thoughts: "I like the articles better than the textbook. Articles have information you need. You can put it together and think about it. We had a great discussion. Everybody got to hear each other's thoughts. Everybody was alert and paying attention. And it's better for everybody to have a different article. That way everybody has something to say. If it's just one article, only a few people talk. Yeah, I plan to slow down on all the sugar and sweets."

Classroom Workshop is not a piece of content or a unit, or another maddening mandate that overloads your curriculum—it's simply a powerful classroom management tool that allows students to work on individually chosen topics and receive individualized attention from the teacher. It's a strategy that secondary English teachers and elementary teachers have employed for reading and writing for many years, guided by experts like Donald Graves, Lucy Calkins, and Nancie Atwell. A Workshop approach is also a regular feature of

science, shop, art, home ec, drama, and just about any other lab or performance class. But we shouldn't allow only a limited group of our teaching force
to monopolize such a valuable instructional tool, particularly when it's so
handy.

Along with providing a structure for students' real-world reading in your
curriculum, there are some further powerful advantages to using Reading
Workshop:

Eight Benefits of Independent Reading Workshop

1. Workshop offers students a wide variety of real-world reading in your
   subject.
2. It signals that reading and studying your subject is important enough
   that you're willing to give students some class time for it.
3. It can be run in short chunks of time, and does not have to involve extensive assessment.
4. Workshop allows the teacher to directly teach learning strategies or
   course content through short minilessons, followed by immediate application of what is taught while it's fresh in students' minds.
5. It enables the teacher to easily observe students' understanding or difficulty with a concept, through the one-on-one conferences that take
   place during reading time. This can alert the teacher to re-teach difficult material, correct misconceptions, or add information that she
   discovers the students need.
6. Through a Workshop structure, the teacher can provide students with
   individualized support. As more schools introduce differentiated instruction and nontracked classes, classroom workshop is one of the
   most effective tools for addressing students' greatly varying needs.
7. Workshop promotes student buy-in because it enables the teacher to
   introduce individual choice into the instructional mix. Research studies tell us that student choice is a major motivator for reading—but
   also that school rarely provides this opportunity (Worth and McCool
   1996).
8. Workshop enables the teacher to employ interactive student involvement as a significant element of instruction—through immediate application after a minilesson, through dialogue with the teacher during
   conferences, and through sharing time at the end of the Workshop session. Again, the research tells us how important this is. The Consortium on Chicago School Research found that across the grades (at least
   through grade eight), Chicago students' scores on standardized reading

187

INDEPENDENT

READING

WORKSHOP IN

CONTENT

AREAS

tests were 5.2% higher than average in classrooms with high levels of interactive instruction, and 4.5% below average in settings where the amount of interactive instruction is low (Smith, Lee, and Newmann 2001).

How to Make Sure Reading Workshop Works

- The classroom has a good assortment of readings, from library resources to copied articles, to bookmarked websites (see page 63–67).
- The teacher provides an opening "minilesson" on content or a reading strategy.
- The teacher gives brief descriptions of the various reading selections, so that students can choose meaningfully.
- Individual students decide which selection they will read.
- Reading time is provided in class.
- While reading, students take notes or jot responses, applying the concept or reading strategy just taught.
- During reading time, the teacher conferences with individual students to answer questions, provide help to those who are confused, and gain information on students' level of understanding.
- The teacher briefly records observations as he or she observes, to develop a record of students' progress and/or needs.
- At the end of the reading period, several students report on what they've learned, or how the reading strategy worked.
- Other students are encouraged to respond or ask questions so that the reporting becomes a learning activity for everyone.
- Assessment is brief and simple—give points for participation, completed notes, and presentations.

Conducting Minilessons

Minilessons are important not just for teaching or re-teaching content, but also for showing students how to use Workshop time effectively, and for initiating activities that help students focus on and process the ideas they are reading about. So these lessons are key for both content and effective classroom management. Minilessons should, indeed, be mini. The idea is to briefly refresh or focus kids on one important thing that will be relevant to the reading they're about to do—and then let them get reading so they can apply it. Minilessons can be divided into three main categories: 1) the rules and procedures of Workshop, itself, which you will conduct primarily at the start of the year, when you first introduce the structure; 2) reading and thinking strategies (many of which we've provided in Chapters 5 and 6); and 3) lessons tying in course content.

In *The Art of Teaching Reading,* Lucy Calkins outlines a generic minilesson structure that makes sense at any grade level, and in any subject:

☞ First, the teacher establishes a connection with material that the students have recently been working on, or a concept or process they've struggled with: "I noticed yesterday when you were working on those problems in class . . ."

☞ Then the teacher explains the concept and models her thinking or application of it.

☞ Third comes active student involvement. Students give it a try as a whole group, using the process or jotting down their own understanding of the idea.

☞ Finally, link the lesson to today's reading—"So as you're reading these articles, be sure to think about . . . and explain in your journal some spot in your reading that connects with it."

Here are a few typical minilessons for helping workshop to run smoothly:

☞ **Minilesson on how to choose reading matter wisely.** Model the process yourself, showing kids how to read a few sentences to see if the piece focuses on what they need to learn, and to find out whether it is too hard or too easy (a variation on the Think-Aloud strategy described in Chapter 5). Use several examples, one very technical and difficult, one for elementary grade students, and one that is just right. Perhaps also include one that turns out not to be relevant to the topic you are interested in. Students can be helped to skim over the reading to get a quick sense of what it's about, and whether it's likely to be relevant, or of interest to them.

☞ **Minilesson on what to do if the student needs help but the teacher is busy.** Kids need to understand that you can't help everyone at once, and they need to have useful alternative activities while they wait for you. So brainstorm with the students some of their options: quietly ask a fellow student for help; write in your journal about what is giving you trouble; look up confusing words in the dictionary; find another article on the same topic and see if it explains the

189

INDEPENDENT

READING

WORKSHOP IN

CONTENT

AREAS

concept more clearly or answers your question; etc. List these items on a large piece of newsprint and post them on the wall so you can refer to them instantly when a student gets antsy.

☞ **Minilesson on how to ask for help in a conference with the teacher.** Students having difficulty often express only a global sense of being stuck or lost. Model for them how to pinpoint where the confusion lies so the conference can zero in on their real needs. This will probably involve solving a problem or answering a quiz question and doing a think-aloud, in which you talk through each step of your thinking. Build in a couple of spots where you portray yourself as confused and describe the confusion in detail—"Wait a minute. I'm not sure if I should add here, or subtract. What was that rule again?" Also explain to students the kinds of questions you'll be asking them in conferences, and again model the sort of responses that are helpful.

☞ **Other valuable minilessons on helping students use Reading Workshop effectively:**

> What to do when finished with your reading (record thoughts in a reading log, list vocabulary words learned from the reading, complete a project on the reading, go on to choose a new book—whatever you the teacher have determined to be the most productive next steps).
> What needs to go into each student's reading folder.
> How to work quietly with other students, if student-to-student conferences are a part of the process.
> Lessons on any of the other aspects of Workshop which we are now about to describe.

Keeping Students on Task During Reading Time

Effective and creative classroom management is key to making Workshop go well. A valuable strategy used by teachers experienced with this structure is something called "status of the class" (named by Nancie Atwell, whose professional text, *In the Middle: New Understandings About Writing, Reading, and Learning,* has been *the* Workshop bible for many teachers across the country). After completing a minilesson and reviewing students' reading choices, the teacher asks each student to briefly—in a simple phrase—state what he or she has chosen to read during the Workshop period. Some teachers jot these choices on a list with the students' names pre-printed, while others have the students themselves record their reading in a log in their reading folder (see below). This process establishes a quick contract with the students about the work they are about to do, and also lets the teacher know if particular students need help or are unsure of how to proceed. These will be the first ones she gets to for conferences during Workshop time.

191

INDEPENDENT

READING

WORKSHOP IN

CONTENT

AREAS

Conducting One-on-One Conferences During Reading Time

When helping individual students during Workshop, ask questions to assess their progress and needs. Ask them to summarize one main idea from the material they've been reading, explain one important concept, or indicate a question they have. If you've just taught a new concept or a learning strategy, you can ask about it—"Can you tell me about the last comment that you wrote in your journal?" Ask what help the student wants from you, so that you give responsibility to the student. Then respond briefly and teach just one thing, so that the conference remains short and the student can learn but not feel overwhelmed.

Your aim in the conferences is two-fold—well maybe three-fold: first, to provide help where it's needed; second, to see for yourself quickly and promptly whether the kids are getting it; and third, keeping them on task by maintaining your presence around the room. That's why it's much better for you to go to the students, rather than have them come up to your desk. And also why it's important to keep the conferences short. If you see that a student needs a great deal of help, this isn't the setting to get that done. We're also looking for efficiency, here. If you notice that most of the class is experiencing the very same problem, it's a time-waster to go through the explanation with each individual. Instead, call a brief halt to the reading and do an extra minilesson on the spot. Or use some debriefing time at the end of the Workshop session. Minilessons can come before or after reading time. The idea is to give kids exactly what each one needs, when they need it.

Recording Your Observations of Students' Reading and Understanding

Meeting with students during Reading Workshop enables you not only to assess students, but to inform yourself about their learning needs and their achievements. But you'll need some tools to help you keep track of all the data in simple and manageable ways. Many teachers have students keep folders that contain not only their ongoing work, but handy forms that summarize their progress—sheets that list the books and articles they've read, learning goals that they've set for themselves, skills and concepts they've mastered, and reflections on their learning. A helpful resource for this recordkeeping is *Classroom Based Assessment* by Bonnie Campbell Hill, Cynthia Ruptic, and Lisa Norwick (1998). In it you'll find a great variety of such forms, provided on a CD-ROM disk so you can alter them to suit your own needs. One inspired and easily recreated tool is a sheet with squares the size of small sticky notes, plus space above each square to enter a student's name. After you talk with a student, simply jot on a sticky note a few words about what took place or what you observed in the conference and slap it in the student's square. As these notes accumulate, transfer them to separate sheets for each student, and presto, you've got a continuous anecdotal record of each student's progress without any extra time or effort expended.

Making Student Sharing and Presentations Really Work

The goal of student sharing at the end of Workshop is not merely to monitor whether the kids did the reading, but to make the classroom a more active learning community. As the research reminds us, creating a community of learners is one of the keys to better reading and higher student achievement. In our highly individualized and competitive culture, however, we're often working against the grain when we attempt to promote such community. Students who are new to Workshop are accustomed to just sitting absently as their friends deliver their reports. To reverse this, teachers need to make explicit that class members will be asked to respond, to ask questions, and to connect what they've heard to their own reading.

Thoughtful teachers address this in a variety of ways. Some appoint specific respondents, or ask the presenter to choose several people to respond—**before** the report is delivered. Some teachers provide minilessons on how to respond, modeling constructive ways to pose questions or add ideas to what has been said. Some even go so far as to have presenters design quiz questions on their material.

What About Assessment?

If you do a good job with Workshop and provide lots of fascinating stuff for kids to read, you won't, in the long run, need to grade their reading. And since our goal here is to create habits of intrinsically motivated literacy, a nonevaluated reading period is really what we'd all probably prefer. However, we know this is the real world, and kids are so accustomed to receiving some sort of grade for everything they do that it can be hard to wean them from that. Still, the more we can reduce the role of grading, the more Workshop will be serving its long-range goal—and the less burdensome it will be for you, the teacher.

So our suggestion is: Have students keep reading journals in which they both record ideas on material they've read and respond with their own thoughts. The double-entry journal outlined on p. 118 is a very serviceable model for this task. It's not difficult to quickly review the journals later and give simple checks or points for completed entries. Just don't discourage yourself by taking home the journals from all your classes at once. Spread out the paper load by rotating your collection dates. You'll get a clearer picture of the progress and understanding in each class that way, as well. And *don't* mark or grade those learning logs for grammar, spelling, or neatness. The journals are informal notes, tools of thinking, not formal papers for a public audience. Enough said.

There is still one big question about Workshop that teachers most frequently ask: How do I possibly find time for Independent Reading Workshop—how do I fit it into my schedule? After all, very few of us have big chunks of time lying fallow in our teaching days, waiting for some activity to occupy them. So first, if time is tight, focus the readings on content that you know you must teach, but as much as possible, look for short real-world articles and essays that cover the topic rather than just the textbook.

Start with short SSR (Sustained Silent Reading) time periods for reading and expand them if it's working well and achieving your learning goals. Many teachers struggle at first with fitting Workshop into their schedule, but increase its use as they find they can spend less time on lecture and cover the same topics more effectively with this interactive strategy. "Coverage" is, in some ways, an imaginary issue. If you skim over everything lightly and the students don't get it, they'll still do badly on the final exam. And conversely, if they've really grasped some central concepts of your course through their own choice of lively readings, they're more likely to become engaged and learn more from even the pedestrian stuff.

Use Reading Workshop at least once a week when first getting started, to make sure students are familiar and comfortable with the process. Then later, you may vary the frequency of Workshop according to need and the amount of time you have. If you simply can't find time at least once a week, then use Workshop frequently for a period of four-or-five weeks and then let it rest, so you achieve some sense of continuity and focus on real reading for periods of

193

INDEPENDENT

READING

WORKSHOP IN

CONTENT

AREAS

time during the year. In addition, teachers often use the basic Workshop time pattern even when having students read from whole-class assigned textbook material, to help get them accustomed to it, and to take advantage of the many benefits that Workshop offers.

Tips for Helping Workshop Run Smoothly

Start with short time periods for reading and expand them if it's working well.

Do short minilessons to help students use the Workshop effectively—for example, on how to choose reading matter wisely, and how to participate in a teacher-student conference.

Make minilessons work by connecting clearly with recent work, by modeling, and by including active student involvement.

Keep students productive during reading time by conducting a "status of the class" check-in before students begin to read, and by conferencing with individuals.

Conduct effective one-on-one conferences on students' reading by asking questions that probe students' thinking and use of reading strategies.

Use student folders to keep the kids' responses and recordkeeping organized.

Document your students' reading and understanding by using forms and folders that allow for quick entry of information by both you and the student.

Make student sharing and presentations interactive by having the rest of the class ask questions and give comments.

A final challenge: teachers may wonder, "Sure, I can make this work with a topic students will find exciting, like body chemistry, but what about something more technical, something like, say, 'moles' in chemistry?" Okay, we realize that because the Workshop hasn't been employed as much as it could be in most subjects, collections of good, interesting, short articles aren't pre-collected for us. It will take time for good teachers to build up their article sets and begin sharing them more widely. Still, let's take up this challenge, as an example of how we might proceed.

For those who have forgotten their high school chemistry, let's pause for a little minilesson. A mole is a standard number for counting atoms (or any other objects), specifically 6.022×10^{23}—a pretty large number. It's a handy

195

INDEPENDENT

READING

WORKSHOP IN

CONTENT

AREAS

number for chemists because the amount of any element, in grams, that is equal to the element's atomic mass has exactly that number of atoms. If that sounds confusing, an example can help: 12 grams of carbon 12 contains exactly one mole or 6.022×10^{23} of atoms. This standard number allows a chemist to determine the relative amounts, by weight, of each chemical that they need for a chemical reaction, and the amount of the chemical (or chemicals) that will be produced. For example, to produce methane gas, CH_4, by combining carbon (C) and hydrogen gas (H_2) you don't just take one gram of carbon and four grams of hydrogen and mix them together. Instead, you'd combine one *mole* of carbon to each two moles of hydrogen gas (two, not four, because each molecule of the gas has *two* hydrogen atoms, and you need four hydrogen atoms to each carbon atom to make methane). Okay, stay with us one last step. To get one mole of carbon, you'd weigh out 12 grams of it—because 12 is carbon's atomic mass. And for two moles of hydrogen gas, you'd need 4.03 grams—1.00794 is hydrogen's atomic mass, times two atoms of hydrogen in each molecule, times two moles. In learning about chemical reactions, students are typically asked to calculate just how much of each chemical will go into and come out of a reaction. And real chemists use this kind of calculation when they design chemical manufacturing processes so that all the raw material gets used up.

Now how about some readings to connect this technical concept to the real world. Steve spent an hour on the Web and easily located the following:

☞ An article in *ChemMatters* magazine (published by the American Chemical Society for high school students and teachers, with sample issues and articles at www.acs.org) on making ink from oak tree galls—lumps formed when insects lay eggs on oak trees. Turns out this is how ink was made for centuries; this type of ink was confirmed to have been used by Leonardo da Vinci, Bach, Van Gogh, the authors of the Dead Sea Scrolls, and the drafters of the U.S. Constitution. The article explains the chemical reactions involved in turning the gallotannic acid in the galls into ink, and the specific lab steps for making it. The amount of materials to be combined depend on knowing the chemical reaction and calculating the molar amounts of the various chemicals needed for it.

☞ A group of clearly written pieces on chemical engineering careers, located on the website of the American Institute of Chemical Engineers. We include this piece to show students how the technical concepts they are learning can prepare them for highly paid careers in fascinating fields. Jobs include process design engineer, environmental engineer, process safety engineer, business coordinator, patent law attorney, etc. Average starting salaries in the years 2000 and 2001 are quoted ($51,572 for a graduate with a bachelor's degree), and diversity statistics are included—36% of undergraduate chemical engineering students are women, and 27% are under-represented minorities.

☞ A "Periodic Table of Comic Books" (at www.uky.edu/Projects/Chemcomics), which catalogs comic book references to the various elements in comic books going back to the 1940s. While the site is more focused on fun than chemistry, it does include the atomic number and atomic mass for each element, and some of the comic book segments make use of real concepts and processes in chemistry.

Obviously, we could keep going with this list. We've varied the kinds of readings to cover a range of issues: a specific technical application of the concept of moles and molecular weight, the use of such knowledge in possible student futures (of which many students have little knowledge), and a bit of sheer fun that a group of university chemistry students have had with one part of the topic. Nowadays, such searches are unbelievably easy compared to life before the Internet. There's no reason for us to hesitate using it to engage kids with our subjects by providing choices among real-world articles, giving them time to read them, and freeing you the teacher to help individual students.

Notes

American Chemical Society. 1998. *ChemCom: Chemistry in the Community.* 3rd edition. Dubuque, IA: Kendall/Hunt.

Atwell, Nancie. 1998. *In the Middle: New Understandings About Writing, Reading and Learning.* 2nd edition. Portsmouth, NH: Heinemann.

Calkins, Lucie. 2001. *The Art of Teaching Reading.* New York, NY: Longman.

Hill, Bonnie Campbell, Cynthia Ruptic, and Lisa Norwick. 1998. *Classroom Based Assessment.* Norwood, MA: Christopher Gordon.

Rall, Judie. 2001. "Why Soda Pop Drains You Dry," at www.unhinderedliving.com/soda.html.

Selegue, John, and F. James Holler. 2002. *The Periodic Table of Comic Books.* At www.uky.edu/Projects/Chemcomics.

Smith, Julia, Valerie Lee, and Fred Newmann. 2001. *Instruction and Achievement in Chicago Elementary Schools.* Chicago, IL: Consortium on Chicago School Research.

Sun Media. 2003. "Oreo Cookies—Inedible?" at chealth.canoe.ca/index.asp. Under chealth news, nutrition and fitness.

197

INDEPENDENT

READING

WORKSHOP IN

CONTENT

AREAS

Tinnesand, Michael, ed. 2001. "An Ironclad Recipe for Ancient Ink." *ChemMatters,* Oct. pages 8–9.

"What Do Chemical Engineers Do?" 2000. at www.aiche.org/careers/. American Institute of Chemical Engineers.

Worth, J., and L. S. McCool. 1996. "Students Who Say They Hate to Read: The Importance of Opportunity, Choice, and Access," in E. Leu, C. Kinzer, and K. Hinchman, eds., *Literacies for the 21st Century,* 245–256. Oak Creek, WI: National Reading Conference.

CHAPTER NINE
Book Clubs

Scott Sullivan's students are just finishing a round of Book Clubs at Highland Park High School. A couple of weeks back, Scott invited his class to select from a group of six nonfiction titles, representing a wide range of interesting topics and reading levels (all included in the book list in Chapter 4).

Nickel and Dimed: On Not Making It in America, Barbara Ehrenreich
Postville: Culture Clash in the Heartland, Steven Bloom
Stupid White Men, Michael Moore
Into Thin Air, Jon Krakauer
Media Unlimited, Todd Gitlin
Rocket Boys, Homer Hickam

Having done Book Clubs before, the kids got right to work. They formed into small groups based on their book choices: four kids selected *Stupid White Men,* five chose *Postville,* and so forth. Looking at a calendar, they divided up their book, assigning themselves a certain number of chapters for each upcoming club meeting. On those appointed days (two consecutive Mondays and Thursdays), the groups ran their own discussions for half an hour, drawing upon notes they had taken while reading the book as homework.

English

Toward the end of the Book Club cycle, Scott threw the kids a tantalizing final assignment. "What if the high school decided to delete one book from the required curriculum next year—and solicited suggestions for another book to replace it? Would you argue for your book being required reading for everyone in the junior class—or not? What arguments would you make, pro or con? And how would you present it to the English Department Chair, who would make the decision?" The first reaction was venting by some kids about how they would like to delete Toni Morrison's *Beloved* from the school list ("Too hard! Too boring!"). Steering back to the positive side, Scott offered a couple days for groups to think further about their book, establish their position, do some additional research, and prepare some kind of presentation to make their case.

Now, it's report time, and the group that read *Stupid White Men* goes first. Michael Moore, they explain, is a hard-core, left-wing critic of the establishment, who is pretty funny but also says really mean things (e.g., "Hey, this is America, we don't prosecute felons if they're rich or married to a governing Bush."). To decide whether his work merits inclusion in the school curriculum, the kids have done their homework. They rented and watched Moore's film *Bowling for Columbine,* which won the Academy Award for best documentary in 2002, and also studied the text of Moore's incendiary acceptance speech at that awards ceremony, during the Iraq war. Their conclusion: *Stupid White Men* is too biased, too one-sided. If this book were to be included on the required list, it would need to be paired with another book from the far right-end of the political spectrum.

Another Book Club reports on *Postville,* which tells what happens when members of a Jewish fundamentalist sect called the Lubovitchers arrives in a small Iowa town to set up a kosher slaughterhouse. The ensuing neighborhood tension ends in a town hall meeting, basically deciding whether or not to repudiate the newcomers. The students in this Book Club, several of them Jewish, are very enthusiastic about adding Bloom's book to the school's reading list. They note that Highland Park's theme for the junior year is "culture clashes"—a perfect match for *Postville*'s subtitle. But there's more: the students make a connection between the book and the "Seeds of Change" program, which has recently visited the school. This traveling band of Israeli and Palestinian teenagers meets with other young people, showing them how to find friendship across ethnic and religious lines, even if their parents are stalking and slaying each other. Concluding the group report, the teenaged David gestures idly toward his ancient teacher, 35-year-old Scott Sullivan, "It's too late for you guys to change," he concludes, "only us kids can do that."

Book Clubs Across the Curriculum

All across the country, every month, hundreds of thousands of thinking Americans gather regularly in voluntary adult reading groups. There are countless variants—literary book clubs, beach-book clubs, bible study groups, self-help book clubs, professional journal study groups, Civil War history clubs, and on-line book chats. The number of such groups has doubled in the last decade, doubtless owing to television's *Oprah Winfrey* and *Today* shows, which have showcased Book Clubs and sparked the formation of even more reading groups in living rooms, community centers, bookstores, church basements, and, here in Chicago, a few bars.

Over the past 10 years, Harvey has been working to transfer this naturally occurring literacy structure into schools, across all grade levels. His book, *Literature Circles: Voice and Choice in Book Clubs and Reading Groups* (2001), has been used widely by teachers to set up similar reading discussion groups in their classrooms. While implementation has been most common in language arts, where reading trade books is a normal part of the curriculum, teachers in other content areas have begun to import this model into their teaching, too.

More appropriately labeled "Reading Circles" or "Book Clubs" when we look across the curriculum, these structured discussion groups combine two powerful educational ideas: **collaborative learning** and **independent reading.** Simply defined, Book Clubs are small, peer-led discussion groups whose members have chosen to read the same article, chapter, or book. These groups can be organized in a wide variety of ways, but the consistent elements are:

Students choose the reading materials

Small groups (3–6 students) are formed, based upon choice of texts

Grouping is by text choices, not by "ability" or other tracking

Different groups choose and read different materials

Students keep notes to help guide both their reading and discussion

Groups meet on a regular, predictable schedule to discuss their reading

Discussion questions come from the students, not teachers or textbooks

Personal responses, connections, and questions are the starting-point of discussion

A spirit of playfulness and sharing pervades the room

The teacher does not lead any group, but acts as a facilitator, fellow reader, and observer

When Book Clubs finish a cycle, groups may share highlights of the reading with classmates through presentations, reviews, dramatizations, or other media

New groups form around new reading choices, and another cycle begins

Evaluation is by teacher observation and student self-evaluation

In other words, if you walk into a classroom where Book Clubs are meeting, you'd expect to see perhaps five or six small groups of students sitting together and talking quietly about an article, chapter, or book they have chosen. Along with the reading material, students will have brought some form of notes (a journal entry, a special worksheet, notes on sticky notes, some annotations on the text itself) which they created while reading, and are now serving as a source of discussion topics. The teacher circulates through the room, visiting groups, but does *not* lead the discussions or "teach" any group.

Visiting a History Book Club

That's just what's happening today, in Nancy Steineke and Mike Dwyer's class at Andrew High School. Their American Studies program puts two teachers and 56 kids together for two periods a day to study integrated American literature and U.S. history. Right now, the kids are dividing into their "1929–1969" Book Clubs. Groups of three or four students are pulling desks together, each preparing to discuss their chosen historical novel set during the Depression, World War II, or the Cold War Era. Among the choices were sets of books that Nancy and Mike have been assembling over the years:

> *The Eye of the Needle,* Ken Follett
> *Summer of My German Soldier,* Bette Greene
> *Snow Falling on Cedars,* David Guterson
> *The Great Escape,* Paul Brickhill
> *The Journey Home,* Yoshiko Uchida
> *Wings of Honor,* Tom Willard
> *Fail-Safe,* Eugene Burdick and Harvey Wheeler

These seven book choices not only cover a variety of topics from the historical period, but also provide a range of difficulty, from a quick-reading book aimed at younger readers *(Summer of My German Soldier)* to quite challenging adult trade books *(Snow Falling on Cedars)*. As students browse the choices, each can find a just-right book, some shorter and easier, some harder and longer. But there's also a parity in this: everyone will be reading and discussing a whole novel about the historical period. In this way, Book Clubs help Nancy and Mike differentiate instruction in their classroom, not by putting kids in permanent "tracks" and labeling them, but by using temporary, kid-driven forms of grouping and re-grouping.

Now, as the Book Club meetings begin, students place their books (with post-it notes sticking out of the edge) and their personal learning logs on the table in front of them. The first order of business is a two-minute warm-up conversation, much like the personal chit-chat that adults typically do before undertaking a small-group task. Each day, Nancy offers a generic topic ("the best movie you've seen lately" etc.), and the rule is that every kid in the group must say something. By now, the students prefer picking their own subject, and the group of girls in the back is definitely warming up with their home-grown question: "What do you look for in a boy?"

Now, Nancy and Mike call time and signal the switch to book-talk. Since this is the last of several meetings, and the kids have now finished reading their books, there is much talk about endings, big themes, and resolutions. The *Fail-Safe* group is having an especially lively conversation. A couple of kids are truly disturbed by the ending, in which the U.S. government allows New York City to be destroyed by a nuclear bomb as payback for its accidental attack on Moscow. Bill and Alice are amazed that the Russian and American governments would accept such a double tragedy instead of engineering some kind of diplomatic escape. Chris, the group's resident tough guy, just shakes his head and says: "An eye for an eye, man." "But they're not soldiers, all those innocent people in New York," protests Farina. And then an extended argument develops about military versus civilian casualties in a war—and whether there is ever any such thing as a "non-combatant."

Circulating through the room, you notice that the students are using several tools to support their discussion, to remind them of ideas they want to share. Kids have marked important passages of their book with small post-it notes, jotting a few key words or a question on each, so it hangs out of the edge of the book. In their journals, they have also made a drawing or illustration, some kind of graphic representation of each section of the book. When the time seems right, they'll show their picture around, as another way of spurring conversation. And finally, each student maintains and draws conversational material from two lists in their journals: one of "Personal Connections" (what the book means to me), and another of "Historical Connections" (tracing the setting and events back to topics studied in the history class and textbook).

How do Mike and Nancy assess this activity? First, they check kids' notes, journals, and books each day, making sure that everyone is prepared. This doesn't mean collecting and scoring everything: it means walking past each kid and grading "over-the-shoulder." They listen in on conversations and make notes about the quality of students' thinking. And at the end of a round of Book Clubs, they require an individual project. For the 1929–1969 Book Clubs, the students are to write an essay—but definitely not a traditional book report. As Nancy says, "Hey, I don't need any plot summaries—I've read all these books." Instead, the kids have a four-part assignment: 1) recount in detail one conversation that you started in your Book Club; 2) recount another conversation that started with someone else's question; 3) describe one significant historical connection you made between the novel and the period we studied; 4) write about one other element of the book that struck you as interesting or important.

Getting Started with Book Clubs

Let's say you've read the story about Nancy and Mike's Book Clubs, you've started building a classroom library in your subject area, and you have assembled some multiple-copy sets of books. Now you're ready to devote class and homework time for groups to read a trade book in your field: a biography, a historical novel, a popular trade book with good subject matter content. How do you organize, monitor, and assess this work? Here's a quick rundown of the key steps.

Training

We can't plunge kids into Book Clubs without knowing how they are supposed to operate; we need to show them first. You can do that by enlisting a couple of colleagues to offer a live "fishbowl" demonstration right in your classroom—or show a videotape of an adult Book Club, or of a successful student group from another class, or from your own class last semester. Or, you can ask a group of students themselves (pick the most collaborative ones) to try their best at a discussion in front of the class, using a short article everyone can read first. After whatever demonstration you decide to offer, ask kids to list the specific social skills they saw in action—what did they see people doing that helped the discussion work? You can also collect negative examples (Don't interrupt! No putdowns!) and convert them into positive statements. You'll eventually come up with a list of social skills/Book Club behaviors like this:

Come prepared
Take turns & share air-time
Listen actively: make eye contact, lean in, nod, confirm
Pull other people into the conversation
Ask follow-up questions
Piggyback on the ideas of others
Be tolerant of other people's ideas
Speak up when you disagree
Disagree constructively
Stay focused, on task
Support your views with the article/book
Be responsible to the group

If your students are already experienced in cooperative group work, this review of social skills may be all the warm-up they need. On the other hand, if collaborative learning is a brand-new way of operating, more preparation will be required before jumping into multi-day, peer-led discussion of whole books.

You can further practice peer-led discussion using smaller samples of text, convening several meetings, with varying groupings of students, over a couple of days. We like to use very brief pieces of text (news clips, even cartoons), quite small groups (pairs or threes), and short amounts of time (2–3 minutes) for kids to practice these peer-led discussions. A good way to begin is to give everyone the same minitext, have them read and make notes, and then discuss in their groups. Next, hold a whole-class debriefing, using your home-made list of social skills as an anchor. What worked and what didn't? Did everyone participate? How did you handle disagreements? What do you need to do differently next time? What was a question that really sparked someone's group? Practice with three or four "shorties" and debriefings, until kids get a fair proportion of the social skills going (not 100%, they are beginners, after all). Then you can move on to bigger selections—chapters or entire books.

Group Formation

In their pure form, Book Clubs are built on reader's choices of books. However, your kids may not be ready for the pure version. You may need to make some artful interventions to ensure that all groups will be functional, with a good balance of social and reading skills. We do not want you to try this activity and encounter one or two nightmare groups careening off task, undermining your enthusiasm for Book Clubs before it can even take root. So here's how many of our Chicago colleagues manage for "modified student choice."

Offer students five, eight, or 10 different books (or articles) to choose from. The choices should cover a range of reading levels, from thin and easy to thicker and harder, to accommodate the diverse reading levels that probably exist in your class; remember, Book Clubs are independent reading that should be recreational-level, for comfortable, fluent reading. To help kids find the right book, give a quick (30-second) overview of each title you have read yourself; for others, see if a student has read the book and can talk about it, or read aloud the blurb from the back cover, or print out reviews from Amazon.com. Give students a couple of days to browse the books, suggesting that they read the first couple of pages of each book to see if the interest and readability are right. Then it's time to ballot: ask students to write down their top three choices from the alternatives. Then take the ballots home, and taking your time, form wholesome (meaning, "likely to function well") groups. If someone doesn't get their very first choice this time, because you could foresee a crashing and burning Book Club, you can reassure them that next time they probably will.

We particularly like groups of four, because they provide for a good range of different views, while still placing significant responsibility on each member. In a group of six or seven, one or two people can always hide, hitch-hiking on the efforts of others. On the other hand, groups of two or three are too small to have enough diversity, and too vulnerable to absence and other afflictions. Pragmatically, we try to form groups of five if possible, knowing that on any given school day there will usually be four members actually present. Of course, we do form larger or smaller groups when the book choices point that way, but we encourage the kids to be vigilant about the potential difficulties. Six is O.K., but seven and above we usually split into two smaller groups for increased individual responsibility.

Scheduling

Book Clubs need not eat up huge amounts of class time, since after initial training, the reading and note-writing is done mostly outside of class, as homework. The big scheduling questions are: how much time should we allow for students to finish a whole book, how many meetings should they have along the way, and how long should those meetings last? At BPHS, we have a couple patterns that work for us: one is to divide the book into thirds, and meet three times over a three-week period, for a half-hour each time. Often we use Fridays for this: read and talk about the first third of the book for this Friday, the second for next Friday, and final third for two Fridays from now. With *Fast Food Nation,* which is fairly long and packed with facts, our teachers broke the book into five sections, and kids had five meetings over a three-week period. The more we use Book Clubs, the more we understand how important it is not to drag out a book for too long; better to hustle through it than to read just a few pages a day, thus losing the momentum of really reading. At Lake Forest High School, Maggie Forst moves things along even more quickly, giving her Book Clubs two whole class periods a week for discussion, so they can get on a roll and finish books faster.

Five Kinds of Notes

For student-led Book Clubs to work, it is vital that kids "harvest" their responses while they are reading. Kids need to grab those thoughts right away and save them—after all, they may be reading at home, in the evening, a day or three days before the next meeting of their Book Club. And the last thing we want is for kids to come to their Book Clubs and say: "I can't remember anything to talk about." That's why we use one of five different tools to help readers capture their responses while reading (or just after reading a section) and bring them to the meeting. Four of these have already been outlined in the strategies chapter:

Bookmarks (p. 116)
Post-Its (p. 114)
Double-Entry Journals (p. 118)
Text Coding (p. 115)

The fifth tool, especially designed for Book Clubs, is called Role Sheets. With this device, we encourage students to focus on one particular kind of thinking that smart readers use. A Role Sheet not only stores ideas to bring to your group, it also helps set a purpose for reading when you sit down with the book. Here's a set of roles we often use for middle-school and high-school kids who are reading nonfiction; you'll notice that many of them overlap with various strategies in Chapter 5.

Connector

Your job is to find connections between the material your group is reading and the world outside. This means connecting the reading to your own life, to happenings at school or in the community, to stories in the news, to similar events at other times and places, to other people or problems that you are reminded of. You might also see connections between this material and other writings on the same topic, or by the same author. There are wrong answers here—whatever the reading connects you with is worth sharing.

Questioner

Your job is to write down a few questions that you had about this selection. What were you wondering about while you were reading? Did you have questions about what was being described? Why someone said or did something? Why the author used a certain style or structure? How things fit together? Just try to notice what questions pop into your mind while you read, and jot them down, either while you read or after you're finished.

Passage Master

Your job is to locate key sentences or paragraphs that the group should look back on. The idea is to help people notice the most important, interesting, funny, puzzling, or enjoyable sections of the text. You decide which passages or paragraphs are worth reviewing and then jot down plans for how they should be shared with the group. You can read passages aloud yourself, ask someone else to read them, or have people read them silently and then discuss why the passage stands out.

Vocabulary Enricher

Your job is to be on the lookout for especially important words—new, interesting, strange, important, puzzling, or unfamiliar words—words that members of the group need to notice and understand. Mark some of these key words while you are reading, and then later jot down their definitions, either from the book or from a dictionary or other source. In the group, help members find and discuss these words.

Illustrator

Your job is to draw some kind of picture related to the reading. It can be a sketch, cartoon, diagram, model, timeline, flowchart, or stick-figure scene. You can draw a picture of something that's discussed specifically in the text, or something that the reading reminded you of, or a picture that conveys any idea or feeling you got from the reading. Any sort of drawing or graphic representation is okay—you can even label things with words if that helps. Whenever it fits in the conversation, show your picture without comment to the others in the group. One at a time, they get to speculate what your picture means, to connect the drawing to their own ideas about the reading and the subject at hand. After everyone has had a say, you get the last word: you tell them what your picture means, where it came from, or what it represents to you.

Researcher

Your job is to dig up some background information on any topic related to this reading. This might include the geography, weather, culture, or history of the setting; information about the author, her/his life, and other works; information about the time period portrayed: pictures, objects, or materials that illustrate elements of the text; the history and derivation of words or names; music that reflects the subject matter or the time. This is not a formal research report. The idea is to find some information that helps your group understand the material better. Investigate something that really interests you—something that struck you as strange or curious while you were reading. Here are some places to look for information: the book's introduction, preface, or "about the author" section of the book, library reference books, magazines, an on-line computer search, encyclopedia, interviews with people who know the topic, other articles, novels, nonfiction, or textbooks you've read.

⌒

These jobs are useful because (shades of Chapter 2!) each one embodies a kind of thinking that mature readers actually use. So the roles can be a "back door" way of introducing or reinforcing good reading-as-thinking strategies. There are several ways to put the roles to work. You can simply name and explain these jobs, putting them onto classroom posters or have kids list them in the front of their journals, as a reminder. Or, if you want to be really official, you can make the roles into full-page handouts, color-coded by job, leaving most of the page blank for kids' notes.

When students use Role Sheets to capture connections or questions, we don't want to limit them to only that kind of thinking. We always want kids to talk about everything that struck them in the reading, not just their assigned role of the day, so the group conversations can be free-flowing and spontaneous. That's why we instruct kids to put their Role Sheets *face-down* when they start a meeting, and use them only if they completely run out of things to talk about. The roles should also rotate every meeting; we don't want one person to get typecast as a questioner or illustrator; instead, all the members of a group should try all the different kinds of thinking that good readers do.

If you use the worksheet form of roles, restrict their use to a brief training period. We have consistently found that when Role Sheets are used for too long, the conversation around them can become mechanical and dull. Anyway, kids will have more to draw upon when they use one of the other four "harvesting" strategies, each of which invites a whole range of reader responses instead of limiting it to one sort of thinking.

The Teacher's Role

When student Book Clubs are meeting, the teacher's role is to assist, observe, and facilitate. Generally, this means circulating around the room, visiting groups for a few minutes each. Obviously, if you have groups that are struggling or off task, you'll be going there first. Tell kids beforehand that when you sit down in their group, they should keep talking, not look to you for direction, topics, or feedback. You may eventually share an idea or question, but you'll do it as temporary group member, not the boss. If they really need help, you can "donate" a rich question, give them a conversational spark, but then move on immediately. Kids must take responsibility for running these discussions; we cannot get tricked into spoon-feeding them topics. When groups have learned the norms and are humming along, you can take observational notes to aid in your assessment of the kids' work—or join a group for a longer time, as a real member.

Projects

Book Clubs often create valuable and useful projects, like the book recommendations Scott Sullivan's kids made to the English Department Chair. Such real-world projects can also give students a chance to use the tools of drama, art, writing, websites, PowerPoint, music, design, or other expressive outlets. We recently enjoyed a social studies class where, after reading opposing materials about global warming, two teams of students each prepped their in-house lobbyist to "Brief the President." At the appointed moment, each lobbyist was separately ushered into the Oval Office, where a straight-faced classmate impersonated the Chief Executive and the lobbyist was allowed five minutes to make her strongest case. In the first briefing, the President sat in stony silence as a worried Sierra Club scientist begged for government intervention. A few minutes later, the President slapped the subsequent lobbyist on the back when she asserted that "global warming is a cuckoo left-wing plot." The student playing the President's aide immediately improvised mixing cocktails, and all three clinked imaginary glasses in an comic tableau of old-boyism.

Assessment

We find that teachers' number one question about subject-area book clubs is: "What about assessment?" Yes, they can envision students meeting in small, peer-led conversations about books, but they worry about justifying the time expenditure, documenting the benefits. Of course, when we devote classroom time to *any* activity, we always want to know if it worked, if kids learned from it. But with student-centered, collaborative activities like Book Clubs, we are especially concerned that kids are accountable for careful reading, preparing thoughtful notes, and joining fully in a group conversation.

There are other assessment pressures, too. The school that employs us probably requires that all major classroom activities be represented by some

Social Studies

kind of mark in our grade books. And then there are parents, especially the ones in our nightmares, who appear at a quarterly conference to demand: "Show me exactly why my little Dixie got a C in history!" And if all these worries weren't enough, we educators are now living through "The No Classroom Left Intact Act" (or something like that), and its mad quest for "scientific proof" of every subatomic particle of learning in the entire school universe.

So, for a variety of good and not-so-good reasons, Book Clubs must be assessed. We also realize that overly intrusive assessments can undermine the spontaneity and trust that small-group conversations require. After all, adults who attend monthly Book Club meetings do not receive grades as they put on their coats to head home. In fact, most grownup reading groups actually tolerate a very wide range of behavior without penalty. It would be more natural and lifelike to have evaluation-free Book Clubs like the ones adults enjoy, but we are in the school zone now, where one seemingly inescapable function is to rank, rate, judge, and label kids' work.

O.K. Now that we are done regretting this truly regrettable reality, how can we assess Book Clubs without wrecking them? First of all, you can give kids 10 points for every time they arrive prepared with their reading materials and their notes, in whatever format you have assigned (bookmarks, post-its, annotations, Role Sheets). This is all-or-nothing grading, done by walking past the students, grading over their shoulders, 10 or 0, no 5's, no arguments. Some of our colleagues in Chicago use a rubber stamp with the day's date to acknowledge completion; others carry a clipboard with a class list and quickly check kids off as they scan. The quickest system: assume everyone gets 10 points a day, and only record the zeros of the unprepared.

Don't read (and certainly don't "correct") these reading notes; they are meant to spur memory and aid discussion, not to be a formal paper. If you try to grade them qualitatively, you'll get sucked into a time-eating spiral. If you are worried about kids creating fake notes, then collect one a day at random, just as a preventive. When a cycle of Book Clubs is completed, have students place all their notes in a folder—or a Book Club Portfolio, if you want to get more formal. This provides a written record of each student's reading and thinking all the way through a book. If students have used post-it notes to mark their responses, put page numbers on each one first, and then take them out of the book, stick them on a plain piece of paper in page number order— voila, documentation!

Now assessment can get more interesting and substantive. Once your classroom Book Clubs are up and running, you have the opportunity to visit groups for a longer time—say eight or 10 minutes—to sit and observe how kids are discussing and what ideas they are sharing. Some of our colleagues use a group observation form which includes these elements for each student.

Name of student: _____

Prepared? ❐ Yes   ❐ No

Participated? ❐ Yes   ❐ No

One memorable comment or quote: _____

_____

_____

The kind of thinking this represents: _____

_____

_____

One noticeable social skill: _____

_____

_____

Often, these teachers say: "If I visit your group for 10 minutes, and you don't open your mouth once, it counts as 'not participating' (tough love, we know)." You may be surprised to find that in such a short visit you can easily discover who is prepared, recall one important comment from each member, determine what kinds of thinking the kids are doing, and also notice the social skills they manifest—or lack. When you have this kind of written record for each student, perhaps two or even three times during the course of a book, you are developing some pretty deep assessment of what they are learning—and creating another useful document for students' folders.

Part of any valuable evaluation plan is student self-assessment. You can design assessment forms, much like the teacher version above, in which students periodically stop to reflect on their group's process in writing, followed by a discussion of the "findings," and later, a whole-class debriefing. At Washington Irving School, Kathy La Luz aims a video camera at one Book Club each day, and that group is obligated at its subsequent meeting to review the tape, discuss strengths and weaknesses, and make plans for improvement. At Andrew High School, Nancy Steineke uses student observers, having a single group member step out of the conversation for just one meeting, to track the group's reading strategies or social skills, jotting notes on a simple form that is later shared with the group. Nancy talks in detail about such assessment strategies in her book *Reading and Writing Together: Collaborative Literacy in Action* (2002).

Finally, if you must give kids an overall grade for a cycle of Book Clubs, you can assign a group or individual project, as we discussed previously. But it isn't necessary. In the adult reading groups that are the template for school-based Book Clubs, do people put on puppet shows and make dioramas? Uh, no. What real readers generally do is find someone to talk to for a while, and then they start another book. In school, we sometimes insert a project at the end of a Book Club cycle because we need to grade *something,* and grading kids on their small-group discussions seems "too subjective." And after all, we can tell a B+ project from a B− project at a hundred yards.

But if our desired outcome is for kids to engage in sustained and thoughtful peer-led discussion about books they have chosen and read carefully, then why grade some surrogate, tacked-on project? Let's get brave and grade the thing itself. All we need is a legitimate scoring rubric, a performance assessment tool that includes valid criteria for evaluating the work of a Book Club. And the best way to create such a tool is with students. After they have had some experiences with peer-led reading discussions (perhaps during the training period, when they were using short pieces) you can ask them: what do effective Book Club members do? What are the specific traits or behaviors they demonstrate? Kids will typically brainstorm a list with items like these.

Use your indoor voice
Do the reading
Involve other people in the discussion
Take your turn
Do your job
Bring your notes
Don't dominate
Have original ideas
Don't spoil the book by reading ahead
Build on other people's ideas
Support your points, using the book
Make good drawings
Speak up for yourself
Respect other people
Be responsible to the group

Next, put kids in small groups with this instruction: "Now, we don't want a scoring guide with 17 criteria on it—that would be way too complicated and time-consuming. So decide which five or six elements are most important, and decide exactly how you want to word them. You may find that some items on our list are saying the same thing in different ways, so you may want to put them together in one statement." Give groups some time to create their short list of key Book Club skills, and then add one more job: "Now, take 100 points and allocate them to your criteria. You will decide if some behaviors are more important than others by the points you assign them." We like to have groups put their proposed rubrics on overhead transparencies, so their reporters can later explain their models to the whole class.

Finally, groups report back for a whole-class consensus-building meeting, where we make the big decision: which will be our official criteria, and how many points will each be worth? After some usually lively debate, the class must agree and adopt a rubric. They tend to look something like this:

Come prepared (reading done and good notes)	20
Be an active listener	15
Share responsibility for the discussion	15
Ask good follow-up questions	10
Support your ideas with the book	30
Keep all notes, records, and forms	10
TOTAL	100

There's no "correct" rubric or point allocation to work towards; as long as your model includes some valid criteria for book discussion, and everyone agrees to abide by it, you're set. Indeed, the whole rubric-creating exercise itself is a conversation about good reading and discussion habits—one of those rare moments when assessment actually does feed instruction. Now, the next time a Book Club cycle is finished, the kids use the class-adopted rubric to score themselves on their overall performance. You can score them also and reconcile the two, or just review the students' scoring, to adjust ratings up or down if needed.

If you use all these assessment ideas, look at what might wind up in a student's Book Club Portfolio:

Daily check-ins, with points if needed
Copies of all reading responses/notes/sheets/post-its

Teacher observation logs
Peer observation form
Videotape of a group meeting with written reflections
Final assessment rubric form from student and teacher
Optional ingredients (projects, etc.)

Now that's what we call evidence, accountability, and ta-da, grading. Of course, the best assessment of all, the one that really matters is this: after doing Book Clubs, do young people want to read more books? We think they will.

Notes

Daniels, Harvey. 2001. *Literature Circles: Voice and Choice in Book Clubs and Reading Groups,* 2nd Edition. York, ME: Stenhouse.
Steineke, Nancy. 2002. *Reading and Writing Together: Collaborative Literacy in Action.* Portsmouth, NH: Heinemann.

CHAPTER TEN
Inquiry Units: Exploring Big Ideas

O h, we tried that inquiry stuff before!" remarks a skeptical colleague in the teachers lounge, as a couple of friends talk over the recent inservice on interdisciplinary study projects. Teachers are justifiably dubious about the staff development fads that come and go in their districts, touted for a year or so in once-per-semester half-day inservice sessions and then forgotten in favor of the next silver bullet that's being lionized in the professional magazines. And even when the new ideas do sound good, it can take hours and hours to plan them, while classes and tests and papers to be graded continue to rush at us.

Yet we have to reach beyond the cynicism (or is it just exhaustion?) that so often comes with our profession, because connecting learning with the bigger issues of life is simply too important to ignore, for our students' growth. One of the most powerful ways to make reading real is to build it into an extended inquiry on a topic of importance for your subject, for students, and the world at large. And it is not just teen topics, such as rap singers or adolescent pregnancy, that energize students and engage them in active inquiry. Vital and absorbing topics abound, and cover important aspects of many of the subjects we teach—democracy, violence, slavery, folklore, pollution, ecosystems, global warming, and human health.

Vanessa Brechling wants her Advanced Algebra students to learn about exponential functions and their practical applications, and so she launches the kids on a study of population trends in various countries. She brings in population reports on Russia, China, India, South Africa, Germany, Japan, the United States. The six-page report, *International Brief. Population Trends: Russia,* for example, was issued in 1997 by the U.S. Department of Commerce, Economics and Statistics Administration, and contains plenty of fascinating information: explanations of recent declines in Russian birth rates and life expectancy, and death rate of infants and women in childbirth. Graphs show the strikingly low numbers of people born during World War II, and a previous dip among somewhat older people born during the famine and disruptions of the 1930's. Life has not been easy in the land of our former nuclear rival.

Math

Vanessa's students choose which countries they want to work on, with groups of three to five focusing on each country. Each group reads some of the reports on their country and then creates a list of factors they think have had the most influence on that particular population. In Russia, for example, poor health care in the more remote regions appears to play a major role, as has an increased rate of abortion. In some underdeveloped countries, AIDS is a large factor, though high rates of childbirth still insure population increases there. The students' task is to create a mathematical model of the population trend in their specific country. They begin by graphing the existing data and relating the graph to the factors they identified in the population reports. The graph provides the students with a visual representation of the population trends. Then they are asked to find mathematical equations to fit the data in the graph. The equations need to incorporate both the general trend of population growth, which is best described by an exponential model, and any specific changes in growth patterns that may have occurred due to wars, the AIDS epidemic, changes in birth control policies, etc. Through their investigations, the students learn about using various forms of mathematical models to represent numerical changes in these patterns over time. Ultimately, the kids make predictions about future population trends for their countries.

The level of engagement in this project is high. Students take pride in choosing their countries and learning about them. They decorate their graphs with national symbols—flags, pictures of major exports, scenery, and wildlife. They have fun while performing mathematical analyses similar to those done by government statisticians. They use the reports to find explanations for increases or drops in population. They get the satisfaction that comes from investigating actual phenomena and making sense of it. And they explain their charts proudly to visitors.

By the completion of this project, Vanessa's class has covered a variety of topics on her Advanced Algebra curriculum list. The students have learned how to:

1. Recognize and become familiar with exponential growth patterns over time
2. Identify and graph nonlinear functions
3. Fit data to an exponential model (or other nonlinear models, if appropriate)
4. Use mathematical models to make predictions about the future.

In listing these curriculum elements that are covered by the project, Vanessa is doing something we call "backmapping." Rather than march through these goals one at a time, with an isolated teaching activity for each one, she plans an activity that she knows will be interesting and that involves plenty of math. Then she works backward to see which goals and standards it embodies, and checks these off on her curriculum guide. That way, she can be sure that such an extended project is not taking time away from the items she needs to teach, but simply getting them taught in a more meaningful way. With the pressures on content teachers to cover district and state requirements, this approach helps us see that inquiry units needn't "take time away" from our curriculum, or add to our work load, but simply do the job in a different and better way.

Why Is Extended Inquiry Important for Reading?

Jeff Wilhelm and Michael Smith describe a particularly powerful reason for launching inquiry projects in *Reading Don't Fix No Chevys.* Boys, they found, especially value activities that have clear goals, and that yield immediate satisfaction rather than only future benefit. The 49 boys they studied, from a wide variety of backgrounds and schools, rarely experienced these things in their school reading. But when Jeff, for his own classroom, framed *Death of a Salesman* within a larger inquiry asking, "What are the costs and benefits of the American emphasis on sports?" both the boys and girls became much more deeply involved. We'd love to see Jeff and Michael's study replicated with young women, since a more real-world approach seems to affect the girls' performance just as much as the boys'. Students started with a pre-reading questionnaire on their own attitudes about sports, and then went on to read sports-oriented short stories and poems, copies of *Sports Illustrated,* newspaper sports sections, and athletes' endorsements in advertising, along with

Some Advantages to In-Depth Inquiry Projects with Real-World Reading

Students are engaged with large, important ideas and issues.

A wide variety of engaging readings can be naturally included.

Student choices and questions can easily be accommodated.

Content-area subject matter can be connected with student concerns and larger world issues.

Clear and significant outcomes of their inquiry give students a sense of immediacy and accomplishment in their learning.

discussing Willy Loman and Biff's interest in sports. They investigated particular questions related to the issue, and concluded by making video documentaries and other visual displays. Three girls in the class even successfully campaigned to change the school's fall homecoming so it would recognize many activities, rather than just football. Jeff reports that "Every student completed the final project with uncharacteristic energy and passion" (2002, pp. 85–87).

Starting on Your Own

In a school that supports grade-level faculty teaming, teachers can easily work together on projects because they share the same kids and enjoy common planning time. They can divide up subtopics and each teach about one of them. Individuals can take charge of particular activities and the students cycle through all the classrooms. Teachers can re-shuffle the kids according to the kinds or focuses of presentations they choose. However, while more and more schools are creating smaller learning communities to enable such cooperative work, the great majority of us do not have this opportunity. We teach alone, and our kids move through complex schedules so that no more than a handful share any two teachers together. So what do inquiry units look like in a single-subject classroom?

Actually, we've already described several in this book—like Melissa Bryant-Neal's anatomy students studying and reporting on diseases of the digestive system, or Sarah Lieberman's eighth graders analyzing what makes an abolitionist to prepare for studying biographies of pre-Civil War figures. At Nia, a small school in Chicago, Jacqueline Sanders leads her eighth graders through an economics unit she calls "Where does the money go?" "You've been complaining that when you ask for that new Playstation, your parents put you off. Do you wonder why?" she asks. "What do you think we'd need to know to understand whether your parents really can't afford those gifts, or are just putting you on?" The kids take some guesses about what rent and food costs are—a kind of KWL on family budgets. Ms. Sanders then distributes newspapers and sends the kids to the want ads to choose a job with a salary they think is adequate, and to write a resumé and cover letter applying for it.

The resumés require a pause for a minilesson, a look at examples, and some classroom writing time. Then work on family budgeting begins, based on the pay offered in the job ad. The kids learn that after dividing their annual salary into monthly gross pay amounts, they've got to subtract withholding taxes (for which Ms. Sanders gives them a flat rate, to keep things simple). Next, it's time for apartment hunting in the newspaper (searching as single individuals, rather than family couples, to avoid hard feelings about who gets paired with whom). But now there's more tough news: they'll need to post a security deposit, with some landlords asking for two months' rent these days. Some students now realize they're in much too low a pay bracket and go back to choose another job—an interesting lesson about goals for their future.

For food costs, the students return to the newspaper. Motivated now to economize, the kids compare prices at Aldi's, Jewel, and Dominick's. Next come utilities, with a discussion to clarify what these are. To give the kids a break, Ms. Sanders assumes that heat and hot water are picked up by the landlord, so the kids just need to cover telephone and electricity. Interviews with parents reveal these costs. Using IRS instruction booklets, they figure their final income tax returns. And at last they can determine if there's anything left over for treats and gifts. Since the seventh graders are working on a simpler version of the same project, the eighth graders also serve as "H & R Block" consultants to do the younger kids' taxes for them.

Obviously this project integrates economics, reading, writing, and math. While many good teachers have created projects similar to this one, we want to emphasize the range of reading for such a unit:

Newspaper want ads, apartment ads, and grocery ads
Sample resumés on the Internet
Booklets on wise shopping practices and guidelines for family budgeting
News articles on the truth or illusion of price discounting in many stores
Articles on the comparative cost of living in various cities
IRS form 1040-EZ instruction booklet
Bills from home for electricity, telephone, grocery, car insurance, cable, and other household expenses.

Moving to Team Projects—Challenges and Successes

While it's easy to feel jealous of our colleagues who get opportunities to work together, cross-disciplinary projects present plenty of challenges and pitfalls. When the faculty at Best Practice High School tried their first such project it fell pretty flat, because of predictable but unanticipated design flaws. Fortunately, they didn't let one flop discourage them, and applied the many lessons learned as they designed a whole series of very successful projects. That first, ill-fated unit, dubbed "Here We Are," examined the many aspects of the changing neighborhood where the new school was located. The project included walking tours of the area and interviews with residents and representatives of organizations that were active there. Nevertheless, it dragged on for weeks, with minimal student engagement or serious inquiry.

What went wrong? First, it was much too ambitious and multifaceted a topic for the teachers' and students' initial try. Teachers shared a strong belief in the value of integrated curriculum, but had had little opportunity to try it or figure out the strategies to make it work. Problem one was that this was not the kids' own neighborhood, since they came from all over the city. Then, the teachers had not activated the kids' prior knowledge about neighborhood issues, or sought out the kids' own questions about the subject (contrast Jeff Wilhelm's use of an opinion questionnaire at the start to get students' juices flowing). Nor had the teachers themselves given the project a clear focus by posing a controversial question of their own making. When the project wasn't working, they valiantly urged the kids to complete their research, delaying deadlines and stretching out the time allotted to the whole thing. A second project that compared aspects of various cultures did grow out of students' own choices and questions, but still suffered because kids lacked the background knowledge they needed for deepening their questions; and the teachers were overloaded searching for material on a number of cultures all at once.

Successive projects began to address these needs, with strikingly improved results. A smaller effort, which teachers named "Island Nations," connecting world geography, English, and art, did much better. The students worked in small groups to design their own civilizations, each imagined to be living on an island. The geography teacher provided information about how geographic features such as mountains and rivers affect people's activities, beliefs, and livelihoods. In English, students drafted documents they imagined their societies would generate. In art, they made flour-and-salt maps of their islands, along with flags for the countries they had created. The various geographic features they'd given the islands shaped many of the characteristics of their civilizations.

Later on, to prepare for more meaningful, student-negotiated projects for the following year, the teachers conducted surveys, asking students to list their questions about themselves and the world (suggested by Jim Beane and Michael Apple, in *Democratic Schools*). These questions then guided the teacher teams as, with more lead time over the summer, they designed activities and gathered material for the next year's projects. The following are some of the

Geography

English

Art

units that Best Practice teachers have since conducted, with consistent success, in grade-level teams:

☞ **"Better Pastures,"** a simulation exercise in which an ex-urban community must decide what to do about the closing of a nuclear power facility in their area—choosing the best alternate power supply, deciding on new use of the land, etc. Students take on the roles of various interest groups in the community and present their arguments to the "city council." They must do a considerable amount of reading to understand the perspective of their group (for example, the Pottowatomie Native Americans living in the town) and prepare their presentation to the council.

☞ **"Isms,"** a study of various -isms such as sexism, racism, able-ism, age-ism. Each teacher on the team takes several days to provide information and concepts on one of the -isms, so that students gain knowledge about each one. Then each student chooses one aspect of one -ism to study in more depth, and creates a presentation about it. Kids acquire the background knowledge they need, as well as exercising choice about what they wish to learn in more depth.

☞ A unit focused on **Research Skills.** Because teachers were concerned that students would need better research skills to do well with their other projects (Best Practice students do four integrated projects each year), they decided to concentrate one project on research itself. However, since student engagement is crucial, they identified several different focuses ("I-searches," science fair projects, and creative thinking projects) and students were divided up by their interest in these areas. As the various skills were taught, the kids used them to gather information on their chosen topics. This project culminates each year in a "Learning Fair," at which students and adult visitors circulate through the gym, observing the displays, hearing the creators presentations on what they've learned, and then providing written feedback on pre-designed rubrics.

So Just What Do We Mean by Inquiry Units?

There are actually a wide variety of structures for inquiry projects, serving many instructional purposes. Considering the projects we've observed at a variety of schools, we list key planning elements in the box on p. 225. And we list some of the main characteristics to consider as you plan your own inquiry projects, recognizing that creative teachers work many variations on the structures, adjusting activities to suit the learning needs of their classrooms. The following are some elements.

Elements for Planning Inquiry Projects

Extended Time: Students read, gather information, discuss, and write (or create other communicative materials) about a single topic for an extended time, over several class periods.

Focus on a Larger Issue: The topic involves a question or focus that connects with the larger world or a particular interest that students have.

Choice: The topic and questions around it are often (though not always) generated by the students. Other elements of choice are introduced as much as possible—choices among subtopics, readings, other students to work with, kinds of research tasks (such as interviews, Web searches, calls to experts in a particular field), and various ways for students to represent their learning.

Combining Disciplines: The topic often crosses curricular boundaries. Some projects intertwine subjects deeply into an integrated whole, while others operate through "parallel play," i.e., if several teachers are involved, each guides students through an aspect of the topic related to her subject.

Support: Teachers provide activities and steps to help students become engaged, think critically about the topic, and work through stages to get it done. Typical strategies to teach: how to tell quickly if a book is useful; how to design good interview questions; how to take useful notes; how to decide whether information is important or tangential to your topic; etc.

Prior Knowledge: The teacher provides information or material that gives students prior knowledge when it is needed to help them pursue and think about their topic more deeply and meaningfully.

Readings: The teacher provides reading materials, or supports the students in finding them (suggesting Internet websites, providing book lists).

Teacher's Role: While the teacher provides many structural supports, she is more a facilitator than a giver of knowledge. Many teachers struggle with the relinquishing of control that this involves—though well-planned projects actually provide a more meaningful and productive kind of control.

Teaming: Where possible, teachers conduct projects in interdisciplinary teams, each one helping students with a different aspect of the project.

Grouping: Students often work in small groups on their inquiries.

Outcomes: Students complete presentations, activities, or displays to represent their learning, share these with the rest of the class, or with a wider audience, respond to questions, and receive feedback from them.

Kinds of Inquiry Projects

☞ Inquiries on subtopics of traditional school subject matter—such as digestive diseases, within human anatomy, or abolitionist biographies, within U.S. history

☞ Inquiries focused on a large question, like Wilhelm's "What are the costs and benefits of the American emphasis on sports?"

☞ Information-gathering on a subject that crosses several subject areas and/or goes beyond traditional subjects, such as students delving into their own family histories

☞ Simulation activities in which students take on particular roles, research how their characters would respond to a particular situation, and then enact the situation as a culminating role play

☞ Variations on a theme, such as "jigsawing" to cover a variety of aspects of the topic

☞ Wider topic choices, with the structure based instead on processes, as in the Best Practice research skills unit

Tips for Making Inquiry Projects Work

Whatever variation you choose, based on your students' needs and your subject's demands, here are some important strategies we've learned for insuring that inquiry projects really work and don't get bogged down or turn into traditional, mechanical, plagiarized research papers:

☞ **Help the students identify a large, multi-faceted, open-ended question,** something people can disagree about, to focus and motivate their inquiry. This can be a single question for the whole class, like Wilhelm's question about the meaning of sports, or "Why do we always have wars?" or separate questions for each small group or individual. It's most meaningful if the questions are ones students have posed, but your own can work too, if you choose well. Use "front-loading" activities like questionnaires or comparisons of brief, controversial cases to make the questions real and urgent for the students—"If we can treat diseases with animal genes, will we still be 'human'?" "How do advertisers deceive us with numbers?"

☞ **Create opportunities for student choice, even when you need to keep the focus on required course material.** Sometimes enthusiastic teachers pre-design a project so completely that students just march through the steps, rather than questioning and inquiring with real care. But even limited choices, such as Melissa Bryant-Neal's options among digestive diseases, mean a lot to students, signaling that their judgment is valued and their voice heard.

At the same time, have materials ready in a number of likely areas so that you're not searching frantically at the last minute to find readings for 30 different projects. Since finding good material the kids can understand is one of the most challenging of research tasks, you'll want to have books, articles, and websites ready, or check on where they can be found on the Internet.

If students are unfamiliar with the subject, arrange for them to do some reading of short pieces, or other information-gathering, before they choose and begin specific projects. It helps to build prior knowledge so that students make choices they are truly invested in.

☞ **Don't worry if you can't fit in every subject area under an interdisciplinary project.** It's better to meld two or three disciplines into one naturally flowing inquiry focused on a real question, rather than stuffing a project, Christmas-tree-like, full of activities. An activity like the "Better Pastures" unit at Best Practice High School, combining community politics (social science) with electrical energy sources (science) makes much more sense than one in which students measure lengths of hypothetical whales, listen to whale music, write whale poems, study whale anatomy, and argue about international laws on whaling, just to jam in all the traditional subject areas.

☞ **Consider telling students they can only choose a topic if at least two classmates are interested in it as well.** That way, even with a variety of topics or questions going at once, the kids can support each other and you can handle the demands for help. However, you'll often have the bright loner who demands to do something special on his or her own. Your own good judgment as a teacher will guide you here.

☞ **Provide guidance for each step in the research process, and monitor kids' progress.** If they're floundering on their own, students will only learn and succeed if you help them. Conduct minilessons on how to take notes, how to ask good interview questions, how to organize information, how to create a PowerPoint presentation—whatever your project requires and your students need.

☞ **Build in a meaningful process for sharing the knowledge that students have gained**—for example, in an effective "Learning Fair," students not only create charts and demonstrations, but also present explanations and answer questions as visiting "judges"—parents, community members, other teachers, other kids—circulate and fill out response sheets. Melissa Bryant-Neal also requires her classes to ask questions of presenters, write entries in their journals after each presentation, and make lists of new vocabulary they've learned, so that the presentations become real learning experiences for the audience and not just recitations for the teacher.

☞ **Don't start too big!** A project that takes three or four class periods can be plenty. Then if your structure works well, go ahead and expand it next time around. Team up with one or more teachers in another subject area, if at all possible. This will support integration of subjects and give each of you some welcome support.

Accountability and Assessment

While inquiry projects approach learning through larger questions, district curriculum guides and state standards usually list more discrete skills and topics that teachers are expected to cover. How can teachers square this circle, make sure they are covering what's required, and prepare their students for district or state tests? Barbara Brodhagen (1995) describes a simple strategy in *Democratic Schools* to resolve this puzzle, and we call it "backmapping." Simply make yourself a two-column chart, and in the left column, list all the skills and content items you find that your inquiry project covers. Then in the right-hand column, list items from your state or district standards that match those in the first column. For Jackie Sanders' "Where Does the Money Go?" budget project, the chart would look like this:

My Goals for the Unit	Chicago Learning Outcomes—Eighth Grade
Consumer knowledge	Social Science: exhibit an understanding of economic principles as an informed consumer.
	Social Science: recognize the preparation needed for the world of work.

Applying math to real-world situations	Social Science: recognize how the allocation of resources affects the attitudes and behavior of people at the national and international levels.
	Math: make connections between related mathematical concepts and apply these concepts to other content and vocational areas.
Resumé writing	Language Arts: read and write independently for personal and academic purposes.
Calculating percentages	Math: extend the use of numbers in real-life situations to include integers and beyond.

Ms. Sanders will not have a difficult time justifying her kids' work on her unit, either to district administrators, parents, or her own sense of responsibility as a teacher.

Assessment need not be a complicated challenge either. Melissa Bryant-Neal's evaluation of students' presentations on digestive diseases, for example (see pp. 175–176), employs a rubric like the one on page 229.

For the larger junior class Learning Fair at Best Practice High School, visitors are handed rubrics and asked to provide written feedback to at least five students. Once students understand how rubrics work, they can be helped to create their own rubrics at the start of a project, as a way to both guide their work and create opportunities for individual goal-setting.

Can I Fit This In?

A chemistry teacher worried about covering all the topics for the district test, an English teacher with a prescribed list of novels to get through, a math teacher concerned about the kids' transition to advanced algebra and trig—all may wonder how to make room for these ambitious projects when there's already so much to cover. And we won't tell you that in-depth inquiry projects don't take time—they do. But the reasons for doing these projects are irresistible.

First, the effect on students' approach to learning and reading is just too large and too important for them to miss out. These projects give students valuable experience in what it's like to be responsible, independent thinkers. We teachers often use the phrase, "lifelong learner," but need to take action to turn it into reality for kids. And these projects are often memorable, among the few learning experiences students remember long afterward. Too often, kids experience school reading as drudgery to get around however they can. As one of the students put it in Smith and Wilhelm's study (perhaps exaggerating

OBJECTIVES	LOW PERFORMANCE—2 POINTS	NEEDS SOME WORK—4 POINTS	GETTING THERE—6 POINTS	MASTERED—8 POINTS	EARNED POINTS
Case background detail	Fails to give background about the case, or gives very little	Addresses patient profile somewhat, yet misses 2 or more necessary components	Addresses patient profile in detail, yet misses 1 of the necessary components	Addresses patient profile in detail: history, family, social, symptoms, mediations, lab data	
Scientific accuracy	Many inaccuracies, terms not defined, group does not seem to understand main ideas	Some inaccuracies & terms not explained. Group could respond to questions but not in detail	Mostly accurate & research evident. Some terms a bit confusing but main ideas clear	Well researched & accurate. Group could define & explain new terms & concepts, answer questions.	
Research questions	Many questions unanswered or incorrectly answered with little effort to tie to case	Very little detail on questions & some inaccuracies	Most questions answered accurately, with some detail missing	All questions answered accurately, in detail, & group can relate them to the case	
Teamwork	Group effort extremely unequal. One member dominated presentation and/or 1 person failed to participate	Some group members seem more prepared & researched more than others	Group mostly equal but at times 1 member dominated presentation or 1 left out	All group members participated equally & helped each other research & explain case	
Presentation style	Mainly reads from paper, rarely interests audience, lacks inspiration; little confidence in subject	Reading often from paper, little eye contact, gets some audience attention but doesn't inspire discussion	One of the qualities missing and lacking some confidence	Gets audience attention, interests class in case, inspires discussion, shows confidence in subject	
				Score:	

a bit to justify his own attitude, but still capturing a truth most of us can remember from our own high school years),

> Yeah, just fix the teachers some BS. Everyone does it. I mean, there is, like, not one person in this school who does their reading. Even the kids that get 4.0 GPA, they BS. . . . My BS just isn't that good so I don't have a 4.0. (2002, p. 102)

So it boils down to a trade-off. We can "cover" all the material, with most of our students passing a test and immediately forgetting most of what was taught; or we can let a bit of it go—not all, but a bit—and fit these valuable experiences in, so that more of our students deeply understand some topics, and come to value the subjects we teach.

Project work may be even more essential for our struggling students. If they've had some time to read and inquire in depth on topics that matter to them, it's much more likely that they'll understand and engage with more of the standard textbook material we do have to cover. The choice is simple: stick to the textbook and lose most of these students permanently; or incorporate some inquiry projects that get students engaged and keep them going through the drier spells.

The national standards documents, such as the National Science Education Standards, and the National Standards for United States History, desperately plead that students be given opportunities to ask important questions, read a variety of real-world materials, think critically, and inquire more deeply into specific topics, rather than skim lightly over endless parades of facts. While state test-makers have not always honored these recommendations, we know that such in-depth inquiry is vital for the preparation of competent experts in our fields.

Anyway, the projects don't have to take forever. Melissa Bryant-Neal's digestive system disease reports required a total of two double-period classes—one for her to introduce the structure and get the kids going on their research, and a second one for the groups to finish writing their reports and present them orally.

As tight as our curriculum and time schedules may seem to be, in-depth inquiry projects are some of our most powerful teaching strategies for making reading and learning matter for our students. At Addison Trail High School in the suburbs west of Chicago, the very popular Freshman Studies program focuses much of its entire curriculum on interdisciplinary learning, combining English, history, and biology. Here are some typical student comments at the end of the year:

"When I really thought about this year, I enjoyed most of it. I enjoyed the class and the discussions. Also, there was a connection between the students and the teachers that you don't see often."

"Now that it is the end of the year, I am no longer afraid to go up to the front of the class to give a speech. I am much more confident."

"When I first signed up for Freshman Studies, people warned me not to take the class because there were too many projects. I did anyway, and I am so glad that I did. I will miss this class so much."

Notes

Beane, James, and Michael Apple, eds. 1995. *Democratic Schools.* Alexandria, VA: Association for Supervision and Curriculum Development.

Brodhagen, Barbara. 1995. "The Situation Made Us Special," in James Beane and Michael Apple, eds., *Democratic Schools.* Alexandria, VA: Association for Supervision and Curriculum Development.

Kingkade, Ward. 1997. *International Brief. Population Trends: Russia. Washington, D.C.: U.S. Department of Commerce, Economics and Statistics Administration.*

Smith, Michael, and Jeffrey Wilhelm. 2002. *Reading Don't Fix No Chevys: Literacy in the Lives of Young Men.* Portsmouth, NH: Heinemann.

CHAPTER ELEVEN
Help for Struggling Readers

Sushma Sharma's freshman physics class is working on real-world applications for the equations relating distance, time, and speed of a moving object. The group includes many struggling readers who have not had much success in school. They have difficulty focusing at the start of the period and are easily distracted, particularly when they don't understand something. The problem they are working on describes the diving powers of the peregrine falcon, one of the fastest birds in the world. The falcon can dive at a speed of 97.2 meters per second. Sushma has posed the following question: if the falcon dives from 100 meters in the air at a rabbit down below, and the rabbit spots him starting the dive, how long does the rabbit have to scoot under a rock and avoid becoming dinner?

As we worked with several pairs of students who struggled with this problem, similar conversations were repeated:

Students: "We need some help!"
Steve: "So what do you think is going on in this problem?"
Student: "I don't know."
Steve (groping to see what the student does and does not understand): "Well, what's the scene? What does the paragraph say is happening here?"
Students: Silence.
Steve: "Okay, let's read it aloud. You start."
Students read the problem.
Steve: "So now tell me what is happening in this situation?"
Student: "Well, there's a bird, a . . . a . . . (struggles with the pronunciation) falcon."
Steve: "And what is he doing?"
Student: "He's, he's diving."

Again and again, a number of challenges emerge as the students talk. First and foremost, they aren't accustomed to turning the words they read into mental pictures. They don't see what's happening in the problem until a considerable amount of discussion brings the picture into focus—exactly the problem that researchers say is characteristic of struggling readers.

Another issue is the sheer unfamiliarity of the content for these students. They lack background knowledge. They don't have lots of opportunities to watch falcons dive for rabbits. None could recall seeing such a scene on television, though nature documentaries no doubt include such feats. A related set of challenges showed up in a different word problem, one about shining a laser beam at a "reflecting panel" on the moon in order to determine its distance from the earth. Some students didn't realize that a reflecting panel is simply a mirror. Nor were they accustomed to picturing that a beam of light "travels" like an object (or a wave, physicists would add). But again, as a result, they could not *picture* the situation.

Later, when the kids did construct a picture in their minds, they still needed to understand how to search through the paragraph for information that might help solve the problem, and to have confidence that such information would indeed help, even if they weren't yet sure how. And finally, they needed to decide what equation would give them an answer, and why.

These were willing students who wanted to learn, even if they sometimes acted out when frustrated. They worked patiently when the teacher and observer helped. So to help them develop the skills they needed, Sushma introduced the students to a problem-solving process that starts with picturing the situation from the reading and then locating key information within it. Several months later, while not every reading problem was resolved, the students were much more comfortable and successful with their efforts. During a similar in-class session solving problems about wave speed and frequency, the same kids worked steadily and seriously. They still struggled with the concepts and particularly with the vocabulary, but their confidence and commitment were visibly stronger.

We sympathize when teachers say to us, "I'm a physics teacher, not a reading teacher!" There's so much we need to do for our kids, and never enough time to do it all. And yet our close observation of their struggles tells us that to help the students understand and do the tasks we assign them, we must learn how reading works.

Oh, and by the way, if you were unsure about that falcon and the rabbit's fate: the basic equation is *rate = distance/time*. Since we know the rate and the distance, but are seeking to determine the time, the equivalent equation is *time = distance/rate*. We plug in the numbers, *time = 100m/97.2*. Looks like the rabbit has just a little over one second to hide. Thank goodness for Steve's long-ago study of physics.

A number of great teachers have written about their insights as they've helped move struggling and discouraged adolescents to become good, enthusiastic readers. And some great teacher-researchers have developed and brought together the studies that on a larger scale confirm the strategies these teachers have used. They include Janet Allen's *It's Never Too Late,* Kyle Gonzalez's *There's Room for Me Here,* written with Janet Allen, Chris Tovani's *I Read It But I Don't Get It,* Jeff Wilhelm's *You Gotta BE the Book,* Wilhelm and Michael Smith's *Reading Don't Fix No Chevys,* Richard Allington's *What Really Matters for Struggling Readers,* and Kylene Beers' *When Kids Can't Read: What Teachers Can Do.* We can draw on this fund of experience, as well as the successes of teachers we have known and observed, to learn what it takes to make a difference for the kids who need help the most.

To get close to some struggling readers and the efforts of their teacher to help them, we asked social studies/reading teacher Kenya Sadler and four of her seventh- and eighth-grade students at Foundations, a small school in Chicago, to tell us about their work. While Foundations is a school committed to addressing all students' needs, it's on a regular Chicago Public Schools budget, with regular Chicago class sizes and no extra funds for special programs. In fact, because this small school gets less Federal money than many others due to its size, the teachers find themselves stretched even thinner than in many traditional schools. So we'll follow Kenya as her kids work through approaches that make a difference in their reading.

We wanted to hear not from the top students in the school, but from those who have not had it easy. Three of the four we interviewed are kids who say that they do not enjoy reading—though as Smith and Wilhelm found with adolescent boys in *Reading Don't Fix No Chevys,* each had *some* reading topic he or she enjoyed. George reads about sports, Keyah about teenagers' issues, and Marvin follows news about "how kids get treated by adults." Only Samone is actually an avid reader. Nor did we seek out students who would merely tell us what we wanted to hear. When asked whether, in general, Ms. Sadler helps them with their reading, we got some typical teenage skepticism. However, when it came to specific strategies, these students were very clear about the mental tools they've been given.

So what do we learn from the reading experts, the kids, and the ways Kenya has helped them? Of course, all of the strategies we've outlined throughout this book will help students who are struggling. Conversely, the strategies we'll describe now are also effective for all students—but they're especially crucial for kids who see themselves as nonreaders, and who have experienced a lot of failure in school. Here are the approaches that Kenya, her students, and the experts we've mentioned all tell us are paramount.

Key Strategies for Helping Struggling Readers

☞ **Build Supportive Relationships.** Show students that you care intensely about their reading, believe they can succeed, and won't accept anything less. Many struggling readers feel that adults have somehow abandoned them, or pre-concluded that they are failures. Find your own individual ways to demonstrate that this is not true.

☞ **Model Thoughtful Reading.** Use "think-alouds" (see p. 102–103), in which the teacher reads aloud and stops to narrate how her mind works with the material—asking questions, making inferences, and entering the world created by the book or article. Struggling readers are too rarely shown the active thinking that more experienced readers bring to the process.

☞ **Use Activities That Build Engagement with the Text.** Drawing and role plays, arguing positions on real-life issues, helping students visualize the events and situations they are studying, all turn reading from a mechanical activity that kids avoid to one they are willing to work through.

☞ **Promote Self-monitoring.** Students can only clarify confusion if they stop to notice when they're confused. Waiting until a teacher tells them they've got it wrong is too late. Readers can be helped to realize when they're having difficulty and shown effective ways to get back on track.

☞ **Use Materials Students Can Successfully Read.** Students who have experienced repeated failure with reading are only further discouraged when they encounter lots of vocabulary they don't understand. For any given topic, providing materials at a variety of levels helps avoid this teaching trap.

☞ **Provide Books and Articles on Tape.** Listening to, as well as making taped readings connects students to the printed word with the human voice that gives it life in every subject. Recording sections and chapters of both fiction and nonfiction books helps students to become more fluent readers.

Building Supportive Relationships

All the great teachers who describe success with struggling readers focus on the essential process of developing students' trust. We've talked about this earlier in the book, but it's so essential for these students that we need to go a little further here. The psychologist-educator, William Glasser, in *Choice Theory in the Classroom*, explains that people who have repeatedly failed at something usually cope by focusing their lives elsewhere to avoid still more failure. If students in difficulty are going to take the risk and give math or science or a foreign language a new try, they'll need to know that you'll be there to help, and that they're in a safe place where they won't suffer further hurt if they don't succeed on the first try. When Chris Tovani shares with kids her own strategies for "fake reading" from her days as a student in *I Read It But I Don't Get It,* she's making an important move. Of course, she's showing the students she's street smart and not easily fooled. She also explains why the students won't be doing "book reports"—they're not only easily faked but don't help students learn to read better. Perhaps most important, she's placing herself on their level—"I've been where you are. I know what it's like. But I've learned and improved, so you can too." And her admission takes kids by surprise, always a valuable tool for getting people's attention and shifting them to new ground.

There are hundreds of ways for teachers to make supportive connections with their students, and the individuality of these is what makes the message powerful. One-size-fits-all actually doesn't really fit—so each of us needs to find our own way in this work. Kenya Sadler emphasizes her availability for individual help. Students know that they can always find her for reading conferences at lunch, and she takes calls for help on her cell phone at home between 5:00 and 6:00 P.M. When one student, studying author Bill Cosby, insisted on reading a biography with difficult vocabulary, Kenya's lunchtime conference consisted of reading alternate sentences aloud with the student and asking her to summarize her understanding after each paragraph. When kids were assigned to read aloud to an adult at home and one child called to say that no one was available, Kenya served as her telephone audience. Another insisted on reading a book above his comfort level because his friends were reading it too, so she supported him through a series of lunch sessions, rather than pressure him to choose something easier and expose him to the social isolation he feared. "They know I'm there to help," Kenya says. This also communicates high expectations: "The only excuse for not turning in homework is if I don't call you back."

The students we talked with know Ms. Sadler is not only available, but determined that they succeed. "She's twenty-four seven," Marvin announced, confirming that everyone has her cell phone and pager numbers. "You don't dare to *not* do her work. You might blow off some other teacher's assignments sometimes, but never hers, because you'll just get in trouble." *Supportive* is not the same thing as *easy.*

Not all of us can be as available as Kenya Sadler is. With families at home and extra duties assigned by our schools, we don't all have the same flexibilities. However, we can call on the reading specialists and special education teachers in our buildings to pitch in, collaborate on support for particular students, and give us additional ideas for how to help these kids become more successful with our subjects. And we can find other ways to signal our encouragement and support. Even Kenya can't do it all. As we write this, her new baby has her pretty deeply occupied and will probably keep her somewhat sleep-deprived in the coming months.

Modeling Thoughtful Reading

Effective teachers help struggling kids by modeling their own mental processes as they read, rather than just exhort students to do something they don't know how to do. Kylene Beers, in *When Kids Can't Read: What Teachers Can Do,* describes how teachers use "think-alouds" (described on p. 102–103, here) to demonstrate meaningful thinking, giving *instruction* rather than just *instructions.* This is more challenging than it might sound, since so much of our thinking is nearly unconscious as we read. Beers uses the following passage, to challenge students in classes she visits, asking them to figure out what's going on and then notice the mental processes they used:

> He put down $10.00 at the window. The woman behind the window gave $4.00. The person next to him gave him $3.00 but he gave it back to her. So when they went inside, she bought him a large bag of popcorn. (2003, pp. 62–63)

Most of us see a girl trying to keep her date at the movies from paying for everything. Good readers make some spirited inferences to reach this conclusion, perhaps with further speculation about the two people's motives. Struggling readers often don't even see the point in deciphering the puzzle. They need to see how we do this and what we learn as a result. Of course, when we demonstrate this process for reading in math or science, we're actually showing students how to think about our subjects.

Kenya Sadler provides this sort of modeling regularly. "The kids know that I talk a lot in class," she laughs. "But I found that if you let them know there *is* a process, and you know it and can show it to them, they'll use it." For her unit on the Harlem Renaissance, Kenya asked students to read short biographies of important figures, collected in *Black Stars of the Harlem Renaissance,* so she used a piece on Duke Ellington to model her own thinking and questioning. The students were to watch for moments in the artists' lives when a major change might have occurred. Since she'd previously taught the kids to jot their responses on sticky notes at relevant spots in the text, she talked through her own reading and sticky-note writing, wondering aloud what Ellington may have thought about the contrast between his warm reception in Europe and the discrimination he suffered working at the Cotton Club in New York. Later, when the students completed their reading, they transferred their sticky notes to a timeline to trace the struggles and growth of these important artists and innovators.

Interestingly, the think-alouds led the kids we talked with to focus on the sticky notes more than on her oral testimony—which is just fine with us. "The notes help you remember what you read," explained Samone. "If you see something important, you just put a sticky note there." So would you use them on your own? we wondered. The unanimous pragmatic answer: "Yes, especially if it's reading for school, and if there's going to be a test." Well, O.K., most of us adults are similarly practical. We might happily use post-its for our professional reading, but rarely in the novels we read for pleasure.

Activities That Build Engagement

When Jeff Wilhelm realized how extensively his top readers immersed themselves in the stories they read, he encouraged resistant kids to do the same thing (1997). But they continued to resist, because this simply didn't fit in their mental picture of reading. Jeff found two strategies that launched students on the road to engagement by using activity, rather than exhortation: drama and drawing. And he introduced these activities not for after-reading enrichment, but for before-reading introduction. Once students experienced some physical, visual, and auditory involvement, they more readily continued it as they moved into their reading.

Kenya Sadler also finds drawing especially helpful for her seventh and eighth graders. To help groups of kids read their *Harlem Renaissance* articles, Kenya asked them to fold large sheets of newsprint into small squares, and then draw a picture in a square at various stages as they read—no words or captions allowed. Each group then used their pictures to report on their section of the text. We talk about this strategy, "Sketching my way through the text," on p. 120–121.

The students' perceptions of this strategy varied. Samone was positive— "I'd rather draw than write." George, on the other hand, complained that his lack of artistic ability limited his enthusiasm for drawing—reminding Kenya to reiterate that this kind of drawing is a tool for thinking, not a performance to be judged. George explained that when he's confused, he tries writing out a paragraph about the topic to help clarify his thoughts. Marvin, to round out the responses, reported that he found writing and drawing equally helpful. On the importance of engagement, Samone was very clear: "You have to be into it; you can't just look at the words."

Promoting Students' Self-Monitoring

Chris Tovani found that her high school students wanted her to do their thinking for them. Asserted one student,

> I'm sick and tired of you telling the class that it's our job to know when we know and know when we don't know. You're the teacher. Aren't you the one who is supposed to know when we understand something and when we don't? (2000, p. 35)

School too often encourages students to abdicate responsibility and leave all the thinking to their teachers. Students become highly adept at waiting for teachers to simply give them answers instead of taking on challenges themselves.

So self-monitoring is one of the first reading strategies Kenya teaches, showing her students how to use sticky notes to mark the places where they've lost meaning or become confused. If their confusion continues, she tells them, it's time to stop and talk with a partner. If they're still having trouble, they can ask for the teacher's help. Her students were absolutely clear about a sequence for self-help when comprehension breaks down, though their version differed a bit from Ms. Sadler's. Keyah asserted: "If you see a word you don't understand, try to sound it out; then if you're still confused, ask somebody; then try reading around it; and if you still need help, look it up." Samone had her own creative strategy: "If I don't understand a word, I just make it up. And when I see it again, I remember what I made up." Of course, without saying so, she's using context to do this.

Using Materials Students Can Successfully Read

It's crucial for resistant readers to work with books they can read, rather than simply being defeated again and again by ones they can't. While books beyond their level may just lead average and successful students to have less interest in reading, for struggling readers this risks completely locking them out. It's very simple: if a student can't read the material, he can't get anything out of it or get any better at comprehending it. Reading researcher Richard

Allington summarizes the clear conclusions of one thorough study on the issue this way:

> Tasks completed with high rates of success were linked to greater learning and improved student attitudes toward the subject matter being learned, while tasks where students were moderately successful were less consistently related to learning, and hard tasks produced a negative impact on learning. Hard tasks also produced off-task behaviors and negative attitudes. (2001, pp. 44–45)

Kenya Sadler makes sure to provide a wide range of readings for each unit that she plans. This not only allows students to work at their independent reading level, but introduces choice into their reading as well. For example, for her Harlem Renaissance project, Kenya provided the following items:

Black Stars of the Harlem Renaissance by Jim Haskins—all students read selections

The Harlem Renaissance by Veronica Chambers—all students read selections

Bring on That Beat by Rachel Isadora—picture book on Black musicians for all students

Shimmy Shimmy Shimmy Like My Sister Kate: Looking at the Harlem Renaissance Through Poems by Nikki Giovanni—options for any students

The Block by Langston Hughes—options for grades 4–6 reading level

Black American Poets and Dramatists of the Harlem Renaissance edited by Harold Bloom—options for grades 7–12 reading level

Each student reads at least a part of the first three, and then chooses something from at least one of the second three. Kenya used to worry that her seventh- and eighth-grade kids would be put off by picture books, and they do indeed respond skeptically at first. But now she incorporates powerful picture books on important topics at the very beginning of the year, reads several aloud, and keeps plenty out for students to browse, and the problem quickly disappears.

Creating choice can sometimes push us to our limit, however. Kenya wanted her students to make their own choice of a focus for a spring study project. The kids obliged and decided on "medieval times." The topic was very broad, however; she didn't have a wealth of materials ready; the time for planning was slipping away; the challenges of collaborating in a small school were mounting; and so this time Kenya backed off her ambitious plan. It would have to wait until next year.

Providing Books and Articles on Tape

In *There's Room for Me Here,* Kyle Gonzalez, as a new middle-school teacher, describes how taped books can help students become readers. Like most strategies, however, the tapes don't automatically provide a miracle cure without plenty of adjusting by an observant and resourceful teacher. Kyle admits, "Our first day of Sustained Silent Reading (SSR) was an eye-opener: my students were neither sustained nor silent, and they certainly had no intention of reading." She had to gradually discover the type and level of materials her students would read. She began a log to keep track of students' reading and tape-listening, to minimize confusion, and to get kids started quickly at the beginning of the period. Arguments over who would sit in the upholstered chairs led to a rotation chart. Brief check-in conferences during reading time helped keep students going. Kyle gradually found solutions to each problem, rather than reprimand and blame kids when things didn't flow smoothly (1998, pp. 62–66).

Kenya Sadler uses tape recording not only for students to listen to a voice as they read, but for them to become more fluent with their own. For her social studies unit on the U.S. Constitution, Kenya required each student to record a primary source reading for the class. This served a number of important purposes. First, it built up her collection of taped pieces that struggling readers could listen to. Second, it provided important practice in fluency, one of the four main components for improving the reading of students in difficulty (Allington 2001; National Reading Panel 2000). Third, it allowed Kenya to monitor each student's reading. And how does Kenya find time to listen to the kids' tapes? By playing them in her car as she drives to and from school. Yes, we know that some of us need that drive home in silence, just to let our brains rest after an intense day, and that maybe it's wiser to pay closer attention to the traffic, but Kenya's time investment certainly pays off.

The Kids Evaluate Their Progress

So how has reading changed for our four Foundations School students over the past two-to-three years? What is the impact of Ms. Sadler's intensive work, at least as her students see it? Keyah's response: "I read faster and I understand more." Marvin: "I can catch on to what's happening sooner." George: "I realized that sometimes I have to read something several times to understand what's on the page." So he doesn't just let the words go by unthinkingly. Finally, Samone throws us her usual curve ball: "I used to smack my lips at the end of each sentence. Now I don't do that." Huh? But maybe this isn't the trivial matter it first appears to be—she's describing a physical aspect of her growth from an earlier, little-kid stage of oral performance to a more internalized, higher-speed adult reading process, involved with thinking and understanding rather than mere decoding.

Notes

Allen, Janet. 1995. *It's Never Too Late: Leading Adolescents to Lifelong Literacy.* Portsmouth, NH: Heinemann.

Allen, Janet, and Kyle Gonzalez. 1998. *There's Room for Me Here: Literacy Workshop in the Middle School.* Portland, ME: Stenhouse.

Allington, Richard. 2001. *What Really Matters for Struggling Readers.* New York, NY: Longman.

Beers, Kylene. 2003. *When Kids Can't Read: What Teachers Can Do.* Portsmouth, NH: Heinemann.

Bloom, Harold, ed. 1995. *Black American Poets and Dramatists of the Harlem Renaissance.* New York, NY: Chelsea House.

Chambers, Veronica. 1997. *The Harlem Renaissance.* New York, NY: Chelsea House.

Giovanni, Nikki, ed. 1996. *Shimmy Shimmy Shimmy Like My Sister Kate: Looking at the Harlem Renaissance Through Poems.* New York, NY: Holt.

Glasser, William. 1998. *Choice Theory in the Classroom.* New York, NY: Harper.

Haskins, Jim. 2002. *Black Stars of the Harlem Renaissance.* New York, NY: Wiley.

Hughes, Langston. 1995. *The Block: Poems* (Selected by Lowery Sims and Daisy Voigt). New York, NY: Viking.

Isadora, Rachel. 2002. *Bring On That Beat.* New York, NY: Putnam.

National Reading Panel. 2000. *Teaching Children to Read: An Evidence-Based Assessment of the Scientific Research Literature on Reading and Its Implications for Reading Instruction.* Washington, D.C.: National Institutes of Health.

Smith, Michael, and Jeffrey Wilhelm. 2002. *Reading Don't Fix No Chevys: Literacy in the Lives of Young Men.* Portsmouth, NH: Heinemann.

Tovani, Chris. 2000. *I Read It But I Don't Get It.* Portland, ME: Stenhouse.

Wilhelm, Jeffrey. 1997. *You Gotta BE the Book: Teaching Engaged and Reflective Reading with Adolescents.* New York, NY: Teachers College Press.

CHAPTER TWELVE
Recommendations from Reading Research

Everyone—particularly the Federal government—asks, these days, whether there's "scientific" research to support the many plans, recommendations, and curricula for education reform. Sounds reasonable. Teachers need to better understand how students think and learn. And they need reassurance that the methods they use are the best possible, even though they can see for themselves whether their kids are making progress or not. Fortunately, plenty of this educational research has, in recent years, focused on teenagers' reading habits, skills, and struggles, and it points in some clear directions. Though much of the reading inquiry does focus on beginning reading and younger children, dozens of quantitative and qualitative studies of rigorous design back up this book's prescriptions for older students.

As we write this book, many educators are worried about the impact of the Federal No Child Left Behind law, which has some controversial provisions. The law poses a whole range of requirements for teacher quality, assessment, unremitting progress with every possible student subgroup, remediation and sanctions when that doesn't happen, and, yes, "scientific" research validation of any curriculum practices supported by Federal funds. So what does this mean for our efforts to strengthen reading in the content areas?

Well, first we could easily get worked up over the corrosive aspects of the No Child Left Behind law. We could quote all the distortions of research on the state of education in America that were used to justify the law. We could tell stories about the resulting rule changes in a big school system like Chicago's, changes that are undermining good programs and important innovations— presumably unintentionally. Not surprisingly, these changes usually leave the weaker schools floundering just as much as they were in the past. We could point out that the National Reading Panel, which evaluated the reading research and teaching methods, excluded many of the most respected experts in the field, and defined "scientific" so narrowly that many of the most helpful studies are left out. As a result, some of their recommendations on beginning reading just happen to validate old traditional approaches that committee members favored in the first place. Yet at the same time, there are many places where its report contradicts itself on these matters. And we could note that the few reading programs given the stamp of approval are sold by publishers who just happen to have friends in high places. (See Allington 2002, for a detailed examination of these many problems.)

But for a couple of big reasons, we needn't dwell on these issues. First, this cumbersome law follows a long history of ultimately ineffectual efforts by the political party in power to supervise teachers in their classrooms. We believe it will fail and fade away just as previous ones have, while our schools are left, as always, trying to educate kids and to learn how to do it better. Second, the main controversy in reading focuses on beginning reading, and pits the advocates of heavy phonics and tightly scripted, teacher-proof lessons against those who favor integrating skills more fully with lots of good reading, and who see the need for plenty of flexibility in teachers' decisionmaking in the classroom. But we're talking in this book about older students, most of whom conquered the skill of decoding long ago, though they still may not think deeply about or remember what they read in their courses. And ironically, when it comes to the comprehension and vocabulary skills teenagers need, even the conservative National Reading Panel, which has vetted the research so hypercritically, fully agrees with the recommendations in this book. Here's what the NRP says about vocabulary:

> First, vocabulary should be taught both directly and indirectly. Repetition and multiple exposures to vocabulary items are important. Learning in rich contexts, incidental learning, and use of computer technology all enhance the acquisition of vocabulary.

And here are the main reading comprehension strategies that the Panel says "have a solid scientific basis":

☞ Comprehension monitoring, where readers learn how to be aware of their understanding of the material;

☞ Cooperative learning, where students learn reading strategies together;

☞ Use of graphic and semantic organizers (including story maps) where readers make graphic representations of the material to assist comprehension;

☞ Question answering, where readers answer questions posed by the teacher and receive immediate feedback;

☞ Question generation, where readers ask themselves questions about various aspects of the story;

☞ Story structure, where students are taught to use the structure of the story as a means of helping them recall story content in order to answer questions about what they have read; and

☞ Summarization, where readers are taught to integrate ideas and generalize from the text information

247

RECOMMEN-

DATIONS

FROM

READING

RESEARCH

The Panel also goes on to endorse both "direct explanation," in which teachers demonstrate "strategic thinking" to understand a text, and "transactional strategy instruction," which means:

> . . . the teacher's ability to provide explicit explanations of thinking processes. Further, it emphasizes the ability of teachers to facilitate student discussions in which students collaborate to form joint interpretations of text and acquire a deeper understanding of the mental and cognitive processes involved in comprehension. (2000, pp. 10–12, "Findings" section)

If you've been reading this book, all of this sounds pretty familiar, yes? The one area where the Panel hesitates is on the effect of "independent silent reading." While hundreds of studies show correlations between reading more and reading better, the National Panel worries that these studies don't actually prove causation. Again, however, this doesn't really create an issue for us here, though we believe the Panel ignored some powerful evidence. For one thing, no one could possibly argue that students shouldn't read about the subject they are studying! And the Panel never looks at how subject-area learning is influenced by what students read—the hard-to-use textbook or engaging, real-world nonfiction books and articles.

So we can go on to look with some confidence at what the research tell us about reading in secondary education, particularly as it supports learning in the various subject areas. First and foremost: while traditional textbooks have their place in the classroom (and in Chapter 6 we talked about how to use them more effectively) they should occupy just a fraction of kids' reading lives. For the rest of their middle-school and high-school experience, young people will learn more from their reading in their various courses if they read widely and extensively just as literate adults do, and become genuinely engaged in that reading. Here's what the research urges.

Key Points

1. **Kids should read a wide range of materials in all classes.** Teenagers' reading and learning of school subject matter grows when they read the kinds of materials real adult readers do—including a wide range of text, fiction and nonfiction, articles and books, paper and electronic, informational and poetic, in a wide range of genres. This broad mixture aids learning in all subjects—English to math, history to science, art to foreign language.

In a comprehensive 1988 study of 30 successful secondary literacy programs around the country reported in *Adolescent Literacy: What Works and Why* (Davidson and Koppenhaver 1993) the researchers found a number of common attributes of effective programs. Two key characteristics: giving students access to a wide variety of materials, and spending a high proportion of time on actual reading, as opposed to drills.

> Teachers in successful literacy programs don't wait for someone to supply the books; they get the books. Books, not standard textbooks, are a budget item they request. They are ruthless in their search for books and magazines: they raid locked closets where retired teachers have left books long forgotten, beg from businesses, haunt garage sales, and demand donations from friends whose children have gone off to college . . . (p. 189)

This longstanding finding was reconfirmed in a more recent study, *Literacy Learning in the Middle Grades: An Investigation of Academically Effective Middle Grades Schools* (Strauss 2000). It's essential: kids need to read lots of real-world books and materials of many kinds.

Presently, however, 45% of high school history teachers and 90% of science teachers use only the textbook for their students' reading, and that's by self-report (Patrick and Hawke 1982; Yore 1991). Yet, teachers in many studies have provided reports of effective use of novels and trade books for teaching social science (Spiegel 1987; Crook 1990; Lehman and Crook 1989). In one particularly striking study, Leslie Mandell Morrow and her colleagues observed how students learned more science in a program that integrated literature-based study with the science curriculum (Morrow et al. 1997).

Wide reading is also necessary for developing vocabulary in various subjects. It is estimated that students normally learn vocabulary at the rate of 3,000 to 4,000 words per year, adding up to 50,000 words or more by the time they finish high school (Anderson and Nagy 1992; Anglin 1993; White et al. 1990). Clearly, no directly taught vocabulary program alone—10 words a week with a quiz on Friday—can ever achieve this rate of learning. Instead, kids' word knowledge expands as they read widely, acquiring most of their vocabulary through context and repeated exposure (Anderson 1996). Obviously, we need to support this process.

2. Students should read for the same purposes as literate adults, both for information and pleasure, and a sense of purpose is key to their reading success. The purposes in students' heads make all the difference not only in what they get out of reading and study in math and science and social studies, but in whether they even attempt the work at all.

John Guthrie and Emily Anderson (1999) identify the larger motivations students may have for reading:

involvement in the material itself
curiosity about a particular subject or question
social interactions with others about their reading
the challenge of tackling something difficult
the sense that reading is important
a sense of efficacy, feeling confident about their reading abilities
recognition for doing well (a more extrinsic motivation)
competition, proving oneself better than other students (also an extrinsic motive)

Not surprisingly, it's the intrinsic motivations that lead to greater learning in high-school subject areas. For example, in one study, students who reported being motivated by a strong interest in physics and believed it was relevant to their everyday and future lives "read more widely, talked to their teachers and parents, and thought deeply about physics applications both in class and out of school" (Hynd 1999; Hynd et al. 1994).

Unfortunately, all such motivations for reading decline steadily as students move up the grades (Wigfield and Guthrie 1997; Gambrell et al. 1996; McKenna et al. 1995). Repeatedly, researchers find that especially with adolescents, those who avoid reading see it as merely decoding the words, or looking for answers to the questions at the end of the chapter (Wilhelm 1997; also Lowery-Moore 1998; Beers 1998; Carlsen and Sherrill 1988).

249

RECOMMEN-

DATIONS

FROM

READING

RESEARCH

If we are to reverse this decline, we need to promote the kind of involvement we see in the teens who do read a lot. And between good readers and those who struggle with the process, there's a sharp difference over what reading is even about. Jeff Wilhelm (Wilhelm 1997), interviewing eighth graders, found that good readers enter deeply into the material they read, visualize what is happening, identify with characters and events, and connect the material with real life. In contrast, those who don't read well experience none of these things, and simply do not recognize that they are possible. Avid student readers are reading not because work is assigned to them, but because their reading matters. As one enthusiastic student said, "I think reading is important because it teaches people to understand life more and understand themselves" (Lowery-Moore 1998).

Wilhelm and Smith looked into high-school boys' struggles with reading, in *Reading Don't Fix No Chevys* (2002), and found that while boys in all kinds of schools are less engaged in academic reading than girls are, most boys use extensive literate activity in other parts of their lives—and not necessarily just books about cars and sports. They found that the boys favored stories over textbooks, and preferred reading that provides multiple perspectives, that has an edge or is surprising or funny, and especially reading that feeds into social interaction. More broadly, they found the boys seek. "A sense of control and competence, a challenge that requires an appropriate level of skill, clear goals and feedback, and a focus on immediate experience" (pp. 29–30). Unfortunately, for many boys (and indeed both genders), these purposeful characteristics are frequently missing from reading assignments in school—though they don't really need to be.

3. Students need to read a lot; volume, quantity, and practice count.

It's disturbing to realize the minuscule amount that middle-school and high-school students actually read. According to a National Assessment of Educational Progress report (NAEP 1997), 56% of 13-year-olds and 47% of 17-year-olds read 10 or fewer pages each day. In an earlier survey, three-fourths of fourth graders were found to read for fun each week, compared to only half of 12th graders (NAEP 1988). Yet students who do more reading frequently achieve at higher levels on the NAEP reading test. Another study, involving students' reading logs, showed that high-achieving fifth graders read over 2,000,000 words per year, while low-achieving kids covered only 51,000 (Anderson et al. 1988). And it's hard to avoid the implications: John Guthrie and his colleagues found that higher reading volume related to better reading comprehension in third-, fifth-, eighth-, and 10th-grade students (1999).

The National Reading Panel worried that such data shows a correlation, but not necessarily a cause-and-effect relationship—in other words, it's possible that some kids read more **because** they're already better at it and therefore enjoy it, rather than improving because they read. However, some useful studies help separate these effects. Studies that look at assigned classroom reading time, for example, remove the question of whether the better readers just choose to read more. And indeed, classrooms that provide more reading time yield higher reading achievement (Keisling 1978; Taylor et al. 1990). Careful studies even go so far as to control statistically for past reading achievement, prior knowledge, and motivation (Guthrie and Anderson. 1999).

4. Students should read plenty of books and articles written at a comfortable recreational level, not frustration level.

This can seem counter-intuitive—doesn't it mean dumbing down the curriculum and lowering standards? But research shows that students' reading improves most when no more than 10% of material in a text is difficult for them to understand. In other words, their learning improves as they have more success with reading. Actually, it's logical when you think about it: if kids don't understand what they're reading, then how can anything happen in their heads? When reading is disrupted repeatedly by unknown vocabulary or unclear connections, meaning quickly gets lost (Denham and Lieberman 1980).

Of course, when a student *wants* to try a more challenging book, we shouldn't hold him or her back. However, studies show that high-school students become very frustrated when trying to read textbooks that are difficult to understand (Hynd et al. 1994, 1995, 1997). It's not for a lack of interest in the subject matter though, because when passages are re-written to provide clearer explanation and more connection between ideas, the students learn more (Britton et al. 1996; Beck et al. 1991, 1995).

5. Young people need genuine choice of reading materials: at least half of what kids read should be self-selected, based on interest and curiosity.

If subject-area teachers fear that student choice of reading might lead to nothing but trashy novels and fashion magazines, they can put away their fears. We can understand this by comparing adult Americans' choices to those of teenagers. So what do the adults choose to read? Far more nonfiction than anything else—84% of published books are nonfiction. And the adults pursue a wide range of subjects. In 1994, for example, Rosie Daley's cookbook *In the Kitchen with Rosie* sold 5.5 million copies, compared with John Grisham's top-of-the-list 3.2 million for *The Chamber.* John Gray's nonfiction *Men Are from Mars, Women Are from Venus* sold 2.9 million. In 1995, Colin Powell's autobiography, *My American Journey,* was a blockbuster (Carter and Abrahamson 1998). According to the Associated Press, Hillary Clinton's autobiography, despite her polarizing personality, sold 1.2 million copies in its first six weeks on the market.

Just like adults, when kids make their own choices, they gravitate to nonfiction on topics that matter to them. For example, in the late 1990s three very popular series with teens were the "Cross Sections" books by Dorling-Kindersley (e.g., examining a medieval castle, or an 18th-century warship), Jill Krementz' *How It Feels* books (*How It Feels to Fight for Your Life, How It Feels When a Parent Dies,* etc.), and the "Headliners" books (on past or recent world

Major Conclusions from Six Decades of Reading Research

1. Kids should read a wide range of materials in all classes.

2. Students should read for the same purposes as literate adults, both for information and pleasure. A sense of purpose is key to reading success.

3. Students need to read a lot; volume, quantity, and practice count.

4. Students should read plenty of books and articles written at a comfortable recreational level, not frustration level.

5. Kids need genuine choice of reading materials: at least half of what they read should be self-selected, based on interest and curiosity.

6. The classroom should become a reading community, a group of people who regularly read, talk, and write together.

7. Teachers must help students develop a repertoire of thinking strategies to handle challenging texts, and guide students to be increasingly aware and in charge of their own thinking processes.

8. Students should engage in frequent interdisciplinary inquiries, projects, and where possible entire interdisciplinary courses to explore topics in depth.

9. Students of all ages need to hear powerful writing in performance—reading aloud by the teacher and other students, dramatic interpretation, audiobooks, etc.

10. Adolescent students need opportunities to connect with the adult literate community, starting with teachers as readers who generously share their reading lives with kids.

events). A "Headliner" favorite: *The Los Angeles Riots: America's Cities in Crisis.* Biographies of Hitler and Charles Manson vie with more positive models like Arthur Ashe. When Daniel Fader developed his ideas on students' reading, in the famous *Hooked on Books,* he found, working with reform school boys, that their favorite choice was *Black Like Me* (Carter and Abrahamson 1998).

Several researchers have found that making choices for reading matters a great deal to teenagers. Frustratingly, though, while choice was a major factor in students' engagement, the classroom opportunities for choice and access to a variety of books were both very limited (Worth and McCool 1996; Oldfather 1993, 1994; and Oldfather and Dahl 1995).

253

RECOMMEN-

DATIONS

FROM

READING

RESEARCH

6. The classroom should become a reading community, a group of people who regularly read, talk, and write together.

Many studies have supported the value of collaborative learning. Judith Davidson and David Koppenhaver's study of successful reading programs for adolescents tells how collaboration is key (Davidson and Koppenhaver 1993; see also Alvermann et al. 1999, and Goatley et al. 1995). Valerie Lee and her colleagues with the Consortium on Chicago School Research found that when sixth graders and eighth graders felt that their teachers knew them well and listened to what they had to say, and when they experienced that their fellow students respected and helped each other, their improvement on standardized scores in both reading and math were greater than when these aspects of community were missing from the classroom (1999). Another Consortium study, by Julia Smith, Valerie Lee, and Fred Newmann, showed that students in classrooms that featured "interactive" teaching and learning also did significantly better on standardized tests than those provided with more "didactic" lessons. While the descriptors for interactive teaching covered a wide range of characteristics, activities that involved students interacting together in the whole class or in groups were high on the list. The data were collected on large numbers of students from second through eighth grade, with significant outcomes at each level (2001).

With older students, the effectiveness of group discussions and projects appears to depend very much on how they are organized. They do not go as well when the tasks are competitive (Johnson et al. 1985), when all the students in a group are low functioning (Mulryan 1994), or when low-quality group interactions occur. Collaboration is effective when students work with others they know and like, and strategies must be introduced to insure that everyone in the group contributes. Open-ended tasks and engaging topics help insure that group work succeeds (Alvermann et al. 1996).

7. Teachers must help students develop a repertoire of thinking strategies to handle challenging texts, and must guide them to become increasingly aware and in charge of their own thinking processes.

Richard Allington, in *What Really Matters for Struggling Readers,* emphasizes that our goal for kids' learning is not just factual recall, but thoughtful literacy. This means not just assigning reading to students, but showing them how to do it, helping kids run their minds and think about material—so that it directly aids the teaching of content.

Not surprisingly, the research on this is extensive. Teaching strategies for comprehension—such as questioning the author and connecting material to students' prior knowledge and experience—are central characteristics of the successful reading programs across the country evaluated by Davidson and Koppenhaver (1993). They are the core of "reciprocal teaching," developed by Palincsar and Brown (1984). And their effect on students' understanding of material they read is confirmed by researchers again and again (Pressley et al. 1990; Dole et al. 1996; Pearson and Dole 1987; Pearson and Fielding 1991; Rosenshine and Meister 1994; and Mastropieri and Scruggs 1997). Comprehension strategy instruction even increases students' willingness to study difficult material (Anderson 1992).

But when we speak of *comprehension,* we're not talking just about recalling facts and information. Thoughtful literacy means elaborating ideas, recognizing implications, gaining a sense of the larger meaning carried by particular information—all of which are emphasized as goals by national and state standards for subjects across the curriculum. And teaching comprehension strategies does not mean merely assigning them or just creating more drill sheets. Teachers must model adult thinking and help students engage in dialogue using the strategies. Judith Langer's study, "Beating the Odds:

255

RECOMMEN-

DATIONS

FROM

READING

RESEARCH

Dickens with complete surprise in graduate school. It seems as if, until I was an adult, the reading that affected me most was somehow connected with my family.

Now, my reading is not like that of my friends or my wife. Mostly I read for my work, or during the half hour after breakfast when I sit with the newspaper. I'd rather get up at a brutally early hour than miss that quiet morning reading time. When I do read a novel, I become quite obsessed with it. It seems to disrupt my life, and by the time I've passed the middle, I rush to the end in one mad sitting. Afterward, I ruminate on it for weeks. As a result, I don't read many, but really stew over the ones I do get into.

Teaching Middle and High School Students to Read and Write Well" (CELA 2001), reveals this as a key feature of effective classrooms in schools serving poor and culturally diverse students. Lessons focused on this more elaborated thinking do in fact produce higher comprehension of the material that students read (Dole et al. 1996; Knapp 1995; Pressley et al. 1990; Purcell-Gates et al. 1995), though they do not occur often enough in our classrooms.

8. Students should engage in frequent interdisciplinary inquiries, projects, and entire interdisciplinary courses to explore topics in depth.

Studies of interdisciplinary learning bring up two very different kinds of questions. One asks what we are really aiming to teach and the other asks how effective this teaching is. The first question cannot be answered with statistical numbers. Rather, it asks what we've observed students' needs to be, both developmentally and related to the larger world we're preparing them for. An especially articulate educational thinker for these questions is James Beane. In *A Middle School Curriculum: From Rhetoric to Reality* (1993), Beane explains how the division of the curriculum into traditional university-style subjects fails to serve early adolescents well. Instead, they need to address personal and social issues in a more integrated way. "The centerpiece of the curriculum would consist," Beane concludes, "of thematic units whose organizing centers are drawn from the intersecting concerns of early adolescents and issues in the larger world" (p. 68). Wilhelm and Smith's study, *Reading Don't Fix No Chevys,* also strongly supports this approach. Since extended inquiry projects are often characterized by efforts to gather information on important issues that matter to students and the wider society, they carry with them a larger sense of purpose and immediacy that Wilhelm and Smith found boys particularly sought in their lives, but are often missing from school reading tasks.

As for the second question, a number of studies examine, in individual school efforts and larger multi-school studies, how such broader education can be conducted effectively. In her thorough guide, *Teaching Middle School Students to Be Active Researchers*, Judith Zorfass (1998) reviews a list of studies that confirm the effectiveness of interdisciplinary learning, including reports from the National Dissemination Network, which required very rigorous statistical evaluation before programs could be accepted. A number of research reports describe the content, structure, and positive learning results of interdisciplinary projects in individual middle schools and high schools (Gallagher et al. 1992; Alexander et al. 1995). And still more were designed to involve multiple schools or classrooms, compared to control groups (McConney et al. 1994; Hecht 1994; and Hange and Rolfe 1995). At Maine East High School in the Chicago area, for example, students in one interdisciplinary program not only earned higher grades, but had better attendance than the control group. A second project group, which also tried to integrate computer technology, did not do as well, and the teachers reported that they had simply bitten off more than they could swallow in one year (Hecht 1994).

An additional group of studies focused on "problem-based learning," which is not the same as, but has a lot in common with, interdisciplinary study. Problem-based learning focuses on student-guided inquiry, which is not always the case with interdisciplinary projects, though it is frequently one of their major ingredients. Problem-based learning can be focused on a single subject, though the need to solve a problem often does, in fact, take students

HARVEY'S READING HISTORY

I know my parents provided all the right fairy tales and little-kid books, but I also remember one of my teachers telling my mother at a conference, "He's a good reader but not the best reader in the class." I mean, ouch! Later on, like most male children of my generation, I gobbled up the Hardy Boys books, swapped titles with friends, and collected a pretty long shelf of them. The first book that completely knocked me out was *The Swiss Family Robinson*. Something about that shipwrecked family really appealed to me: they were relentlessly cheerful, cooperative, inventive problem-solvers who viewed every challenge as a learning opportunity—and I read their story over and over. A little later, I fell in love with two big, thick books which would sit under my bed and be best reading companions through my teen years: *The Complete Sherlock Holmes* and *The Complete Mark Twain*. Oh yeah, and *Mad* magazine, of course.

continued

257

RECOMMEN-

DATIONS

FROM

READING

RESEARCH

For much of my adult life, I was a three-month-a-year reader. From September through May, I'd read only professional stuff—journals, books, curriculum materials, research reports—feeling that there was just no time for fun reading or real books. Then in June, my wife, The Mother of All Readers, would feed me her top 10 or 12 books from the hundred she'd read that year. And I'd spend the summer reading on the dock, happily catching up. Recently, I've made more room for reading in my life, all year long. It hasn't been easy—it meant turning off Letterman, and better yet, skipping the morning news programs, which are just designed to keep you in a state of fear and hopelessness anyway. Now, I get up and read for a half hour, mostly fiction, in a genre I'd call "Oprah and Above" (e.g., J. W. Coetze's stunning novel of South Africa, *Disgrace*). The past year, preparing to write this book, has been especially delicious, since it "forced" me to read our own Top 20 and many of the other titles listed in Chapter 4.

beyond the bounds of a given field. Again, however, the outcomes are consistently positive (Stepien et al. 1993; Achilles and Hoover 1996), in some cases significantly compared to a control group (Williams et al. 1998).

9. Students of all ages need to experience reading of powerful writing in performance—reading aloud by the teacher and other students, drama, etc.

The Commission on Reading named reading aloud as "The single most important activity for building the knowledge required for eventual success in reading" (Anderson et al. 1985). Students in grades 7 through 12, when surveyed, indicated that reading aloud was the most effective motivator for getting them to read (Livaudais 1986). A meta-analysis of numerous studies confirmed that at all grade levels, reading aloud leads to gains in reading comprehension, vocabulary, and even grammar and usage (Martinez 1989). More recently, Teri Lesesne, in "Reading Aloud to Build Success in Reading" (1998), explains how these same effects are also achieved through paired student reading and Readers' Theater, in which groups of students prepare and give reading performances.

A number of additional studies support the effectiveness of reading aloud to high-school students. Several focused exclusively on read-alouds as an intervention, showing particularly an effect on students' willingness to read more (DuBois and McIntosh 1986; Carr et al. 1995). Several others observed improvement in student achievement by combining teachers reading aloud with other strategies such as a home reading contract, paired reading, writing, older students reading to much younger ones, etc. (Robb 1993; Turner 1993; Fisher et al. 2002). *Read It Aloud! Using Literature in the Secondary Content*

Classroom (Richardson 2000) provides read-aloud lists for all of the core high-school subject areas.

10. **Adolescent students need opportunities to connect with the adult literate community, starting with teachers who are also readers and who generously share their reading lives with kids.**

Reading aloud is of course one way for an adult, usually the teacher, to communicate to students his or

---

MORE–LESS CHART

To strengthen students' reading as an engine for learning in all subjects, secondary classrooms need:

More	Less
Real books	Textbooks
Teaching of reading	Assigned reading
Student choice of reading	Reading only "the classics"
In-class reading	Take-home assignments
Workshop and Book Clubs	Whole-class discussion
Reading as a community activity	Reading as an individual activity
Reading lots of books	Many weeks on a single book
Reading for enjoyment	Struggling through hard books
Reading as a life activity	Reading as a school activity

---

her connection with reading. Davidson and Koppenhaver's survey of successful adolescent reading programs describes how teachers in these programs often share their internal reading processes so that the students can see how competent adults actually read (1992). Jeanne Ehlinger, in a 1989 study, showed that when a "think-aloud" process for reading was modeled for students, they tended to use it themselves, in their reading in content areas. Seeing how an adult uses her mind as she reads, in other words, influenced the students' learning process. They reported that they found themselves slowing down to think about what they read, and were able to resolve confusions as a result.

Our Own Research: Where Do Avid Readers Come From?

Everybody says our goal in schools is to create lifelong readers. O.K.: has anybody ever asked a lifelong reader how he or she got to be that way? Often it starts with family and community influences. A person may be helped by school or may keep reading in spite of school. Many people have out-of-school experiences and form attitudes that lead them to be readers. Conversely, for many students, after about third grade or so school assignments kill off reading; far from igniting a love of literature, they too often extinguish it. Following is one example.

Linda Brown, a school social worker and neighbor of Steve's, says she loves to read now, but never did until she got to college. Gradually, however, a few

259

RECOMMEN-

DATIONS

FROM

READING

RESEARCH

positive memories surface—*The Secret Garden* was fun in fourth grade because she and some friends presented a skit about it for her class; *A Wrinkle in Time* was a favorite because she got to choose it herself. A self-chosen book she liked in seventh grade was *The Old Man and the Sea*—an unusual preference for a middle-schooler. But her great interests were simply elsewhere: art, the violin, and creative play in the forest preserve behind her house. In high school, she says, she enjoyed math. "Everything else seemed dry." Again, not what most people might say, though none of her teachers ever tried to capitalize on her interests to deepen her reading experience.

Then in college, her studies turned very exciting for her—art history, the classics, psych. "I think it was the good teachers, more than the material itself," Linda reflects. Now, nothing seemed dull—"I just got into learning." Still, only after college did reading come into its own. Linda started attending Shakespeare plays and reading the texts first. She loved Jane Austen and the Bronte sisters. "Finally," concludes Linda Brown, "I got to read for fun!"

Conclusion

We know that bringing real books and effective thinking strategies into the secondary schools will prepare students better for the literacy demands of adult life—and offer the hope of higher test scores, too. But just as importantly, transforming reading can also become an engine of broader school improvement, throughout a building or a district. Making the shift to real reading provides an opportunity for teachers from many disciplines to gather around a common purpose. Instead of teaching the same textbook year after year, teachers become learners again. Sure, the textbook may seem like a safe harbor for a while, but we've all got to leave port sooner or later. As teachers explore and select trade books, articles, and other materials for their classrooms, they enjoy the invigorating experience of engaging new information, new voices, new concepts—just as they expect their students to do. As they read and think afresh, they become more aware of their own thinking and learning strategies, and thus become better models and mentors for their students.

The shift to real books and smarter thinking also provides an impetus for increased faculty collaboration. Instead of laboring in their separate textbook-driven classrooms, teachers will really need each other now. It creates a natural occasion to come together, to share book titles, to develop cross-disciplinary units, to revitalize our own teaching—and our own reading lives.

Bibliography of Research Studies

Achilles, Charles M., and S. P. Hoover. 1996. "Exploring Problem-Based Learning in Grades 6–12." Paper presented to Mid-South Educational Research Association.

Alexander, Wallace, et al. 1995. *Student-Oriented Curriculum: Asking the Right Questions.* Columbus, OH: National Middle School Association.

Allington, Richard. 2002. *Big Brother and the National Reading Curriculum: How Ideology Trumped Evidence.* Portsmouth, NH: Heinemann.

Allington, Richard. 2001. *What Really Matters for Struggling Readers: Designing Research-Based Programs.* New York, NY: Longman.

Alvermann, Donna, et al. 1999. "Adolescents' Perceptions and Negotiations of Literacy Practices in After-School Read and Talk Clubs," *American Educational Research Journal.* 36: 221–264.

Alvermann, Donna, et al. 1996. "Middle- and High-School Students' Perceptions of How They Experience Text-Based Discussions: A Multicase Study," *Reading Research Quarterly.* 31: 244–267.

Anderson, Richard C. 1996. "Research Foundations to Support Wide Reading," in V. Greaney, ed., *Promoting Reading in Developing Countries.* Newark, DE: International Reading Association.

Anderson, Richard C., and W. E. Nagy. 1992. "The Vocabulary Conundrum," *American Educator.* 14–18; 44–47.

Anderson, Richard C., et al. 1988. "Growth in Reading and How Children Spend Their Time Outside of School," *Reading Research Quarterly.* 23: 285–303.

Anderson, Richard C., et al. 1985. *Becoming a Nation of Readers.* Pittsburgh, PA: National Institute of Education.

Anderson, Valerie. 1992. "A Teacher Development Project in Transactional Strategy Instruction for Teachers of Severely Reading-Disabled Adolescents," *Teaching and Teacher Education.* 8: 391–403.

Anglin, J. M. 1993. "Vocabulary Development: A Morphological Analysis," *Monographs of the Society for Research in Child Development.* Vol. 58.

Beane, James. 1993. *A Middle School Curriculum: From Rhetoric to Reality.* Columbus, OH: National Middle School Association.

Beck, Isabel L., et al. 1995. "Giving a Text Voice Can Improve Students' Understanding," *Reading Research Quarterly.* 30: 220–239.

Beck, Isabel L., et al. 1991. "Revising Social Studies Text from a Text-Processing Perspective: Evidence of Improved Comprehensibility," *Reading Research Quarterly.* 26: 251–276.

Beers, Kylene. 1998. "Choosing Not to Read: Understanding Why Some Middle Schoolers Just Say No," in Kylene Beers and Barbara Samuels, eds., *Into Focus: Understanding and Creating Middle School Readers,* 37–63. Norwood, MA: Christopher Gordon.

261

RECOMMEN-

DATIONS

FROM

READING

RESEARCH

Britton, Bruce K., et al. 1996. *Improving Instructional Text: Tests of Two Revision Methods.* Athens, GA: Universities of Georgia and Maryland, National Reading Research Center.

Carlsen, G. Robert, and A. Sherrill. 1988. *Voices of Readers: How We Come to Love Books.* Urbana, IL: National Council of Teachers of English.

Carr, Dorothy, et al. 1995. "Improving Student Reading Motivation Through the Use of Oral Reading Strategies," ERIC document #ED386687.

Carter, Betty, and Richard Abrahamson. 1998. "Castles to Colin Powell: The Truth About Nonfiction," in Kylene Beers and Barbara Samuels, eds., *Into Focus: Understanding and Creating Middle School Readers,* 313–332. Norwood, MA: Christopher Gordon.

Crook, P. 1990. "Children Confront Civil War Issues: Using Literature as an Integral Part of the Social Studies Curriculum," *The Social Studies.* 81: 489–503.

Davidson, Judith, and David Koppenhaver. 1993. *Adolescent Literacy: What Works and Why.* New York, NY: Garland Publishing.

Denham, C., and A. Lieberman. 1980. *Time to Learn.* Washington, D.C.: U.S. Government Printing Office.

Dole, J., et al. 1996. "The Effects of Strategy Instruction on the Comprehension Performance of At-Risk Students," *Reading Research Quarterly.* 31: 62–88.

DuBois, B., and M. McIntosh. 1986. "Reading Aloud to Students in Secondary History Classes," *Social Studies.* 36: 210–213.

Ehlinger, Jeanne. 1989. "Thinking-Aloud: An Examination of Its Transfer to Other Learning Situations." Paper presented to the National Reading Conference.

Fader, Daniel, and Elton McNeil. 1969. *Hooked on Books.* New York, NY: Pergamon Press.

Fisher, Douglas, N. Frey, and D. Williams. 2002. "Seven Literary Strategies That Work," *Educational Leadership.* 60 n. 3: 70–73.

Gallagher, Shelagh, et al. 1992. "The Effects of Problem-Based Learning on Problem Solving," *Gifted Child Quarterly.* 36: 195–200.

Gambrell, Linda, et al. 1996. *Elementary Students' Motivation to Read.* Athens, GA: Universities of Georgia and Maryland, National Reading Research Center.

Goatley, V. J., et al. 1995. "Diverse Learners Participating in Regular Education 'Book Clubs,'" *Reading Research Quarterly.* 30: 352–380.

Guthrie, John, and Emily Anderson. 1999. "Engagement in Reading: Processes of Motivated, Strategic, Knowledgeable, Social Readers," in John Guthrie and Donna Alvermann, eds., *Engaged Reading: Processes, Practices, and Policy Implications,* 17–45. New York, NY: Teachers College Press.

Hange, Jane, and Helen Rolfe. 1995. "Interdisciplinary Curriculum and Instruction: Teaming to Improve Learning and Motivation." Paper presented to American Educational Research Association.

Hecht, Jeffrey, et al. 1994. "Project Homeroom, Project Schoolroom, and Regular School: Innovations in Team Teaching, Interdisciplinary Learning, and the Use of Technology: A Final Report on the Project at the Maine East High School," ERIC #IR017062.

Hynd, Cynthia. 1999. "Instructional Considerations for Literacy in Middle and Secondary Schools: Toward an Integrated Model of Instruction," in John Guthrie and Donna Alvermann, eds., *Engaged Reading: Processes, Practices, and Policy Implications,* 81–104. New York, NY: Teachers College Press.

Hynd Cynthia, et al. 1997. *Texts in Physics Class: The Contribution of Reading to the Learning of Counterintuitive Physics Principles.* Athens, GA: Universities of Georgia and Maryland, National Reading Research Center.

Hynd, Cynthia, et al. 1995. *High School Physics: The Role of Text in Learning Counterintuitive Information.* Athens, GA: Universities of Georgia and Maryland, National Reading Research Center.

Hynd Cynthia, et al. 1994. *Learning Counterintuitive Physics Concepts: The Effects of Text and Educational Environment.* Athens, GA: Universities of Georgia and Maryland, National Reading Research Center.

Johnson, Roger T., et al. 1985. "Effects of Cooperative, Competitive, and Individualistic Goal Structures on Computer Assisted Instruction," *Journal of Educational Psychology.* 77: 668–677.

Keisling, H. 1978. "Productivity of Instructional Time by Mode of Instruction for Students at Varying Levels of Reading Skill," *Reading Research Quarterly.* 13: 554–582.

Knapp, Michael S. 1995. *Teaching for Meaning in High Poverty Classrooms.* New York, NY: Teachers College Press.

Langer, Judith. 2001. *Beating the Odds: Teaching Middle and High School Students to Read and Write Well. 2nd Edition.* Albany, NY: Center on English Learning and Achievement.

Lee, Valerie, et al. 1999. *Social Support, Academic Press, and Student Achievement: A View from the Middle Grades in Chicago.* Chicago, IL: Consortium on Chicago School Research.

Lehman, Barbara, and P. Crook. 1989. "Content Reading Trade Books and Students: Learning About the Constitution Through Nonfiction," *Reading Improvement.* 26: 50–57.

Lesesne, Teri. 1998. "Reading Aloud to Build Success in Reading," in Kylene Beers and Barbara Samuels, eds., *Into Focus: Understanding and Creating Middle School Readers,* 245–260. Norwood, MA: Christopher Gordon.

Livaudais, M. 1986. *A Survey of Secondary Students' Attitudes Toward Reading Motivational Activities.* Unpub. dissertation.

263

RECOMMEN-

DATIONS

FROM

READING

RESEARCH

Lowery-Moore, Hollis. 1998. "Voices of Middle School Readers," in Kylene Beers and Barbara Samuels, eds., *Into Focus: Understanding and Creating Middle School Readers,* 23–35. Norwood, MA: Christopher Gordon.

Martinez, A. 1989. "A Meta-Analysis of Reading Aloud." Paper presented to Phi Delta Kappa seminar.

Mastropieri, Margo A., and T. E. Scruggs. 1997. "Best Practices in Promoting Reading Comprehension in Students with Learning Disabilities, 1976–1996," *Remedial and Special Education.* 18: 197–213.

McConney, Amanda, et al. 1994. "The Effects of an Interdisciplinary Curriculum Unit on the Environmental Decision-Making of Secondary School Students." Paper presented to National Association for Research in Science Teaching.

McKenna, M. C., et al. 1995. "Children's Attitudes Toward Reading: A National Survey," *Reading Research Quarterly.* 30: 934–956.

Morrow, Leslie, et al. 1997. "The Effect of a Literature-Based Program Integrated into Literacy and Science Instruction with Children from Diverse Backgrounds," *Reading Research Quarterly.* 32: 54–76.

Mulryan, C. M. 1994. "Perceptions of Intermediate Students' Cooperative Small-Group Work in Mathematics," *Journal of Educational Research.* 87: 280–291.

National Assessment of Educational Progress. 1997. *Report in Brief: NAEP 1996 Trends in Academic Progress.* Washington, D.C.: NAEP.

National Assessment of Educational Progress. 1988. *NAEP Reading Report Card for the Nation.* Washington, D.C.: NAEP.

National Reading Panel. 2000. *Teaching Children to Read: An Evidence-Based Assessment of the Scientific Research Literature on Reading and Its Implications for Reading Instruction.* Washington, D.C.: National Institutes of Health.

Oldfather, Penny 1994. *When Students Do Not Feel Motivated for Literacy Learning: How a Responsive Classroom Culture Helps.* Athens, GA: Universities of Georgia and Maryland, National Reading Research Center.

Oldfather, Penny 1993. *Student Perspectives on Motivating Experiences in Literacy Learning.* Athens, GA: Universities of Georgia and Maryland, National Reading Research Center.

Oldfather, Penny and K. Dahl. 1995. *Toward a Social Constructivist Reconceptualization of Intrinsic Motivation for Literacy Learning.* Athens, GA: Universities of Georgia and Maryland, National Reading Research Center.

Palincsar, A. S., and A. Brown. 1984. "Reciprocal Teaching and Comprehension-Fostering and Comprehension-Monitoring Activities," *Cognition and Instruction.* 1: 117–175.

Patrick, J. J., and S. Hawke. 1982. "Social Studies Curriculum Materials" in *The Current State of Social Studies: A Report of Project Span.* Boulder, CO: Social Science Education Consortium.

Pearson, P. David, and J. Dole. 1987. "Explicit Comprehension Instruction: A Review of the Research and a New Conceptualization of Instruction," *Elementary School Journal.* 88: 151–165.

Pearson, P. David, and L. Fielding. 1991. "Comprehension Instruction," in M. Kamil, et al., eds., *Handbook of Reading Research, Vol. 2,* pp. 815–860. New York, NY: Longman.

Pressley, Michael, et al. 1990. "Strategies That Improve Memory and Comprehension of What Is Read," *Elementary School Journal.* 90: 3–32.

Purcell-Gates, Victoria, et al. 1995. "Learning Written Storybook Language in School," *American Educational Research Journal.* 32: 659–685.

Richardson, Judy. 2000. *Read It Aloud! Using Literature in the Secondary Content Classroom.* Newark, DE: International Reading Association.

Robb, Laura. 1993. "A Cause for Celebration: Reading and Writing with At-Risk Students," *New Advocate.* 6: 25–40.

Rosenshine, Barak, and C. Meister. 1994. "Reciprocal Teaching: A Review of the Research," *Review of Educational Research.* 64: 479–530.

Smith, Julia, et al. 2001. *Instruction and Achievement in Chicago Elementary Schools.* Chicago, IL: Consortium on Chicago School Research.

Smith, Michael, and Jeffrey Wilhelm. 2002. *Reading Don't Fix No Chevys: Literacy in the Lives of Young Men.* Portsmouth, NH: Heinemann.

Spiegel, D. 1987. "Using Adolescent Literature in Social Studies and Science," *Education Horizons.* 65: 162–164.

Stepien, William, et al. 1993. "Problem-Based Learning for Traditional and Interdisciplinary Classrooms," *Journal for the Education of the Gifted.* 16: 338–357.

Strauss, S. E. 2000. *Literacy Learning in the Middle Grades: An Investigation of Academically Effective Middle Grades Schools.* Unpub. dissertation.

Taylor, B. M., et al. 1990. "Time Spent Reading and Reading Growth," *American Educational Research Journal.* 27: 351–362.

Turner, Thomas N. 1993. "Improving Reading Comprehension Achievement of Sixth, Seventh, and Eighth Grade Underachievers," ERIC document #ED372374.

White, T. G., et al. 1990. "Growth of Reading Vocabulary in Diverse Elementary Schools: Decoding and Word Meaning," *Journal of Educational Psychology.* 82: 281–290.

Wigfield, Allan, and John Guthrie. 1997. "Relations of Children's Motivation for Reading to the Amount and Breadth of Their Reading," *Journal of Educational Psychology.* 89: 420–432.

Wilhelm, Jeffrey. 1997. *You Gotta BE the Book: Teaching Engaged and Reflective Reading with Adolescents.* New York, NY: Teachers College Press.

Williams, Douglas, et al. 1998. "Examining How Middle School Students Use Problem-Based Learning Software," in *98 World Conference on Educational Multimedia and Hypermedia and World Conference on Educational Telecommunications Proceedings.*

Worth, J., and L. S. McCool. 1996. "Students Who Say They Hate to Read: The Importance of Opportunity, Choice, and Access," in E. Leu, C. Kinzer, and K. Hinchman, eds., *Literacies for the 21st Century*, 245–256. Oak Creek, WI: National Reading Conference.

Yore, L. 1991. "Secondary Science Teachers' Attitudes Toward and Beliefs About Science Reading and Science Textbooks," *Journal of Research in Science Teaching*, 28: 55–72.

Zorfass, Judith. 1998. *Teaching Middle School Students to Be Active Researchers*. Alexandria, VA: Association for Supervision and Curriculum Development.

265

RECOMMEN-

DATIONS

FROM

READING

RESEARCH

CHAPTER THIRTEEN
What Our Students Tell Us

We conclude with the voices of students—they are the focus of all the effort we've advocated throughout this book, the people whose lives we so deeply hope to enrich through the teaching of all our subjects in school. Every time we talk to students about their experiences with reading, we discover surprises and learn more about what makes them tick. At the same time, the themes we've sounded in this book appear again and again.

Themes of This Book

1) The "What" of reading: Students treasure the opportunity to choose their own reading, and as a result much prefer reading on their own to reading for school. Universally, kids disdain textbooks, though the good students dutifully plod through them.

2) The "How" of reading: Engaged reading always seems to involve visualizing, connecting with topics and issues kids care about, reflecting in the mirrors of their own lives, but also peering through windows to see worlds that are different.

3) Where we're going wrong: Students often enjoy reading in elementary school, but get turned off somewhere between fourth grade and middle school, where textbooks become more and more the primary material students are asked to read.

4) A reason for optimism: Even those who say they dislike reading will name topics that motivate them to read anyway. These students are waiting for us to show them the connection, the link, the experience that will bring school reading to life.

Here are samples of their testimony.

Aqueela Long

High school freshman Aqueela Long didn't enjoy reading very much until she was placed in a group home for a year, at age 12. "They locked us in a lot.

There was nothing to do but stay in your room or go to the library. They had a little library there, so I just started reading romance novels."

Her school was attached to the group home. "The teachers read to us—*Harry Potter,* for example. But I don't like being read to. You can understand things better when you read, yourself. You can go back and figure things out." Aqueela stopped her reading in eighth grade, but then, she explains, a friend got her back on track by offering books to her. Now, she reads every night, after finishing her homework.

Aqueela still reads romance and mystery novels, but has widened her focus considerably. "I try to read stuff I wouldn't usually read. I like to expand my mind." For example, she doesn't like western tales, but found a biography of Billy the Kid "kind of cool." She really liked *The Other Woman* by Eric Jerome Dickey, just finished *Bad Boy* by Olivia Goldsmith, and now, for school she's reading *The Black Rose* by Tananarive Due, about Madame C. J. Walker, who developed anti-curl hair treatments. She still reads romance novels but says, "Most are overrated, and some are really stupid."

What goes on in Aqueela's head when she reads? "When you get into a book, it's exciting. You don't want to put it down. I like to picture things in my head. It's better than watching a movie because in my head there's more detail. It helps you use your imagination. I can actually picture characters, what they're doing, what they look like."

As for textbooks, she sniffs dismissively, "I'm not going to sit down and read one on my own. Why would anyone ever do that? But it's something you gotta do because you need the grade. But anyway, reading is reading."

William Sims

"I can comprehend what I read, but I just don't like doing it," explains William Sims. This freshman student's reaction to "The Lottery," which he had just finished: "I just skimmed through it. It's just processing the words." He doesn't remember what it's about. "I just remember long enough to do the work," he admits with disarming honesty.

It turns out, though, that some reading is actually much more engaging for him. Books about sports come first. He'd recently finished a biography of basketball player Allen Iverson. "He had a rough time growing up, like my life. I have the same goals as he did, making it to the NBA." Another he enjoyed was ˦ book version of *The Red Dragon,* though he hadn't seen the movie yet. ꜰor one thing, he'd seen the two previous "Hannibal Lector" films, "So I ɑt it was about, and I knew what to expect. I could picture it." He ɹuspense, the action, and the fact that it was "different." *The Autobi-ɟ of Malcolm X* was also a favorite. "A book needs to be interesting to me, to catch my eye—like sports, or something to do with real life. Fiction is O.K., if it's from a movie, so I know what I'm getting into."

William sees himself as a writer, pleased that his eighth-grade teacher bound his writings into a book. He doesn't care if people read it, however, so there's no conscious link to reading. "It's more just to get things off my mind." William enjoyed reading in elementary school, but stopped in junior high. Textbooks are simply not interesting. "I try to remember what I've read as long as I need to, until the test. And then I let it go."

Darne Boyce

Darne claims she doesn't like to read, though it's not really clear why she says this. "It depends on what I'm reading. I like *Chicken Soup for the Teenage Soul,* because it's about what's really happening." She'll read magazine articles, if they're *truthful.* "When I was little, I'd read things that weren't true, and go around telling people what they said. My friends would tease me—'That's not true!' It was embarrassing." Interestingly, however, she enjoys the novels she reads for English, "If they're more like real life." Myths are enjoyable too, except for those that are "too violent."

What goes on in Darne's head when she reads? Her focus seems to be more on the accomplishment than the actual experience itself. "If it's something I like, I feel energetic, and I know I'm going to finish it." Yet she's unavoidably drawn into the story. "Some stories don't tell what the characters are feeling, and so I say, 'She's mad,' or 'She wants to be left alone.'"

Darne's favorite reading topic: math. "When I had problems reading in school, my Mom took me to the Teachers' Store, to get me back on track. I'm good in math, so I got books about it." But at her high school, neither her reading teacher, her English teacher, nor her math teacher were aware of this.

Darne was not a reader in elementary school. "There was no choice and we had to read, so I didn't like it." She couldn't recall material after reading, which affected her grades. A teacher tutored her, and she learned to take notes as she read, which helped. Even now, however, "If I'm reading something I don't like, I just feel sleepy, because it's boring." This happens with textbooks most of the time—except, naturally, for math.

Danielle Crawford

Danielle Crawford has always been interested in science. So when her 11th-grade biology class was given the option of creating a science fair project or doing some other type of inquiry, Danielle chose the former, and focused on astigmatism. "I wanted to find out if astigmatism could be corrected with contact lenses, because I have this problem, myself. I wanted to see if contacts could help me," she explains. To learn about astigmatism, Danielle obtained brochures from her optometrist plus a dozen library books from the library, and found a number of websites about the condition.

Her eye doctor gave Danielle photocopies of the records of three anonymous patients and explained what the notes and diagnoses meant. "The books helped a lot, too, because they had definitions for the technical terms. They were also fascinating because they described other eye diseases, including some that happen at birth. And then an article on the Internet explained how astigmatism is measured."

When asked about school reading, Danielle assured us, "In the reading that I have to do for my classes, textbooks don't really bother me. But I know ones like the history book are boring to most kids. We teens like reading things that are filled with action and are about real life. Sometimes school reading is like that and sometimes it's not."

Danielle's thoughts about her academic past and future: "When I was little, I wanted to do a project about the solar system, so I read about it. And I wanted to know about warm- and cold-blooded animals, and weather—all kinds of things. So I read about them, too. When I graduate high school, I want to study to be a nurse, and after that I plan to go back to school to study optometry and open my own office. Ms. Bryant [her biology teacher] is the person I really look up to. She encouraged me in my reading."

Final Thoughts

So how do we reach these students and make reading matter for them? What can we learn from their stories, and those of so many wonderful teachers described in this book? We've offered many practical strategies, but perhaps more influential than anything we grownups say is what we ourselves *do*—what we read, how we show kids the way our minds work as we read, how we let them see that reading supports and enriches our lives, how we listen as our students develop new strategies and explore new fields of knowledge, how we care about them as they grow through their reading—and how, as we all read together, our subjects truly matter.

Index